Shelley and the Revolutionary Idea

SHELLEY
and the
Revolutionary Idea

Gerald McNiece

Harvard University Press
Cambridge, Massachusetts
1969

Distributed in Great Britain by Oxford University Press, London

Publication of this book has been aided by a grant from
the Hyder Edward Rollins Fund

Library of Congress Catalog Card Number 75–88808

SBN 674–80620–4

Printed in the United States of America

To the Memory of My Father

Paul D. McNiece

Preface

In *The Liberal Imagination* (page 67) Lionel Trilling said, "Surely the great work of our time is the restoration and the reconstitution of the will." Granted the soundness of this comment, I claim that the poetry of Percy Bysshe Shelley has special relevance to the project and to our times. When I first began my study, Shelley's reputation was clouded by hostile criticism which could make his partisans either apologetic and defensive or militant. Though it remains true that many readers are not temperamentally able to like Shelley — often described as a seriously flawed man and poet with major gifts — the situation has changed. The formalist school of criticism has enriched its readings and tempered its judgments with historical, sociological, and archetypal insights. The general modern sense of doubt and disaster has perhaps created a public more receptive to a poetry of ideas charged with high social purpose.

A re-examination of Shelley's ideas, modes, and intentions and an explanation of his particular problems might strengthen his influence. One does not read him for the sensuous intensity of Keats, for the feeling of kinship with nature of Wordsworth, or for the verve and amusingly insolent cynicism of Byron. Shelley is the visionary poet — almost as much of a visionary as Blake, and certainly more classical and accessible. Believer in a new religion of revolutionary idealism, he becomes its high priest, uniting revolution and religion. Even more than the other great Romantics, Shelley was less concerned with writing poems that were finished works of art than with recording his sense of powers and meanings which could remold the world if man could only sustain his communication with them. The poet contends as in prayer with ineffable forces, but the poems which record his experience and express his thoughts are often admittedly inadequate. "When composition begins, inspiration is on the decline," comments Shelley sadly in his treatise on poetry.

One valid defense of Shelley for our times, acknowledging the incoherent, the sentimental, and the strident element in much of his writing, would be to call attention to his energy, saneness, depth, and the consequent usefulness of his ideas about progress, reform, and revolution. My book attempts such a brief, developed not by rigorous formal analysis of Shelley's poems but by describing them rather generally as microcosmic revolutions and by grouping and relating his ideas.

I feel that Shelley has valuable things to say about significant rebellion, that his career as a rebel, his observations of revolution and reaction, and his practiced beliefs ought to instruct our own radicalism and our own conservatism. The world needs rebels, for irrational, inert, oppressive, and unjust men and institutions always exist. But rebellion is not enough. The enemy must be known thoroughly, the plans carefully constructed, the direction and goal defined distinctly, the energies and passions necessary for success continually kindled — but without dogmatism, without senseless violence, without rejecting the wisdom of past experience, without forgetting the humanity of the opposition. I attempt to present Shelley as something of a model for élan, for valiance, even for virtues not often enough credited to him such as a sense of limits and thoughtful consideration of mind and reality. Finally I present and praise him for a quality of heroic persistence in a good cause in a bad time. I have always admired Shelley for the courage and consistency of his political convictions, especially in view of his background and his opposition.

There are a number of ways of looking at Shelley. He has particularly interested biographers and specialists in the history of ideas. His general social and political views have been examined by many scholars. I have therefore covered some fairly familiar ground, but I have new material to add, and I have surveyed Shelley's idea of revolution and its sources more completely and tenaciously than has been done before.

Shelley read many philosophers, and this reading influenced his opinions; but he also read many books about the French Revolution. I have reviewed his reading about the Revolution, placed his association schemes in the context of the revolutionary clubs, interpreted his poetry and his theory of poetry in the light of the revolutionary ritual, and discussed his concepts of the hero and heroine against the background of revolutionary leadership. I have attempted to reveal the vitality of revolutionary influence on his life and writing generally. In the light of this influence I have re-examined his practical interests and observations, and I have studied *Queen Mab, The Revolt of Islam, Prometheus Unbound,* and *Hellas* as reflections or imitations of the idea of revolution.

I began my study of Shelley under Melvin Solve of the University of Arizona, and owe much to his scholarship and his advice. He first proposed to me a fundamental problem in Shelley's thought: the relation between his changing notions of reality and his doctrine of perfectibility.

I had the good fortune for a Shelley scholar of being able to spend three uninterrupted years between 1948 and 1951 in daily reading at the Bodleian Library. I am grateful to the

Rhodes Trust for the opportunity. At Oxford I completed a study of Shelley's politics which provided some of the material for the early chapters. I worked under the supervision of the late Humphry House, who helped get me properly started. Mrs. Catherine Ing also gave useful criticism to my Oxford project. Jerome Buckley and Douglas Bush of Harvard read the work on which this book is based, and I am very much indebted for the generosity of their comments and for advice and assistance concerning publication.

The President and Regents of the University of Arizona granted me the sabbatical leave which enabled me to prepare the book for publication. Within my own department I owe special thanks to the late Desmond Powell for his defense of my projects and to Laurence Muir for seconding my sabbatical application and for making funds available to cover some of my incidental expenses. Carl Ketcham read the manuscript in an early, desperate stage and gave me badly needed encouragement. Mrs. Sylvia Sloan did an admirable job of typing and pointed out some errors and inconsistencies.

Among Shelley scholars, besides Melvin Solve, I owe most to the writings of Kenneth Neill Cameron, Newman Ivey White, Milton Wilson, and Harold Bloom for specific material and for the example of excellent work. Professor Cameron's numerous publications have been especially useful, particularly *The Young Shelley*.

My wife Cheryl performed an essential role by reading and praising my writing. She helped make the book possible as did others of my family, particularly my mother and the good man to whose memory it is dedicated.

G. McN.

Tucson, Arizona
April 1, 1969

Contents

Shelley and the Revolutionary Idea

Short Titles

Barruel
Abbé Barruel, *Memoirs Illustrating the History of Jacobinism,* trans. Robert Clifford (London, 1797)

Clark ed.
Shelley's Prose, ed. D. L. Clark (Albuquerque, N.M., 1966)

Hutchinson ed.
The Complete Poetical Works of Percy Bysshe Shelley, ed. Thomas Hutchinson (London, 1947)

Journal
Mary Shelley, *Journal,* ed. Frederick L. Jones (Norman, Oklahoma, 1947)

Julian
The Complete Works, ed. Roger Ingpen and Walter E. Peck (Julian edition; New York, 1926–1930)

Letters
The Letters of Percy Bysshe Shelley, ed. Frederick L. Jones (Oxford, 1964)

Paine
The Complete Writings of Thomas Paine, ed. Philip S. Foner (New York, 1945)

Political Justice
William Godwin, *Enquiry Concerning Political Justice,* ed. F. E. L. Priestley (London, 1946)

View of F. R.
Mary Wollstonecraft, *An Historical and Moral View of the French Revolution* (London, 1794)

I

Introduction

According to Mrs. Shelley, the poet was from youth a victim of the reaction to the French Revolution. He came to know first hand the scorn and hatred awarded to the partisans of reform. Nevertheless, Shelley sought in his more significant works to set forth the beau ideal of the French Revolution. To him the Revolution offered a "theme involving pictures of all that is best qualified to interest and to instruct mankind." It defined "the master theme of the epoch" (to Lord Byron, September 8 and 29, 1816, *Letters*, I, 504, 508). The abstract ideas exposed by the Revolution to the world of experience became facts of passionate apprehension,[1] and he remained the ardent disciple of revolutionary idealism throughout his life.

Revolt was for Shelley a first principle. His basic impulse was to rebel against restraint, and only thereafter to suggest measures of improvement which his reading and observation afforded.[2] One must agree that Shelley seems to have the sympathies of a natural rebel with the idea of revolution. He accepted its necessity, proved it, as Keats would say, on his own pulses, and experienced intensively the despair which the decline of the Revolution caused. It then became a necessity to understand the reasons for comparative failure and to create the measures or systems which would forestall further failures, or perhaps to find another plane on which an ideal revolution might be enacted where it would be proof against such failures. Shelley defined the abstract principles of a revolution. He tempered them by studying a real revolution and by looking a little closer at humanity.

Shelley's passion for reforming the world was given meaning and direction by study of the revolutionary ideas and events of the age. One might conclude, in fact, that he was more strongly influenced by the history and fate of the French Revolution than by any of his readings in Godwin, Plato, Berkeley, or Spinoza, though all of these thinkers and others too certainly helped him to define a theory of the mind and to elaborate a program for reform, both practical and ideal, which would answer the challenge of revolutionary failure and reaction.

The main problem was that, although Shelley wanted to reform the world, it was a world frightened by the destruction caused by revolution and therefore hostile to enthusiastic social idealism. The prophets of despair were having it pretty much their own way as the leaders of society searched for more effective restraints to subdue the protesting and untrustworthy masses. The older poets — Wordsworth, Coleridge, and Southey — first revolutionary enthusiasts, then Godwinian rationalists and gradualists, and finally opponents of most reform, decided that the French doctrines of perfectibility and abstract rights led inevitably to revolutionary crime and anarchy. Men freed from traditional restraints and doctrines were in danger of being governed by such evil passions as produced the Terror and the invasion of Switzerland. To help solve the dilemma Shelley offered his message of renewed revolutionary faith and the doctrine of the poet as hero. For him the French Revolution had been both a powerful symbol of what human energy could accomplish and a revelation of human corruptibility. To be sure, radicalism had lost its innocence; but from the idealism of the Revolution, Shelley acquired his religion of humanity, and from its history he learned practical moderation.

The French Revolution had been an attempt to create a marriage between ideas and events sponsored by philosophers who held particular concepts of mind and nature. These concepts had weaknesses and inadequacies revealed by the testing of revolutionary action. Belief in a progress based on unhistorical rationalism, sensationalism, and environmentalism had to be rejected without permitting cultural optimism to dwindle and die. As Shelley insisted in a note to *Hellas*, "it is the province of the poet to attach himself to those ideas which exalt and ennoble humanity" (Hutchinson ed., p. 478). To the old virtues of love and hope, he added another — self-esteem. What men think about themselves conditions their outlook on the world. The antidote for the conservative veneration of tradition and fearful distrust of the future is belief in the natural goodness of the creative and sympathetic imagination. Poets, who interpret nature and legislate for mankind, have the power to create "forms of opinion and action never before conceived; which, copied into the imaginations of men, became as generals to the bewildered armies of their thoughts" ("A Defence of Poetry," Clark ed., p. 287). It is the particular task of the poet in an age of strife and reaction to dramatize a new revolutionary creed and to project heroes who alter the sense of reality. Shelley was a revolutionary idealist, but he was also in an important sense a man of action who wanted to see something done immediately. He wrote poetry for the will.

In order to sustain faith and inspire action, Shelley had to redefine the idea of revolution and re-examine human nature. He became a subtler psychologist and less visionary an optimist than he is sometimes thought to have been. He found room for suffering, doubt, and mystery. The French Revolution had been dominated by faith in Reason. The results seemed to show that reason did not have the strength to inspire continuing heroic effort. It did not look deeply enough into the searchless heart of man, nor could it grasp the independent life and purpose in nature. Reason must be replaced by the creative and redeeming imagination. Poetry must replace or enrich technology. Shelley saw that a world governed by imagination will differ essentially from a world which apotheosizes reason. The hero will now be the poet-prophet. Progress will be difficult to measure. Really the only adequate index will be the number and power of the enlightened. Because at present the imagination illuminates life so transiently and selectively, the visionary world which the Platonists of reform hunger to realize in the world of experience cannot command the allegiance of ordinary men as strongly as the fixities and certainties and simplicities of reform programs shaped by men of reason. For a time liberty and fraternity may matter more than equality, since the natural governing aristocracy must discover and serve a nobler purpose than increasing the number of average happy and industrious citizens owning appropriate amounts of property. Equality will continue to be the ideal, of course, but the equal citizens, living in a true spiritual community, will be guided by individualism and adventurous idealism.

The servant of the imagination has passionate assurance but not a definite program. Perhaps he will have to create new rituals charged with revolutionary poetry in order to unite the masses while the man-mending process goes on. At the same time he seeks to influence the readers with the power of imagination to accept the revolutionary vocation by presenting them with "beautiful idealisms of moral excellence." No doubt his apparent failure to affect this highly select audience contributed to the comparative disillusionment Shelley suffered in his last few years.

Because of what William James calls the "trail of the human serpent" everywhere,[3] there arises the problem of distinguishing illusion from reality. Are we to say that fruitful illusions in a world whose meanings and values are constituted by the symbol-making imagination are as good as realities? While there are clear and obvious alliances between belief in imagination and belief in our individual freedom to select a "supreme fiction," Shelley avoids the extremes of solipsism and subjectivism by proposing or conceding some practical disciplines, obstacles, and correctives without giving up the faith that "we might be otherwise." His innocence profited from experience. He learned that none of our passions seem capable of sustaining themselves for long. Individuals and societies may be governed by hate and fear even more effectively than by hope and love as any study of the manipulations of people by tyrants and empirics easily demonstrates. History, "that record of crimes & miseries" (to Thomas Hookham, December 17, 1812, *Letters*, I, 340), is a gloomy study because it reveals the power of hate and fear. Shelley read a lot of history, and he discovered that both history and experience contain a toughness and complexity which resist political idealism. The enemy is strong because "He reigns." That Shelley should be charged with ineffectual and shallow revolutionary idealism is astonishing in view of the bulk and subtlety of his references to the forces of darkness his heroes must contend against. "He works to make the biggest statement he can, to claim the most for man that he is able, but at his most characteristic the statement is circumscribed: the paradise is a limited one, or he fails to achieve it, or it collapses after having been achieved. His hopes are infinite, but he is sober in expectation."[4] Prometheans are made by suffering. Shelley's optimism may have been reduced after 1819, but the agent was awareness of the entrenched power of the opposition not the superficiality of his knowledge.

Work in practical reform also added realism to Shelley's views. He became a careful student of the details of humanitarianism and reform, extremely aware of the strength of conservative dread of change but always insistent on looking beyond the corrupt present with the aid of a philosophy of optimism. The situation demanded change and action.

Instead of continuing to image two warring principles, as in *The Revolt of Islam*, Shelley began to dramatize a conflict between two worlds of vision, the lesser vision of bourgeois science and technology and the nobler one of the poet. Here perhaps was his major theme, and it is still valid. The modern technological bias had enslaved nature to man's material wants and impoverished man's spirit by destroying his sense of kinship and communion with nature. The twin results were the isolation of poets and the plundering of natural resources. Because of man's infected will, technology consistently outstrips the intelligent and imaginative use of the products it multiplies. That is Shelley's classical indictment and the main argument for the moral and imaginative revolution which must precede a successful political revolution. The true politics of intelligent and realistic hope will not base itself on the simple path of subduing nature and multiplying comforts.

The present need is for both better ideas and a renewed will. The problem, as the French Revolution had revealed, was not simply to know the good, but to do the good that is known. To act wisely, Shelley suggested, men must imagine what they know. The imagination awakes the power of will. Service to the method of the imagination and to the symbols it creates will reconstruct the mind and redirect its strategies for shaping reality. Only thus may the worship of reason and the dangerous bias of modern civilization be corrected. Poetry is the instrument of the imagination. In his poetry Shelley set himself the task of recharging the power of revolutionary ideas. Uniting abstract thought, intense feeling, and images of a golden world both sensuous and ideal, he created a medium for experiencing belief in the presence and reality of the revolutionary gods. But these gods and the heroes who serve them by belief and action must struggle for their reality against dark antagonists in a mysterious dialectic. Like all great truths, the idea of the true revolution can be partly embodied but never truly known. It summons the adventurous spirit on a voyage beyond the limits of charted possibility and arms him with the courage and the faith that the continuing voyage demands.

A man acts when he can imagine what once he only knew. While reality is not going to be changed by developing delusions of the grandeur of human destiny, neither need men limply accept the sense of futility created by the shrunken spirit of positivism. Poetry creates the pattern of meaning which can restore the wasteland of our lives and give a constructive human purpose to our further science. Science and poetry must be united in a deeper exploration of the makeup and correspondences of mind and nature. What this new Orphic or Baconian revolution will require may be described as the "matching of two moving processes, one in nature, one in the mind and language, whereby reality may be altered and controlled." [5]

Rather than passive submission to cultural despair the situation demands a thorough re-exploration of our interior forces with the aid of poetry. The interior energies capable of revolutionizing the individual, his society, and the nature from which he seems alienated have hardly been tapped, much less exhausted. These are the grounds for hope. So little has been tried really. Why condemn the moments of visionary optimism experienced in expanded consciousness as unreal and choose disillusionment and futility? "Let us believe in a kind of optimism in which we are our own gods" (to Maria Gisborne, October 13 or 14, 1819, *Letters*, II, 125). The changed ideals of the inner enrichment of life bring a hope which generates fresh efforts, and with effort and struggle come the necessary abilities.

It may be thought that in an age which has witnessed the failure and bloodshed of the French Revolution repeated over and over again as the destructive power created by man's one-sided technological progress has increased Shelley's theses are worth reviewing. Confronted with fantastically more terrifying "Riddles of death" than Shelley or Thebes ever knew, we continue to need a poetry of hope and vision to support some faith that man can rise again. Shelley is an especially important poet for our time, so like his own, because of the vitality of his tested optimism. He confronted the modern crisis of doubt following the collapse of the old world view and its attendant religious doctrines, and reaffirmed belief in the ability of liberated humanity to achieve, even through inevitable failure and suffering, the ideals it could conceive. He placed his "considerable poetic powers" at the service of the essential ideas, perhaps the only ideas capable of resisting the modern failure of nerve and the weakening of our will to believe.

It is no doubt true that Shelley took his vocation of visionary prophet so seriously that he sometimes oversimplified the human problem and situation. He was far too ready to divide society into two classes of oppressors and oppressed. The simplification may have been useful to sustain his reforming ardor, but it ignored the manifold variations of opinion in a nation and gave insufficient attention to the complexity of the motives which move men. The rulers of England were not monsters waiting to hew down the unresisting multitude; they were men dedicated to the preservation of what they conceived to be the natural order of society. They did not regard all men as equal in the sense proclaimed by the French Revolution. Some were born to rule and some to serve. The organization of society was a reflection of natural inequalities, and property was its basis. Shelley had to learn that the government could not immediately begin to regulate the affairs of the nation by those abstract principles which man might only hope to realize in the process of time.

However, one can grow old measuring difficulties or despairing over human frailties. No one needs any lessons in pessimism these days. Our needs are otherwise, and Shelley's idealism and his ability to communicate a sense of high hope and purpose administer to them.

Certainly he may be said to have spoken the truth for his own times. The England which Shelley observed as he came of age in the shadow of the French Revolution clearly needed reform. Revolution had already come in industry and agriculture, but political institutions were fixed by the fear of anarchy like that across the Channel. There was considerable tension and agitation, but little effective organization among the reformers to take advantage of the unrest; and when economic distress was diminished by recurring though temporary prosperity, the working classes would lose interest in political change. Moreover there was little unanimity among the reformers. The more radical urged universal suffrage, the ballot, annual parliaments, and compromising the national debt, while the more moderate and practical men hoped by tinkering with the Constitution to solve the immediate problems without violating the rights of property in the name of abstract panaceas like the rights of man and the will of the people.

The French Revolution became a real experience for Shelley. He felt its whole history and suffered its failure intensely. He dreamed with the radicals but worked with the moderates, like them conditioned by the results of the French Revolution to respect the necessity of evolutionary change. He was basically a man of action who turned to poetry because men had enough knowledge already and now had to learn to act on this knowledge. Thus he urged Byron to encourage action by idealizing the present rather than writing old-style romances.[6] The generous impulses must be generated through the imagination.

II

The Literature of Revolution

In defining the ideal principles of a revolution, Shelley tempered them by studying a real revolution and by looking a little closer at humanity. Though his debt has often been overstressed, he learned a good deal from William Godwin about both political ideals and political realities. Writing to Godwin in June 1812, Shelley acknowledged that it was reading *Political Justice* which made him "think and feel" (*Letters*, I, 303). Godwin's attitude toward the French Revolution was complex; he was neither a wholehearted supporter nor an obstinate opponent. His stance was rather that of an intellectual critic examining a specimen microscopically in search of a fund of generalizations about human change and progress. His usual theme is that revolutions are not truly beneficial, that they mar the "salutary and uninterrupted progress which political truth and social improvement bring." "They disturb the harmony of intellectual nature." Godwin claimed that revolutions created a violent opposition, the results of which were apt to rivet the chains of despotism and obliterate the memory of past improvement. The Terror of 1793 undid the work of decades of philosophical deliberation. He could scarcely conceive of a greater misfortune for a country, Godwin said, than the occurrence of a violent outbreak before citizens were educated in their responsibilities, when masses of ignorant men were "instigated to subvert existing institutions, and violently to take the work of political reformation into their own hands." When a people are unprepared by a love of freedom to enjoy it responsibly, dreadful tragedies will result if innovators get power and prematurely attempt after abstractly excellent systems. Mainly Godwin criticizes the pressures for conformity which revolutions create, so opposite to the philosophic anarchism which was his ideal. Opponents of the prevailing ideals are coerced into unnatural agreement to save their necks. Men are frightened by formulas. Oppressions ten times worse than before are introduced. All subtle inquiry and speculation are suspended. "Revolution is engendered by an indignation against tyranny, yet is itself evermore pregnant with tyranny." Even, gradual progress is the only true way. Men should doubt their own abstract notions and shun the narrow views and angry passions of contending parties. "What I should desire is, not by violence to change its institutions, but by discussion to change its ideas" (*Political Justice*, I, 255–257, 267–270; II, 531, 537, 539). Godwin's views seem at times barely distinguishable from Burke's. The difference in basic stance is, however, considerable. Godwin looks to the future and hopes for evolutionary improvement, Burke to the past, suggesting that the true way of liberty is to tap the wisdom of the ages and cherish every fading monument for the insight it may contain.

However, Godwin also defended the Revolution. He urged the rightness and utility of revolutionary principles. He admired the Revolution as a first sublime attempt to realize the absolutes of human reason. He believed in the ideas, although he denounced the tyranny of violence. Revolutions are often "coeval with important changes of the social system." Ultimately they may be necessary even though they do produce deplorable mischief. Unlike despotism, the revolutionary anarchy may be an evil of short duration, and also unlike despotism it "awakens thought, and diffuses energy and enterprise through the community" (*Political Justice*, I, 283–284; II, 369).

Godwin communicated the lessons he had learned from observing the process of a real revolution directly to Shelley. The French Revolutionists had erred, he advised, in not taking a long view of man's orderly advancement by means of the "venerable machine" of human society. He urged Shelley to adopt a moderate approach to the problems of society, to do less propagandizing, and to avoid inciting revolutionary activity.[1] Shelley was clearly influenced by Godwin's advice, but he remained a good deal more of an activist than his mentor. He was less suspicious of revolution, though he adopted some of Godwin's reservations, partly as a result of the other's direct influence and partly because of his own further study and experience of reform and revolution.

From the *Historical Sketch* of the Marquis de Condorcet, Shelley would have acquired a richer notion of the historical setting of the Revolution than Godwin offered, though, like Godwin, Condorcet moves far beyond the Revolution to predict the advent of a philosophic, temperate, and healthy humanity when miracles of longevity would be obtained by the work of medical science in eliminating disease. Condorcet was an active Girondist, writer, and scientist. Shelley read his *Esquisse* and cited him in the *Queen Mab* notes. Likely Condorcet influenced Shelley to view history in stages, as he does in many works, praising or condemning ages according to the degree of liberty attained. In this revolutionist's view of history, all the past is reduced to anticipations of the French Revolution, which ushered in the age of progressive perfectibility. Condorcet sees revolution as the final and necessary result of the multiplication and extension of knowledge, whether it occurs in a rapid, stormy fashion or in a slow, tranquil, incomplete one. The germ of perfection, he said, and Shelley echoed him in *Queen Mab*, is present in every heart, ready for nurturing by the forces of light and liberty. Condorcet wrote his great sketch while a

hunted and proscribed man. His noble peroration, surely stirring to a Shelley, describes social visions which consoled him,
he said, for the errors, crimes, and injustices which still soiled
the land. In the asylum of his imagination his persecutors could
not reach him.[2] There he could forget the avidity, the fear, and
the envy which, in a world of revolutionary terror, torment and
corrupt men, "c'est là qu'il existe véritablement avec ses sem-
blables, dans un elysée que sa raison a su se creer, et que son
amour pour l'humanité embellit des plus pures jouissances." *
Shelley echoed this passage in many descriptions of ideal retreats for contemplation and love amidst the storm of life.

Besides Godwin and Condorcet, Shelley read Burke, Paine,
presumably Mackintosh, and a number of other writers who
discussed the theory of the Revolution or commented on the
events from a philosophical perspective. Though the attitudes
of Burke and Godwin toward revolutionary disorder were similar, Burke's attack on the principles of the Revolution was both
violent and shrewd, and hence likely to have been salutary for
Shelley.

The conception of liberty as the product of ages of law which
Shelley outlined in *The Mask of Anarchy* strongly resembles
Burke's theory and, since Shelley generally had a richer sense
than Godwin of the subtlety and complexity of human nature,
he may well have learned something about the intricate and
varied character of man in history from Burke.

As an empiricist in the British tradition, Burke objects to
the Enlightenment's abstract view of naked humanity. In his
view the organic growth of institutions reveals "the disposition
of a stupendous wisdom," something human and blooded rather
than an abstraction. The true enemy of mankind becomes the

---

* "It is there that he truly exists with his own kind, in an elysium that
his reason has been able to create for itself, and that his love for humanity
embellishes with the purest joys."

system-loving rationalist who murders to dissect. Burke's judgments against "sophisters, oeconomists, and calculators" seem compatible with Shelley's own attack on "mere reasoners" in "A Defence of Poetry" in the higher name of imagination which grasps the inward poetry in all institutions. Burke saw utilitarians and radicals as creatures with "cold hearts and muddy understandings," who sacrificed personality to mechanical notions of man, who used their thin and cruel reason to strip away the vestures of civilization and sentiment which "cover the defects of our naked shivering nature."[3]

Tom Paine, the principal challenger of Burke's antirevolutionary stand, influenced Shelley in some ways even more than Godwin, for he was closer to the center of revolutionary sentiment and action. Godwin preferred to temporize, to advocate a kind of progressive expediency which would wait for the right degree of enlightenment before pressing cautiously for certain limited reforms. Paine was for written constitutions — open of course to revision as experience taught men better — and action right now in the name of just principles. The object of revolutions, he said, is "a change in the moral condition of governments." He does not much hold with the doctrine of gradualism. Men are capable of understanding their interests and acting accordingly. "It is an age of revolution," he proclaims, "in which every thing may be looked for!" Youth, activity, and progress must be ranged against government, tradition, and prejudice (Paine, I, 347, 400).

Another critic of Burke who objected to the Godwinian thesis of gradual evolutionary progress through limited carefully consolidated advances was Sir James Mackintosh. Mackintosh says that revolutionary enthusiasm is necessary to effective reform. Corruption is too strong and the people too feeble for tranquil, objective reforming to make any headway. "Power vegetates with more vigor after these gentle prunings." Only the shock of revolution can insure progress towards free institutions. Tranquillity watches "only the accumulation of abuse." "Whatever is good ought to be pursued at the moment it is attainable," while the public voice is aroused and irresistible. When men's minds are strengthened and energies are stored, then active expression is certain to occur. Mackintosh felt that the French Revolutionists were "the authors of the greatest attempt that has hitherto been made in the cause of man."[4] His intelligent analysis of the necessity of action in times when men's souls are severely tried may well have influenced Shelley to select promising openings for his revolutionary and missionary activities in Ireland and England when he opened his career in 1811-12 as a preacher of the revived gospel of humanity.

Mary Wollstonecraft, a personal witness of both the early greatness and the bloody climax in France, undoubtedly influenced Shelley's attitude toward revolution. The central observation inspired by her experience is that sudden revolutions are always suddenly overthrown, that licentious freedom inevitably produces the "miseries of anarchy." Mrs. Wollstonecraft, who takes a general determinist and historical-rationalist position, says that not individuals or sudden enthusiasm caused the Revolution but gradual intellectual improvement. Successful revolution had been morally impossible in France because of the condition of the French masses, who had moved from the "most fettering tyranny to an unbridled liberty" (*View of F. R.*, pp. 396, 460, 467). Because the morality of the nation had been destroyed by the manners formed under the old government, the people's liberty was soon converted into tyranny. Hence she maintains the necessity of gradual reform rather than sudden revolution, lest the light, breaking in too rapidly on a benighted people, "overpower the understanding it ought to direct." However, Mrs. Wollstonecraft does not altogether oppose revolution. She maintains that when the upper classes are so degenerate that no remedy less than the horrors of strife can cure the ills of society, it is better for the people to act and repel the system of coercion. The social sufferings from oppression of long duration are worse than violent convulsions, which, "like hurricanes whirling over the face of nature, strip off all its blooming graces." The time does come when the "deleterious plants, which poison the better half of human happiness," must be rooted out (*View of F. R.*, pp. 252, 395, 70–71).

In general, it may be said that, while Shelley's reading would make him fully aware of the need for moderation and gradual progress, he was instructed also to see the necessity for revolution, even violent and convulsive, when circumstances demanded. Balance characterized Shelley's theory of revolution, for he was considerably more impressed than Godwin as to the ultimate necessity of revolution and more acutely aware than his teacher of the grip of reactionary conservatism on the minds of men. He came to see that his main task was to prepare men's minds for understanding their role in the coming conflict.

Having considered Shelley's theoretical stance on revolution, we shall examine the grounding in revolutionary fact which he obtained from his reading, partly to indicate the context for his own observations and writings concerning the Revolution and partly to demonstrate the richly detailed nature of his knowledge. We shall analyze the contents of the specific texts which there is good reason to believe that Shelley read, most of them appearing on one of the reading lists compiled by Mary, or being referred to by Shelley or his friends, or offering probable evidence of having been consulted by or having influenced the poet.

Godwin's pages are strikingly bare of specific comment about the Revolution. Such references as he does make support his theories. He protests against the nonsensical pledge of inviolability which the French made in 1791: "Just broken loose from the thick darkness of an absolute monarchy, they assumed to prescribe lessons of wisdom to all future ages." Godwin, who always stressed rational duties rather than rights, professed an ideal progressive expediency governed by the systematic operations of ever-unfolding reason. He also criticizes the precipitancy of the French in declaring war in 1792 and their apparent notion that war might unify and make healthy the public mind (*Political Justice*, II, 257, 284, 149–150).

The more practical Tom Paine, close to the events he describes and more fully imbued with the ardor for change inspired by the times, offers a full historical commentary on the Revolution. He sees, for example, in contrast to Godwin, that the excesses of the Revolution were essentially due to the "provocative interference of foreign powers" (Paine, II, 683). A good deal of factual material on the Revolution was available to Shelley in the *Rights of Man*. Paine offers an outline of the dramatic events of the Revolution, a constitutional analysis of its documents and procedures, and a point by point refutation of Burke's attacks. Criticizing Burke's failure actually to write about the French Revolution itself, Paine contributes a detailed description of its philosophical and factual background and gives a connected analysis of the progress of the Revolution. He begins by discriminating the contributions of individual philosophes — Montesquieu, Voltaire, Rousseau — and the physiocrats, whose general effect, he says, was to diffuse a spirit of political inquiry. He takes up the chain of fulminating events with the American war. When the French officers and soldiers returned from America, "A knowledge of the practise was then joined to the theory" of the philosophes (Paine, I, 301). He pictures the financial chaos of the country in the 1780's, and describes the calling of the Assembly of Notables and the various ensuing disputes over procedure which led to the decision to convoke the Estates-General. He tries to convey the sense of mounting tension seizing the nation over such issues as the seating of the Three Estates and the claim of the Tiers État to be representative of the whole nation. Then he traces the quickly succeeding crisis of the Tennis Court, the rallying of the counter-revolutionary royalists, and finally the fall of the Bastille and the publication of a Declaration of Rights (which Paine prints and analyzes) by the new and united National Assembly. The *Rights of Man* preceded the decline of the revolutionary fortunes and rise of the Terror regime, but in the *Age of Reason* Paine gives the details of his imprisonment in Luxembourg and describes the sufferings and the suspense he endured. He prints the documents covering his defense of Louis XVI against execution and depicts the scene created by Marat. Paine, then, provided detailed though occasionally incomplete and generally biased source material for a student of the Revolution.

In her *View of the French Revolution* Mrs. Wollstonecraft covers only the first few months of the Revolution in detail but discusses its whole course in her general remarks. In general her commentary is very shrewd, reasonable, and moderate. She defends the principles of the Revolution and deplores the outrages committed under their protection. She gives rather full coverage of the operations of the Assembly in the first few months, analyzes the debates, particularly those on revolutionary finance, and prints long extracts from the major speeches, such as those of her hero Mirabeau. She stresses the duplicity and treachery of the court party and Louis' counselors. Louis himself she treats more kindly. The reasonableness and moderation of her position is clear in her common-sense observation that the constitution framers would have done better to give the nobles some power to balance the preponderance of the popular representation (*View of F. R.*, p. 102). She gives hostile analyses of the vanity, love of intrigue, and other defects of French character which seemed to her to doom the Revolution. Mrs. Wollstonecraft was resident in Paris during 1793, at the time of Louis' execution, the declaration of war, and the guillotining and other excesses of the Terror. Though the prospect of a golden age faded before her eyes with the miscarriage of a particular revolution, she did describe with enthusiasm the great moments of the early Revolution, the unity of military and people at Grenoble, the Tennis Court scene, the overthrow of the Bastille, and the resistance to foreign invasion.

Shelley likely knew the revolutionary *Sketches* of Mary Wollstonecraft's friend Helen Maria Williams. He sought her out when he visited Paris in August 1814. Like Mrs. Wollstonecraft she deplores the system of terror but hopes for the ultimate termination of the French Revolution in a real extension of human liberty. Miss Williams was imprisoned during the Terror as a British subject, while Mary Wollstonecraft, because of her relation with Gilbert Imlay, an American, was suffered to remain at liberty. Her notes convey graphically the confusion of a lover of liberty during the Terror, aware of the abuses, senseless sacrifices, and ironic reversals. Men were "sacrificing to the infernal deities," when they thought they were addressing "vows to the divinities of heaven."[5] She continues to believe that man's best hopes rest with France, though she has learned the necessity of cautious application of ideas to experience. She criticizes a later French constitution for permitting the exercise of a liberty too extensive for the "present state of political opinion" and knowledge.[6]

Another female authority consulted by Shelley was Sydney Owenson, Lady Morgan, author of various popular novels which he early read with enthusiasm, and, of special relevance, a two-volume work entitled *France*, which was published in 1817 and read by Shelley during the *Revolt of Islam* period. Lady Morgan concentrates on the effects, largely beneficial in her mind, of the Revolution, "the greatest political explosion that time has ever witnessed, or history recorded," [7] on contemporary French life. Her book has a special interest because of her penchant for recording all the small talk of the Revolutionary and Napoleonic eras. It is somewhat striking that Shelley should make so few specific references to the personalities and events of the French Revolution when many of his sources were so full and factual, but indeed he created his own revolutionary events, purged of the dross of actuality and factional corruption.

The violent contrasts of lawless viciousness and heroic virtue which the Terror introduced to the Revolution Lady Morgan sees as a natural product of the terrible corruption, degradation, and immorality of the court of Louis XV. Her book is full of anecdotes concerning the major figures of the Revolution, with detailed description of remarkable instances of savagery or heroism. Condorcet is done a great deal of honor, the manner of his death related, and his "noble disinterestedness and heroic devotion" highly praised.[8] Lafayette, one of Shelley's early heroes, is described in a long idealizing sketch as a natural aristocrat of the most exalted kind, uniting "the gay, gallant, fearless spirit of ancient chivalry, to the modern principles of philosophic liberty." [9] Robespierre's painful last day is described in detail. Perhaps of special interest to Shelley were Lady Morgan's portraits of famous women of the Revolution. They teach, she says, "what noble extremes of heroism female nature was capable of attaining." [10]

Probably the most effective parts of the book are the able, high-principled, and liberal essays by Sir T. Charles Morgan, Lady Morgan's husband, which were printed in the appendix. He discusses the legal developments behind the Revolutionary tribunals and points out that trial by jury had replaced the older forms of justice. (Shelley wrote an essay supporting trial by jury.) Not all had been lost by the Reaction, he says. Once the spirit of the age undermines the revived Bourbon dynasty, French judicial rights can be restored to what they were "during the first pure moments of the revolution of 1789." The excesses of the Terror he blames on the coalition of European monarchs, who also made possible Napoleon's continuing dominion. Napoleon, however, is credited with having preserved many of the benefits of the Revolution; in fact, Sir T. Charles asserts, the revolution is far from being at an end. "A complete counter-revolution is impossible." Revolutionary principles remain ardent as "a spirit of liberty, the eldest born offspring of the art of printing, continues to impress indelible changes upon every nation of the civilized world." [11]

The two-volume study by Madame de Staël, *Considérations sur la révolution française*, could not have failed to interest Shelley. He was familiar with her other works of fiction and criticism. He may even have met Mme. de Staël in Switzerland in 1816, for Byron frequently visited her in Coppet while he was spending a good deal of time with Shelley. Her book on the Revolution had been finished early in 1816, and Shelley might possibly have seen it before publication, for Byron, who was at this period being urged by Shelley to consider the French Revolution as the subject for a great poem, recommended Mme. de Staël's history to Murray for publication.[12] However, as Professor Peyre says, there is no real evidence that Shelley ever accompanied Byron to Coppet, and, though he admired her resistance to Napoleon and her literary talents,[13] there is no assurance that he read her account of the Revolution until 1819. Peacock wrote Shelley in November 1818 and asked him if he would like the book,[14] and Mary records that he read it on November 5, 1819 (*Journal*, p. 126).

Mme. de Staël's political ideals were those of the early period of the Revolution. She favors constitutional monarchy, repre-

sentative government, and leadership by an idealized aristocracy. To her mind the French nobles who adopted the cause
of representative government and equality before the law were
the most virtuous, enlightened, and chivalrous of Frenchmen.[15]
She tells of her sufferings both during the Terror and under
Napoleon. She had been an eyewitness to many of the events
she described and had known the leading personalities well. As
was appropriate to the daughter of Necker, the once-popular
Minister of Finance, Mme. de Staël gives special attention to
the financial failures which led up to the convoking of the
Estates-General. She felt that if Necker's plans for ordering the
finances had been adopted, "a just, gradual, and salutary reform" might have avoided the crises that followed.[16] Mme. de
Staël was an observer who could consistently praise the characters of the King and Queen, yet exult in the beautiful spectacle of the "emotion of a whole people" united in the truly
national movement of the taking of the Bastille on that "day
of grandeur," July 14, 1789.[17]

The more strictly biographical and historical commentary
which Shelley consulted was certainly not all of a kind. It
reflected a considerable range of attitudes, hostile, critical, and
enthusiastic toward the Revolution. He read biographical dic-
tionaries, memoirs, and annals. He found surprising nutriment
in the Abbé Barruel's four-volume denunciation of the work
of the philosophes and the societies in creating the French
Revolution. According to Hogg, this work was a favorite of
Shelley's at Oxford. He says that Shelley went through the
four volumes again and again, and even read aloud with "rap-
turous enthusiasm" the accounts of the German Illuminati.[18]
He was poring over it again with Mary and Jane Clairmont
during the 1814 tour of the Continent. They all returned to
Barruel in October, Shelley reading it aloud October 9 and 11,

the "History of the Illuminati" from Barruel on October 11 (*Journal*, pp. 11, 19). Barruel would offer Shelley a sketch of all the reactionary views with which reviving reformers would have to contend — Christian, monarchical, anti-philosophe. Barruel attacks the Encyclopedists and Voltaire, and, in the course of his voluminous efforts to arouse Europe to the danger of the spread of Jacobinical methods for dissolving society, urges the suppression of all possibly dangerous views. Perhaps not much of a factual nature could be extracted from his diatribes, but he did write an animated and interesting book, full of conviction and rancorous criticism of the Voltairean "crushers." With many flourishes of documentation, Barruel traces the worst excesses of the French Revolution back to some note or implication in some letter of Voltaire or his correspondents. He judges, perhaps accurately, that the irreligious upper classes of France were weakened in their struggle against political revolution by their cultivation of Voltaire and their other destroyers. Likely Shelley found incentive in such comment for directing his own works to an aristocratic audience.

Barruel's bibliography of impiety would furnish the poet with an effective arsenal as his book would equip Shelley with knowledge of proven tactics in employing his weapons. The abbé's description of the Revolution as the result of a long, carefully planned conspiracy against church, state, and society stresses the work of factions and scoffs at idealistic notions about the power in the concerted movements of the people (Barruel, IV, 431). The Terror was simply a natural falling out of factions after an illegitimate ascension to power. His analysis would give a young enthusiast like Shelley a clear picture of the extent and power of destruction associated with the Revolution, however differently he might interpret the causes. The emphasis on results achieved by a network of ideas would have been instructive.

The twenty-eight sketches of the leaders of the Revolution written by John Adolphus feature lengthy citations from documents in order, he says, to permit regicides to witness against themselves (read November 15, 1814, *Journal*, p. 26). Brissot and the other Girondists are seen as republicans desiring war to purify the cause and to hasten the complete abolition of royalty. Lafayette is described as an ambitious egotist without great abilities, who was eliminated during the first surges of Terror by the Brissotins as a devotee of limited monarchy. His role at the Champ de Mars massacre is described. Mirabeau's death is seen as France's greatest misfortune and the beginning of anarchy. The importance to the Revolution of Tom Paine, whom Adolphus describes as a wandering Cain renounced by all men, is developed. His defense of Louis XVI in the Convention is cited (compare the defense of the despot by Laon in the *Revolt of Islam*), and the propaganda warfare to which Paine contributed following Burke's *Reflections* is analyzed. The dramatic moments of the Revolution are recreated, as, for example, Louvet's challenge and denunciation of Robespierre as an unmotivated monster and temporary Messiah.[19] Sensational atrocity stories are collected. The September massacres are described in detail. Activities of the clubs and the nature of the fetes, two features of the Revolution that especially interested Shelley, are frequently discussed. In general, Shelley might have found some leavening in Adolphus for his own intellectualist proclivities; clearly something more than ideas and impersonal forces were at work in the Revolution.

From *A Journal during a Residence in France*, by Dr. John Moore, the poet would get some sense of the day-to-day experience of living in the midst of the most violent period of a revolution. Shelley read it aloud, December 3, 1814, and was reading it again two days later. Mary took it up right after him

(*Journal*, pp. 28–29). Moore's journal entries begin on August 4, 1792, and end in mid-December 1792, but he adds a record of events up to the death of the King. He is mainly sympathetic to the ideal objectives of the Revolution, but repelled by the crimes and atrocities. One should approve 1789 and condemn June 20 and August 10, 1792, he suggests. The Revolution was justified in France by the "abominable system of oppression" under which the French people labored.[20]

The book performs the practical service of identifying and evaluating the contributions of the main actors in the drama. The most interesting and relevant debates in the National Assembly, the clubs, and the Commune are reviewed fully with ample quotations. Moore's work has a special value perhaps in re-creating a sense of the tone and atmosphere of daily living in periods of peculiar fear, doubt, and tension. He describes conversations with people in the streets of Paris and tries to convey the manners and feelings of ordinary folk rather than merely record public events. When he focuses his attention on the famous men, he views them intimately. His judgments of their deeds are linked with descriptions of them in action. He also takes the reader to the machinations behind the large public scene to show the alignment of personalities and the development of situations such as led to the deposition of the King, the murdering of the Swiss guards, and the massacres in the prisons. Animated descriptions of the crucial actions are imbued with a strong sense of the pathos and the energies developed.

Moore arrived at a balanced view of the achievements of the Revolution. He saw much to deplore. The Revolution had attained its original objectives but had sacrificed the spirit of order, tranquillity, and lawfulness needed to consolidate its gains. Many had come to feel that the old despotism was preferable to the later anarchy and carnage. Perhaps, Moore judged, if the nobles had remained to exercise their useful moderating influence, the disasters might have been avoided.[21] Shelley must have read the book sympathetically, for Moore was a shrewd observer, who held on to his ideals while lamenting their abuse. Perhaps he taught Shelley a little pity for the detested kings and priests who are shown paying a cruel price for the old days of corrupt ease and splendor.

Two of the works on Shelley's list have more the quality of romances than of serious studies of the Revolution, but the romantic element is the romance of truth, the human fear, hatred, and joy expressed in the alternating despair and enthusiasm of particularly gifted individuals who played significant roles in the great drama. *Mémoires d'un détenu* (read August 25, 1816, *Journal*, p. 61) describes the fourteen-month imprisonment of a Girondist sympathizer named Honoré Riouffe. Riouffe reveals the Jacobin Terrorists as poorly prepared leaders of the moment, who were distracted from philosophic and legislative good faith by their egoism, lack of knowledge of human nature, and saturation in an atmosphere of systematic illusion.[22] He describes how he was seized in Bordeaux and brutally transported back to Paris where he was imprisoned with the great Girondists and other potential victims of the guillotine who had been herded together for the sacrificial butchery. Riouffe watched them go out bravely to their deaths, he says, like four thousand Socrates.

Louvet de Couvrai was a moderate and Girondist. Shelley read him in 1814 apparently, along with Mary, who then began a "Life of Louvet" (*Journal*, p. 25). His specialty was the *thèse de complot*. He thought the Commune and the Mountain were plotting to re-establish royalty in France. This rather common suspicion that the Jacobins were disguised royalists or Orleanists may have been in Shelley's mind in describing the quick return of royalty in *The Revolt of Islam*. Louvet does succeed in creating the atmosphere and caliber of incident characteristic of fiction in his presentation of the Revolution as a suspenseful drama. He unites two themes, the Revolution and the pangs of separated lovers, in an account of his exciting life as a fugitive from the Jacobins during the Girondist proscription, ever close to being taken, sustained by high principles, the beauties of nature, and thoughts of his beloved Lodoiska. As a novelist, journalist, and lover, and a republican and revolutionary who remained faithful to his principles when other French republicans were being converted to royalism by the Terror, Louvet would have had a strong appeal, and the romance element in his narrative influenced Shelley's story of Laon and Cythna in *The Revolt of Islam.*

Louvet covers the period of defeat, despair, doubt, and fear before the fall of Robespierre. We are conducted by the narrator through various provinces, and we learn incidentally something about the extent of the Revolution and the network of relationships and affiliations with Paris. Actually, fact and romance are nicely balanced in Louvet's work. He describes with enthusiasm the burgeoning national energy produced in the great moments of the Revolution, but he also offers considerable insight into practical affairs. The alignment of factions is carefully analyzed. Louvet also distinguishes between the "people" and the masses, "la foule idiote" who supported Robespierre and the Terror. Like Shelley, Louvet was a somewhat aristocratic republican who could accept a vision of what men may be but was less receptive to man as he is.* As he said, after

---

* Shelley told Hogg that he was above "the bigotry of commonplace republicanism" (December 3, 1812, and February 7, 1813, *Letters,* I, 335, 352). "Perhaps you will say that my Republicanism is proud; it certainly is far removed from pot-house democracy, and knows with what smile to hear the servile applause of an inconsistent mob." Shelley said that his ideal Republic would closely approach and copy the best elements of the old "aristocracy of chivalry and refinement."

recounting various disasters, "oublions la foule égoiste, et ne nous souvenons que des héros." * True revolutionary virtue is attained only by a few. Like other republicans Louvet pays the standard tributes to Charlotte Corday, who rid the world of the deformity Marat, and to Mme. Roland.[23]

Less flattering views of Shelley's revolutionary heroines were read by the poet in the *Female Revolutionary Plutarch,* an anonymous three-volume collection of biographies and essays about women who figured prominently in the French Revolution. The collection is mainly a gossip book, both violently antirevolutionary and anti-Napoleonic, and it is inscribed to the revered memory of Marie Antoinette. Shelley apparently amused himself with it in the troubled November of 1814, for he is recorded as reading it aloud on November 20 and 21 (*Journal*, p. 26). Biographical sketches are provided of Josephine, Marie Antoinette, Mme. de Staël, Mme. Tallien, Mme. Roland, and various other republican, royalist, or imperialist ladies. There are articles on the guillotine, on female clubs, and on revolutionary religions — all supported by numerous letters, speeches, and other testimonies. A long succession of tales of the brutal guillotining of virtuous young women, devoted to their husbands, brothers, or fathers is featured. The massacres in the prisons are described with a special and somewhat suspicious zest for the details of butchery and vengeful cruelty. The debauched citizenry dance like cannibals in the blood around the guillotine. Prisoners, we are assured, were nourished by the work of the guillotine, dishes of "ci-devant." All the aristocratic ladies are seen as chaste heroines, while all women of the other party, no matter how slight their revolutionary tincture, are described as shockingly immoral if not as known whores. Mme. de Staël was an ugly and infamous profligate. Mme. Roland was at best an insignificant person

---

* "Let us forget the selfish crowd, and let us remember only the heroes."

killed by her vanity, at worst a salacious intriguer. Englishmen who might nourish hopes for reform are warned against innovation and reminded that 18,613 French citizens, reformers and reformed, died at the guillotine.[24]

Another attack on revolutionary procedures, if not principles, was available to Shelley in a careful work of scholarship, Bryan Edwards' three-volume *History of the West Indies*. The bulk of Edwards' book is devoted to uninflammatory matters such as the geography, topography, industry, and early history of the West Indies. Shelley is recorded as having read it during December 1814 and January 1815. Mary's notes suggest a rather careful and thorough study (*Journal*, pp. 32–34). It was probably the third volume which engaged most of Shelley's considerable attention, for it offers a full account of the savage Negro revolt in Santo Domingo in 1791. Over one hundred thousand slaves and freed mulattoes rose up against the greatly outnumbered colonists and committed unexampled cruelties because, Edwards claims, men like the Abbé Grégoire and Robespierre in remote Paris had incautiously urged schemes of liberation and progressive improvement. Edwards supports his attack on abstract visionaries with strongly imagined scenes of mass murder, savage butchery, ferociously broken bodies. Such are the results of "the monstrous folly of suddenly emancipating barbarous men." Men too readily create visionary systems which inflame the imagination and introduce a "spirit of subversion and innovation." They find too late that the worst of governments is preferable to primitive anarchy. The abstract attacks on slavery made the slaves and mulattoes so restless and seditious that a fire was eventually kindled "which nothing but human blood can extinguish."[25] One important section of Edwards' book is devoted to the early career of Toussaint L'Ouverture. Shelley kept the West Indian situation in mind, for in his account of world-wide revolutionary advances in the

"Philosophical View of Reform," he considered progress there.

Rabaut St. Étienne's volume in the *Précis historique* made available to Shelley a systematic, practically day-by-day presentation and analysis of the development of the Revolution by a writer interested in the complications of revolutionary finance and the details of legislation and constitutional theory. Rabaut emphasizes the role of the National Assembly. He analyzes the economic plight of France which created the Revolution, describes the injustices of taxation and the expenses of the court, and, in short, reveals the build-up of an impossible situation whose tensions could be relieved only by revolution. He is as fond as Shelley of stormcloud imagery in tracing the workings of change.

He sees the Revolution as a practical, working realization of long-held hopes. His book was written before the Terror, and Rabaut's story and his useful chronological table of events go very little beyond the establishment, on September 2, 1791, of national fetes to conserve the memory of the Revolution. However, all of the principal events of the great early years of the Revolution are objectively described — the summoning of the Estates-General, the Tennis Court fracas, and Mirabeau's celebrated challenge. The famine march on Versailles, the gradual arming of the popular will by despair, the preparations for the taking of the Bastille — these are circumstantially narrated with special attention to the ability and will of the people, their great enthusiasm for the cause, their unity and power at the decisive moments. Rabaut celebrates the sense of a new public will, a united nation, happy and free, which emerged after the fall of the Bastille, and he claims that the overly publicized excesses resulted from popular fear, despair, and doubt over the chances of obtaining justice from the treacherous royalists. Force was their only weapon against duplicity. The real beginnings of antimonarchical sentiment are traced to the flight and recapture of the King, now generally considered, this author comments, to have abandoned the nation. Rabaut ends on a strong note of hope.[26] The French Revolution will succeed because "elle est l'ouvrage des siècles, de la nature, de la raison et de la force." Her history is "un recueil de prophéties." *

Rabaut St. Étienne did not live to see the success he hoped for. His capture and death by the guillotine were described by Jean Charles Lacretelle, who completed in a quite different spirit the history of the Revolution which Rabaut St. Étienne had begun. Shelley read the combined work in 1816–17. He studied it for ten days (*Journal*, pp. 65, 78–79, 81) at the time he was working on *The Revolt of Islam*. Lacretelle, writing after Napoleon's rise, calls the Revolution an interregnum.[27] He offered the poet a great deal of philosophic commentary, mostly antagonistic to the Revolution, but he also gave full coverage of parties and personalities. Like Moore, he writes much about the issues, struggles, and debates in the National Assembly, and he covers more extensively than any other of Shelley's sources the revolutionary situation in the departments. His record of events is more circumstantial than in the other books Shelley read. While he was writing *The Revolt of Islam*, the poet could consult remarkably full and lively descriptions of June 20, August 10, the trials and executions of the King and Queen, the September Massacres, as well as detailed accounts of the later history of the Revolution up to 1799 and Napoleon's assumption of power. Lacretelle was interested in causes and motives. He shows how the Constituent Assembly paved the way for August 10 and what he called the triumph of savagery and mediocrity. He analyzes the defects of policy and temperament of the Girondists. He explains how the ap-

---

* "it is the work of centuries, of nature, of reason, and of strength." Her history is "a collection of prophecies."

proach of the foreign armies and the civil war in the Vendée brought about the September Massacres. He describes how the seat of power shifted from the Assembly to the Jacobins and the Commune, how attempts to stop the progress of tyranny merely redoubled the violence. After reading this dramatic account of the fear, hatred, and anarchy of the Terror, Shelley must have understood better Napoleon's rise and his role in the Revolution.

It is clear, after examining the various books dealing both directly and indirectly with the French Revolution that he read, that the poet had available accurate, detailed, analytic, and even quite sophisticated sources of information and insight, though very little that he read was free of bias of one kind or another. In view of his considerable reading, it may be thought surprising that there is no great wealth of detailed reference to men and events of the revolutionary era in Shelley's writings.* Perhaps he neither heeded nor saw "what things

* One may note, however, the stress on direct testimony in Mary's *Journal*. They interviewed their voiturier (March 22, 1818) about the old revolutionary times in Lyon, a center of civil strife, mass executions, and reprisals, which Shelley had recently read about in Lacretelle's history. Various revolutionary and Napoleonic events and associations are recorded in the *Journal*. Shelley noted (August 19, 1814) that Napoleon and his guards had slept at the same inn as they in Guignes, only a week or so before. They commented on the war-ravaged country they passed through, and they noted testimony concerning the unpopularity of Napoleon.

Some more immediate of Shelley's connections to the Revolution may also be cited. Hogg mentioned the large number of French émigrés Shelley met at the homes of Mme. Boinville and John Shelley (Wolfe ed., II, 79). Professor Peyre thought Shelley owed more to the conversations of Mme. Boinville than to reading books about the French Revolution (Peyre, p. 50). There is a good account of the Boinville circle in Cameron, *The Young Shelley*, pp. 218–221. Later, in Italy, Dr. Vaccà, Shelley's physician, may well have imparted some fresh feeling for the drama of the Revolution. The activities of Vaccà, who is said to have taken part in the storming of the Bastille, are described in H. R. Angeli, *Shelley and His Friends in Italy* (London, 1911), p. 111. Mary Shelley called him "a great republican" (*Letters*, ed. Jones, I, 95).

they be" as he fed his imagination on the "shapes that haunt thought's wildernesses" (*Prometheus Unbound*, I, 742, 746). There may be little reason why he should make numerous notes on the French Revolution since it had become history and because he was more concerned with its effects than with the details of events. Nor should it be argued that his passion for abstract ideas would weaken his grasp of revolutionary fact, for the poet observed closely and wrote considerably about the complexities of English problems during the active decade of his adult life.

Shelley did write about the Revolution of course. Minor references and allusions are numerous, and a few times he considered the full course of the Revolution in reviews of some length. Moreover, he did travel through France, before and after Waterloo. In the bizarre letter which he wrote to Harriet during his elopement with Mary, he described their passage (during the period in 1814 between Elba and the Hundred Days) through French territories blasted by the indescribable desolation of the war (August 13, 1814, *Letters*, I, 392). On a visit to Versailles in 1816, the tourists noted various Revolutionary landmarks and recalled the dramatic events. The Shelleys were curious to see where the King and Queen appeared before the Paris mob, and they tried to discover the chambers where the rioters found the King. Shelley said, "The vacant rooms of this palace imaged well the hollow show of monarchy." Examining a book depicting the splendors of the decayed past he came to comprehend "the present desolation of France, the fury of the injured people and all the horrors to which they abandoned themselves, stung by their long sufferings" (*Journal*, pp. 62–63). It was shortly after making these observations that Shelley recommended the French Revolution to Byron as "the master theme of the epoch," a fit subject for epic treatment (September 8, 1816, *Letters*, I, 504).

Shelley began to explain the Revolution in his earliest writings. In his Irish pamphlet, the "Proposals for an Association," he said that when the French, long degraded by despotism, first learned the novel principles of equality in America, they vented their anger violently on the "monopolizers of earth." Unfortunately they had too soon revealed how far they were from being ready for the state of equal law "which proceeds from consummated civilization" (Clark ed., p. 67). This judgment, closely similar in basic content to his later ones, is the first product of Shelley's study of the French Revolution. During the following years he read many of the books and pamphlets analyzed in this chapter. Having known Godwin and studied his writings with greater care, having traveled and speculated, having come into close association with the liberals and journalists and essayists who were working to keep revolutionary hopes alive, Shelley reached a perspective on the Revolution which seems both mature and consistent.

In the Preface to *The Revolt of Islam*, Shelley reviewed the whole course of the Revolution in order to determine, he said, whether the old ardor and hopes might be renewed in this chastened and wiser world. The fall of the Revolution, he writes, was caused by the lack of correspondence between existing knowledge and institutions. Burdened by the weight of the past as the French were, the expectations of "unmingled good" were excessive. The slave cannot become a free man overnight. Lady Morgan similarly commented that the terror and carnage of the French Revolution taught a lesson in the necessity of gradual training in the exercise of freedom. Much time must pass and "many revolutions" occur before the stains of slavery are erased and the freeman can "forget that he had once been a slave." [28] France attempted to realize a social goal which could result only from centuries of long, systematic progress. When this exaggerated optimism was swamped by dark realities, gloom and misanthropy replaced "sanguine eagerness for good." The mistakes of the French seemed to Shelley to be the best proof of the necessity of reform, and now that the panic caused by the Terror was "gradually giving place to sanity," the time had come for men of good will taught by experience to revive the spirit of reform (Hutchinson ed., p. 33).

In the "Philosophical View of Reform" Shelley once more described the tyranny which uprose as the product of ages of monarchical poison. When men long enslaved revolt, they reveal the lessons of revenge and hatred learned under their old masters. Not the danger of change but the necessity of it is thus demonstrated (Clark ed., p. 235). Tom Paine too had attacked the notion that the Revolution in itself produced the outrages against humanity: "They learn it from the governments they live under; and retaliate the punishments they have been accustomed to behold." The cruel spectacles of the *ancien régime* had destroyed feelings of tenderness and excited those of hatred and revenge. Paine, like other dedicated supporters of the cause, interprets the outrages and excesses as the clearest indications of the necessity of the Revolution. "The moral principle of revolutions is to instruct, not to destroy" (Paine, I, 266–267; II, 587–588).

Very little that Shelley wrote is without some reference to the French Revolution. He created ideal revolutions which reflect a social vision instructed by his study of the defects of the real revolution. He also authored works which have a more direct and immediate relationship. Shelley wrote a *Declaration of Rights,* which, according to Cameron and the Julian editors, is indebted to French declarations of August 1789 and April 1793 (*The Young Shelley*, p. 152; Julian, VIII, 298). Closer to Paine and the French, at least at this stage, and imbued with greater faith in the present powers of reason and human nature, he did not share Godwin's hostility to declarations of rights and institutions. Shelley, too, was the author of a tyrannicidal version of the *Marseillaise*.

While Shelley was first corresponding with Godwin, in January 1812, before the mission to Ireland, he was working on a novel, which he called *Hubert Cauvin*, designed "to exhibit the cause of the failure of the French Revolution." He told Elizabeth Hitchener that the work described the "state of morals and opinions in France" during the latter years of the monarchy, and would focus on some of the "leading passions of the human mind." He claimed to have written two hundred pages (January 2, 1812, *Letters*, I, 218), and a few days later he expected to have it finished within a month. At Keswick, Shelley argued the issue of morality vs. expediency with Southey, and in a letter of the time to Elizabeth Hitchener, he associated his novel with the subject of the debate. *Hubert Cauvin* was to demonstrate the influence of expediency, insincerity, and mystery in producing the "violence and blood" of the French Revolution (January 7, 1812, *Letters*, I, 223). Probably the book dramatized the struggles of an ideal revolutionary hero much like Laon in *The Revolt of Islam* with corrupt, practical, and worldly men. These were Shelley's ruling passions: to discover why the French Revolution failed and to find ways of correcting the flaws in man, society, and programs for improvement which caused such failures.[29]

Here was the central dilemma for a reformer of the time. Why did the French Revolution swerve from its ideal path and convert its energies into Terror and militarism? Was it not dangerous to advocate social and political changes that might lead to similar bloodshed, anarchy, and ultimately tyranny? As Mary Wollstonecraft's book told him, most of the revolutionaries were motivated by selfishness. They worked for "pay and plunder," while spouting of patriotism and progress. There were men of talent available; but in the "wretched struggles of selfishness," which disfigured the Revolution, no one appeared of transcendent worth, animated by a pure love of country and humanity, and capable of the systematic management which might bring "pacific progress" to the Revolution through "moderation and reciprocity of concession" (*View of F. R.*, pp. 293, 301–302). Shelley, accepting the necessity of revolution, decided that the great need was to produce such men, either, as he first concluded, by philanthropic associations, or by a poetry which would help equip the natural aristocrats of society with imagination, the agency and expression of all genuine social and moral improvement.

He considered the objections to the Revolution which came up in the course of the great pamphleteering debates of the period, and sanctioned some of them, at least in part, by modifying his own views of immediate action. He agreed with Godwin's apology for the Terror that it is "to despotism that anarchy is indebted for its sting" (*Political Justice*, III, 188). In his revolutionary epics the hero learns through suffering. Prometheus' conversion is gradual, for Shelley had learned from the French Revolution that change for the good must fail when the will is not "morally prepared for it." [30] Furthermore, the genuine defects of human nature which projectors of Utopias overlook are laid bare by the shocks of revolution. Parties become more disputatious in times of revolution, causes for dispute multiply, and the manners of the disputants sharpen disagreement and hatred. Ultimately the independence of the citizenry is severely threatened, and the cool operations of reason are suspended. The vision of a society of sages governed by virtue dims. Shelley came to see that tyrant and victim are capable of changing places. Man in a "reciprocal world of evil, giving and receiving," loses his visionary identity.[31]

Shelley attempted to anchor his visions to the bedrock of

human nature by continuing his early announced study of the "leading passions of the human mind," to examine the corruption within men — their insincerity, inhumanity, and love of violence and mystery, which wrecked the Revolution (to Elizabeth Hitchener, January 2 and 7, 1812, *Letters*, I, 218, 223). Hatred and revenge were the passions that had ruined the prospects of the French, and with them, as Shelley affirmed in his long poetic studies of the character of the true revolutionary hero, true freedom can never coexist. Movements imbued by the spirit of ideal good and brotherly love may degenerate into their opposites. The books about the Revolution which Shelley read generally confirmed this fact. Having perceived the grounds for despair, the poet did not avoid the issue, but rather dramatized its pathos in his presentation of a love followed evermore by a desolation. In fact, he emphasized in *The Revolt of Islam* and *Prometheus Unbound* the suddenness of this conversion from one state into the other.

Other specific explanations of the eclipse of the ideal revolution also known to Shelley probably moderated or informed his position. He certainly was influenced by the objections to revolutionary change of Malthus, whose theories seemed to undercut radically the optimistic visions of the millenarians. Shelley made several attacks on Malthus' views, but ultimately acknowledged his acuteness. Malthus explained the failure of the Revolution and the falling out of its factions as caused by ever-present poverty. Once an established government has been destroyed and it is seen that human misery due to natural shortages is not appreciably diminished, resentment naturally falls upon the successors to power.[32] Clearly Shelley accepted the view that too much had been expected from the Revolution, that hopes had been pitched too high and thus despair had come too easily over excesses blamed on the alterations it introduced. He spoke early of "overstrained hopes of liberty" which the issue of the Revolution had too readily extinguished ("Proposals for an Association of Philanthropists," Clark ed., p. 67). Without accepting the conservative denunciations of any interference with traditional forms, he granted readily enough the contention that the French were too immature for a republic. His principal sources confirmed the charge. One of these sources may be cited at length.

Mme. de Staël, whom Shelley apparently read rather late, to be sure, reviewed nearly every conceivable cause for the fall of the Revolution. She stresses the misery, ignorance, and resulting lack of moral feeling of the people. The French Revolution, like any successful revolution, had to begin in the higher orders of society because the people were incapable of mounting such a movement; but those orders must maintain control and not be sidetracked by "philosophic fanaticism." The Girondists especially had failed in their responsibility by permitting themselves to be governed by factional hatreds; they despised both the constitutional monarchists and the Jacobins. In the turmoil a way was made for the intervention of the undisciplined and ferocious lower orders to be felt. Instead of taking advantage of the rare "moment of happiness and power," the enlightened members of the upper classes had let the reins slip insensibly from their hands.[33] Equality was permitted to replace liberty as the true object of the Revolution once the people achieved ascendancy. Paris was allowed to dominate the affairs of the Republic.

Perhaps expectations had been pitched too high. The thinkers of the Enlightenment, inexperienced in practical politics and too abstract in their views of human nature and social change, had kindled the lively imaginations of the French in this novel field of politics where they foresaw "countless advantages" to be gained. Unfortunately the early leaders lacked the practical sagacity, energy, unity, and discipline of the Jacobins, who were "organized as a government more than the government itself."[34] Once the generation of the Revolution had been stricken with fear and despair by the terrible civil disorder, they were no longer capable of establishing freedom and just institutions to curb the masses depraved under former institutions. Energy was plentifully available, but not the virtues essential to true liberty. "Other virtues can be only the gradual result of institutions which have lasted long enough to form a public spirit."[35]

Shelley's principal informants, those who influenced him most, did not draw back from the cause because of the violence it entailed. He probably learned more in these matters from studying the Revolution and witnessing the results of reaction than he did from reading or listening to Godwin, forever the opponent of any change not demanded by reason. Maturity and greater practical and political sagacity must have made the poet aware that violence may not be altogether avoidable when reactionary views were solidly entrenched and the habits of despotism were continuing to corrupt the capacities for improvement. Rabaut St. Étienne had expressed the belief that revolutions of opinion are always bloody, since there are always strongly entrenched interests to be combated. Normally truth operates very slowly, but in times of conflict, of intellectual and emotional excitement, it is possible to make much more rapid progress.[36] Shelley's own excursions into practical reform seem to have been motivated by this sense of the need to seize the moments of crisis which arouse hope and energy. The people will not revolt, said Mackintosh, until their resentment is uncontrollable and the great passions essential to successful revolt are generated, a state "too violent to subside in a moment into serenity and submission."[37] Paine forgave the French people for his sufferings by returning to the Convention: "It is not because right principles have been violated that they are to be abandoned" (Paine, I, 516). The example of France should encourage reform, not repress it. This seems to have been the lesson Shelley ultimately drew from the Revolution. It was more than an instructive failure. It had created and nourished hopes that could never die. His study of its course confirmed him in his mission to humanity. He accepted the idea of revolution and turned his attention to the task of rectifying its errors through his own writings.

III

On His Own Times

Shelley did not dedicate his powers to the cause of political justice simply because Godwin, Paine, and other philosophers of the Revolution had called him to his duties as man and citizen. He read much, and his readings gave purpose and unity and intensity to his natural characteristics — an extreme sensitivity of imagination, a hatred of oppression and injustice, and an overpowering impulse to self-expression. Nevertheless, his poetic visions are anchored in his views of events and conditions of contemporary society. The creed of revolt which he had acquired from study was confirmed by his observations of conditions in England and on the Continent between 1810 and 1822. He believed strongly though not always consistently in the power of environment to shape character. To comprehend his schemes of reform and his moral and political ideals more fully, it is useful to examine what he reacted against and what form this reaction took.

England was at war with France most of the time from 1793 to 1815, at war against the danger of spreading revolutionary doctrines as well as against French imperialism. The horror inspired by French turbulence and bloodshed created a general and irrational fear of all change. Since reform in France had led to a republic and massacre, proposals for reform in England were interpreted in the light of this revelation. Talk about a juster representation should be checked by a glance across the Channel. The French Revolution had also been at first conducted by moderate men, men devoted to progress and enlightenment, but they had been unable to control and restrain the blind forces of anarchy which had been unleashed when the ancient order of law, tradition, and precedent was swept away.

French terrorism turned the English against reform. After the French Revolution the poorer classes no longer seemed a passive power: they were dreaded as a naturally discontented leviathan that was just learning its strength. The art of politics no longer seemed the art of keeping the attachment of people who cherished their customs and religion and the general setting of their lives. It was the art of subduing "a vast population destitute of the traditions and restraints of a settled and conservative society, dissatisfied with its inevitable lot and ready for disorder and blind violence." The man without property had no stake in society. He belonged to a new class crowded into factories and mill towns and bound to society only by the cash nexus. Two revolutions had come together. "The French Revolution had transformed the minds of the ruling classes, and the Industrial Revolution had convulsed the world of the working classes." [1] Public opinion was colored by the dread of any change which panic-stricken prejudice could term foreign or Jacobinical, and the moderate, generally practical aspirations of English reformers were effectively repressed for a decade.

The English government initiated a policy of domestic repression in 1793 which, though generally popular, was bitterly opposed by a small remnant of the old Whig party which soon earned the name of English "Jacobins" by opposition to the war and the government's repressive measures at home. They were led by Charles James Fox, hailed by Shelley in "An Address to the Irish" as a great and good man, the "friend of freedom" (Clark ed., p. 48). Charles Howard, Duke of Norfolk, was the devoted supporter of Fox, and patron of Shelley's father. Shelley's interest in the cause of the moderate French revolutionaries would not necessarily have been discouraged at Field Place. Norfolk's liberalism, however, did not weaken his attention to his own extensive borough interests. In 1790 Timothy Shelley had been returned to Parliament from Horsham. The election had been disputed by interests opposed to those of the Duke of Norfolk, and the investigating committee ruled that Timothy Shelley and an associate had not been duly elected. Thomas Charles Medwin, the Duke of Norfolk's steward, had rejected legal votes and received illegal votes for the sitting members. Timothy Shelley later (1802–1818) represented the borough of New Shoreham. The franchise of that borough had been opened in 1777 to about 1200 freeholders after an investigation of the formerly corrupt electorate, and, according to Oldfield, "the borough has since been represented by independent country gentlemen, and every election has been conducted with constitutional decorum." [2]

Norfolk, who had never relinquished his design to secure Horsham to his interests, finally succeeded in buying out the opposition, and thus became sole proprietor with the right to nominate the returning members. Hence, when Shelley was sent down from University College, the Duke was ready to assist in his rehabilitation by placing him in the House of Commons as member for Horsham. Shelley, however, indignantly rejected a proposal which might shackle his mind and his vote. [3] Godwin's *Political Justice* had become his gospel, and the gospel contained this text:

There is a degree of virtue which would probably render me disinclined to fill many eminent stations, to be a great lawyer, a great senator, or a great minister. The functions of these situations in the present state of mankind are of so equivocal a nature, that a man, whose moral views are in the highest degree sublime, will perhaps find in himself little forwardness to exercise them. He will perhaps conceive that in a private station, unincumbered with engagements, unwarped by the sinister motives that high office will not fail to present, he may render more lasting services to mankind. (III, 329)

Shelley rejected an active career in politics. The disciple of the "religion of humanity" could best arouse his brethren to a consciousness of the power for good in the human will by the diffusion of knowledge. This decision did not imply, however, any indifference to political reform.

The reform movement had revived in 1807 after the long years of the anti-Jacobin reaction. The election by Westminster of Sir Francis Burdett, an ardent parliamentary reformer, gave the reformers what they most needed, "a fearless spokesman in the House of Commons, a leader around whom advanced reformers might gather outside the walls of Parliament."[4] Burdett thoroughly justified the hopes of his supporters by taking a prominent part in all reform discussions in Parliament. In January 1809 he seconded Wardle's motion for an inquiry into the transactions which brought the Duke of York, the commander of the army, into temporary disgrace. The Duke's mistress was said to have received various sums of money, particularly from army officers, for exerting her influence on him. The case is said to have given the reform cause a powerful stimulus.[5] Timothy Shelley voted with the minority against the Duke.[6] In June 1809 Burdett made a celebrated speech on parliamentary reform in which he set forth a moderate program. The popular enthusiasm for Burdett is reflected in the second poem of *Victor and Cazire*, dated April 30, 1810:

Then to politics turn, of Burdett's reformation,
One declares it would hurt, t'other better the nation,
Will ministers keep? sure they've acted quite wrong,
The burden this is of each morning-call song.

The *Wandering Jew* was dedicated to Burdett as homage to "the active virtues by which both his public and private life is so eminently distinguished" (Julian, IV, 349). In January 1812, Shelley assured Elizabeth Hitchener that he could demonstrate for reform in Ireland with safety, because Burdett after all had escaped being punished by the Prime Minister Perceval (*Letters*, I, 221–222). His esteem for Burdett did not later diminish. He put his name at the top of the list of people to whom he wanted copies of his 1817 reform pamphlet to be sent as "from the author." Mary told Leigh Hunt late in 1820 that Prince Mavrocordatos had related to them some infamous tidings of English conduct in Greece which they would like to have publicized by Grey Bennett or Sir Francis Burdett in order to give another knock to "this wretched system of things." [7]

Shelley's earliest criticisms of society are the fruits of his readings in abstract revolutionary philosophy. "I have been led into reasonings which make me *hate* more & more the existing establishment of every kind. I gasp when I think of plate & balls & tables & kings" (to Elizabeth Hitchener, December 26, 1811, *Letters*, I, 213). Commenting on the Prince Regent's fete in June of 1811, Shelley declared that such heartless expense was the prelude to a revolution, "the natural death of all great commercial empires" (to Elizabeth Hitchener, *Letters*, I, 110). In February of 1812 Shelley sailed to Ireland. Believing that the Irish crisis might be the beginning of a revolutionary revival in Europe, he wrote and distributed two pamphlets denouncing English misrule and discussing prospects for reform in Ireland. Apparently he thought to capitalize on the moral and revolutionary energies and hopes aroused by the lesser goals of Catholic emancipation and repeal of the Act of Union. On February 28, he spoke at a gathering of friends of Catholic emancipation, apparently stressing rather too much the need for emancipation from Catholicism to please his auditors, but on the whole making a good impression by his enthusiasm. In one newspaper account of this address Shelley was highly praised: "To this gentleman Ireland is much indebted, for selecting *her* as the theatre of his first attempts in this holy work of human regeneration" (Julian, VII, 320, from *Weekly Messenger*, Dublin, March 7, 1812).

Why did Shelley select this particular time and place to introduce himself to the public as an active political radical? At Field Place he would doubtless have heard much of the problems of Ireland, for Catholic emancipation stood first in the Whig political program from 1807 to 1812, and was consistently championed by them in Parliament. The Whig position on this problem was one of the factors which kept them out of office until 1829, for Catholic emancipation was not popular with the general public. Timothy Shelley's patron, the Duke of Norfolk, had been a Catholic, and even after he left the church he had urged emancipation in the House of Lords.[8]

Clearly Shelley knew something about Irish disabilities and was prepared to sympathize with the emancipationists, even though his indoctrination in Godwinism had led him to conceive of far nobler aspirations. The Irish campaign was his first opportunity to work for the revolution after his own emancipation from parental rule, but in fact, he went to Ireland at a propitious time. In 1800 the British government had secured firm control of Irish affairs by the Act of Union. Pitt reconciled Irish Catholics to the Union by letting it be known that union would be followed by a measure of Catholic emancipation. The obdurate opposition of George III, however, prevented Pitt from carrying out his plan. Before the Union it was obvious that to open Parliament and the higher offices of the state to the Roman Catholics in Ireland, where they were three-fourths of the constituent body, must eventually result in a Catholic Parliament and the end of the ascendancy of the Anglican establishment. But after the Union there seemed to be no reason other than the King's obstinacy for withholding emancipation. The pro-emancipation forces had gained steadily in strength and more than once seemed on the verge of attaining their goal. Every year Parliament was petitioned by the Catholics. In 1812 a majority of the House of Commons voted favorably for the petition, and in the Lords a similar motion lost by a single vote.

In short, it was widely believed at the time Shelley sailed to Ireland that Catholic emancipation must soon be granted. In March some limitations imposed on the powers of the Regent would expire, and he had generally shown himself to be friendly to the political hopes of the Whigs, the pro-emancipation party. Thus, there was justification for Shelley's declaration in his first pamphlet: "The present is a crisis which of all others is the most valuable for fixing the fluctuation of public feeling." Shelley seems, however, to have shared the doubts of many observers in the Prince's fidelity to the Whig's expectations, now that he was no longer counseled by that "great and good man Charles Fox" ("An Address to the Irish," Clark ed., pp. 48, 58). He of course was less interested in the constitutional crisis than in the larger cause of "virtue and wisdom" which the Irish affairs seemed likely to serve, and he told Elizabeth Hitchener that he felt gratified at having met many people who shared his faith in equality and believed "the necessity of reform and the probability of a revolution undeniable" (February 27, 1812, *Letters*, I, 263).

When he came to consider measures of practical reform, Shelley pointed to the repeal of the Union, "the most successful engine that England ever wielded over the misery of fallen Ireland," as the most important objective. The Union had lured the Irish Protestant aristocracy to England, and with them their friends and connections. The wealth of Ireland was being dissipated in England. The Irish Catholic leader O'Connell would not have agreed with Shelley, for he had decided that Ireland's cause could be forwarded only by intensive concentration on the more practical goal of emancipation.[9] The Act of Union had made Catholic emancipation a real possibility, and repeal would simply have restored the Irish Protestants to power. Shelley looked to the progressive spirit of the age, and decided that the Catholics were certain to be emancipated in the near future, and that the other Irish disabilities would surely be removed eventually, even if the Prince should prove false. But the achievement of these secondary aims should not be regarded as ultimate. He wrote with a view not only to Catholic emancipation, but to universal emancipation. Ireland should be regarded as the starting point of a movement that should *truly* emancipate the human spirit, not only in Ireland, but elsewhere — a movement that could be grounded only in wisdom and virtue and that would take longer than one generation to reach its goal. "I regard the admission of the Catholic claims and the Repeal of the Union Act as blossoms of that fruit which the Summer Sun of improved intellect and progressive virtue is destined to mature" ("Proposals for an Association of Philanthropists," Clark ed., p. 62).

In Ireland, Shelley got a clear idea of the immediate necessities of reform. He was somewhat humbled by the sight of overwhelming misery and poverty. Abstractions had been brought to life by his own observations of the effects of tyranny. He told Godwin, "I had no conception of the depth of human misery until now" (March 8, 1812, *Letters*, I, 268). Also he had learned that genuine and lasting enlightenment was far more a matter of the distant future than he had previously supposed. As Newman White has well said, Shelley discovered in Ireland the difference "between a clear abstraction of justice in a benevolent, philosophic mind and its effective application to conditions in a wretched community." [10] He had desired to "sink the question of immediate grievance in the more remote consideration of a highly perfectible state of society," but he had discovered that his scheme of organizing the ignorant was ill-timed. Yet the vision of the "mass of animated filth" which comprised the miserable poor of Dublin increased his eagerness. He must teach the lessons of virtue to those who, often without being aware of it, grind their fellow beings into worse than annihilation. "Popular insurrection and revolutions," he assured Elizabeth Hitchener, must be discountenanced, at least until the results of an appeal to the rulers were in (January 7, 1812, *Letters*, I, 221). He must address himself to the educated classes, the reading public of England. Perhaps Godwin had revealed the true way: "Infuse just views of society into a certain number of the liberally educated and reflecting members; give to the people guides and instructors; and the business is done. This however is not to be accomplished but in a gradual manner" (*Political Justice*, I, 104). Had he been like Godwin a direct witness of the French Revolution, he might, he acknowledged to his mentor, have been more cautious in his Irish venture (January 10, 1812, *Letters*, I, 227).

In November 1811 Shelley had commented briefly to Miss Hitchener on the disturbances in and around Nottingham, known to history as the Luddite risings. He observed that the workers had been reduced to starvation and troops had been called out. Southey assured him that revolution was inevitable: "this is one of his reasons for supporting things as they are" (to Elizabeth Hitchener, December 26, 1811, *Letters*, I, 213). When Shelley returned to England, nourishing his increased doubts as to the omnipotence of truth in contemporary society (to William Godwin, March 18, 1812, *Letters*, I, 277), he found that the agitations were undiminished; the militia had been called out in the cities. The rioters and machine-breakers seemed to him to be motivated by hunger, not by any desire for political reform; therefore, he felt that any change they might produce would most likely be devoid of principle and method. Reform was the true and only worthy goal. These demonstrations, though they served to reveal the realities of class oppression, could not produce lasting mitigation of social evils.

In March 1812 Parliament passed the Frame-Breaking Bill, making the destruction of any manufacturing machinery a capital felony. Lord Byron perhaps first came to Shelley's attention by his attack on the bill in his maiden speech. The frame-breakers were guilty only of the capital crime of poverty, he asserted, and added the argument, which the Hammonds regarded as more likely to have touched the heart of the government, that juries would refuse to convict.[11] But Byron was mistaken. Eight Luddites were hanged at Chester and eight at Manchester. Seventeen more were hanged in Yorkshire in January 1813.

Shelley had no desire to see a revolution begin in the lower classes. The role of the Paris mob seems to have been in his mind. It was his task, he conceived, to enlighten the governing classes so that a wise reform might be initiated from above. His point of view is apparent in the correspondence with the publisher Hookham concerning the relief of the dependents of the Yorkshire Luddites. The Shelleys suggested that Hookham start a subscription, to which they would contribute (January 31, 1813, *Letters*, I, 351). But a few days later John and Leigh Hunt received their heavy sentences for libeling the Prince Regent. Shelley wrote to Hookham: "Although I do not retract in the slightest degree my wish for a subscription for the widows & children of those poor men hung at York yet this 1000£ which the Hunts are sentenced to pay is an affair of more consequence" (February 15, 1813, *Letters*, I, 353). The Hunts were important moderate reformers, and the *Examiner* had a wide circulation among the educated class.

In the records of Shelley's life and thought between the summer of 1813 and the autumn of 1816 little evidence can be found of a continued interest on his part in the state of society or in important public events. Compared with Byron, at least, he gave little heed to the drama across the Channel. Elba, the Hundred Days, Waterloo, and the beginnings of the conservative reaction passed without significant comment from Shelley, though Mary noted the principal events in her *Journal*. His troubled personal life may partly account for this diminished attention. The absence of economic disturbances until the impact of postwar dislocations probably figured as well. Also he was beginning to shift his direction somewhat, as a poem like *Alastor* may seem to suggest. Shelley "had now begun to feel that the time for action was not ripe in England, and that the pen was the only instrument wherewith to prepare the way for better things" (Julian, III, 120; Mrs. Shelley's note). He made a conscious attempt to close his mind to the excitements of contemporary issues. "In considering the political events of the day I endeavour to divest my mind of temporary sensations, to consider them as already historical." Such objectivity was not easy, for as Shelley commented to Hogg in August 1815, "the human beings which surround us infect us with their opinions: so much as to forbid us to be dispassionate observers of the questions arising out of the events of the age" (*Letters*, I, 430). The desire to take an active and leading part in reform revived from time to time in Shelley's later years. He went on, however, in his letter to Hogg to note with philosophic mildness the "enormities" committed by the Allied troops in France as the statesmen began to restore the principle of legitimacy. When his sympathies were detached from the struggle, Shelley could sound like an intelligently conservative aristocrat. As he observed in November 1816, the "utter overthrow" of the old order could leave England "the prey of anarchy"; the "illiterate demagogues" would lead a dangerous mob. Such views were perhaps calculated partly to appeal to his correspondent Byron (*Letters*, I, 513). He is closer in his views to the general temper of enlightened opinion than he has sometimes been credited with being.

The slight doubt in British minds a hundred years ago lest reaction, if it were pressed too far, or reform, if it were allowed too free a scope might not lead to revolution, was a factor of great importance. It accounted for much of the moderation exhibited alike by advocates and opponents of change, a moderation which was largely responsible for the peaceful consummation of those great changes which in fact constituted, without violence, the English Revolution, political, industrial, and social, of the nineteenth century. The danger of revolution was in some degree as much a cause of change in England as the fact of revolution was abroad.[12]

When in late 1816 popular unrest began once more to provide a fund of political energy and hope for reformers, Shelley's active and practical interest in contemporary problems was restored. Of course, some of his personal stress had abated. With the end of the war, various inevitable dislocations of industry and commerce had disrupted the English economy. The laissez-faire theory that the best interests of society and industry would be promoted by unlimited competition merely intensified the general misery; for the emphasis of industry was upon production. Distribution was neglected. Shelley's later comment in "A Defence of Poetry" was very much to the point: "We have more moral, political, and historical wisdom than we know how to reduce into practice; we have more scientific and economic knowledge than can be accommodated to the just distribution of the produce which it multiplies" (Clark ed., p. 293). The ideas of Malthus satisfied the consciences of the rich by convincing them readily that charities and poor laws could only add to the miseries of the laboring classes specifically and society generally by stimulating the growth of population.

The working classes, imbued with the doctrines of Cobbett and other reformers and spurred by misery, became potential revolutionaries. The connection between distress and reform was rapidly becoming obvious, and after Waterloo political reform became a serious object to the working classes. During the first Jacobin terror it had been possible and easy for a magistrate to incite a working-class mob to harry a working-class reformer. "But a great change had come over the working classes in the last twenty years. They had learnt much from Cobbett, more perhaps from suffering, and by 1817 there was a widespread desire for the franchise." [13] What the workmen wanted was a better standard of living, higher wages, and lower prices. The reformers, who were usually of the middle classes, told them that these basic desires could be realized only by the conquest of political power. But the reformers were themselves disunited. Hampden clubs and clubs of Spencean Philanthropists had sprung up all over England and Scotland and had tried to make use of the general unrest. The former, led by Major Cartwright and the veteran champion of parliamentary reform, Sir Francis Burdett, advocated manhood suffrage and retrenchment of government spending; Spence and his disciples demanded the expropriation of the landholders, the

restoration of collective ownership of the land, and the establishment in each parish of a system of common cultivation. The
Spenceans were in fact revolutionary anarchists, and they were
prepared, as is apparent in the Spa-Fields affair and the Cato
Street Conspiracy, to translate opinions into actions. Their violent activities for a time prejudiced educated opinion against
every species of reform, even the mild, constitutional program
advanced by the Burdett group. The history of the French
Revolution was still strongly imprinted on the public mind.

The general distress growing out of the complexities of the
English situation attracted Shelley's attention once more to the
problems of practical politics in the autumn of 1816. In a letter
to Byron on September 11 he commented that, while distress
is said to be severe, there are so far no "glaring symptoms of
disaffection." Shelley hoped that wintry burdens would not
propel the desperate populace into "premature and useless struggles" (*Letters*, I, 505–506). By mid-November he had begun
talking of the "tumultuous state of England." It was in this
November of 1816 that William Cobbett reduced the price of
the *Political Register* and became overnight with his "Twopenny Trash" one of the most powerful leaders of popular
opinion. Shelley may have had Cobbett in mind when he
commented that the popular party has suddenly acquired surprising strength and there is considerable danger that demagogues preaching violence may gain the ascendancy. But so
far the people remain calm and "reform may come without
revolution." Much depended, Shelley thought, on the actions
which Parliament might take when it met January 28. He
hoped that anarchy and the rule of "illiterate demagogues"
might be forestalled by a "most radical reform of the institutions of England" (to Lord Byron, November 20, 1816, *Letters*, I, 513).

Any reform that might have been possible was spoiled by

the Spa-Fields uprising, sponsored by the Spenceans, who, waving tricolor flags, plundered weapons from gunsmiths' shops and attempted abortively to capture the Tower of London. The Spenceans were acquitted of treason, defended by Shelley's chancery counselor, Wetherell, though they might well have been indicted for riot had the government preferred lesser charges.[14] The revolutionary atmosphere was further intensified when in January the Prince Regent was shot at as he returned in his coach from the opening of Parliament. Parliament reacted to the general crisis thus brought to a head by suspending habeas corpus in February. Cobbett and other radicals who had been inaccessible to prosecution as long as they avoided libel, blasphemy, and incitement to violence took flight to America. "Ought we not to be happy?" Mary Shelley wrote to Hunt, "and so indeed we are, in spite of the Lord Chancellor and the suspension act."[15] Shelley wrote Byron on April 23 to express his political disappointment: "As to this country, you will have heard that the ministers have gained a victory, which has not been disturbed by a single murmur; if I except those of famine, which they have troops of hireling soldiers to repress" (*Letters*, I, 540).

In the "Address to the Irish" Shelley had prophetically counseled his readers to distrust anyone who came among them advocating violence: "Always suspect that some knavish rascal is at the bottom of things of this kind, waiting to profit by the confusion" (Clark ed., p. 46). On April 23, 1817, a man named Oliver, hired by the Home Office to uncover rebellious activities, began a tour of the industrial districts, posing as a reformer who had been delegated to unify the popular forces. In Nottingham he persuaded one Jeremiah Brandreth to join in a plot to seize arms from the military and then march to London, uniting with the large contingents expected from other regions on the way, there to contend for a change in the government. Under this stimulus a small band of laborers led by Brandreth set out from Pentridge in Derbyshire, but, after a night's straggling march, the insurgents were dispersed by the first show of armed resistance. Oliver's role as *agent provocateur* was soon revealed; nevertheless, the captured rebels were tried in October for treason. November 7, 1817, Brandreth, Isaac Ludlam, and William Turner were executed. The day before, the Princess Charlotte, the Prince Regent's only child, had died.

In his "Address to the People on the Death of the Princess Charlotte," Shelley contrasts the Princess' peaceful death with the brutal slaughter of the condemned men. He ascribes this climax of repressive tyranny to the workings of the national debt. The old aristocracy, composed of "men of pride and honor," had been replaced by organized oppressors called "public creditors." Finally the people began to protest and to demand representation. The government merely marshaled forces to crush such liberties. A ready field was available in the disaffected working class, "the helots of luxury." Spies, "selected from the most worthless and infamous of mankind," were sent forth to find and, if it could not be found, to create discontent. The idea that any extension of political freedom or lessening of economic burdens would introduce anarchy was to be impressed on public opinion. "A few hungry and ignorant manufacturers, seduced by the splendid promises of these remorseless blood-conspirators, collected together in what is called rebellion against the state. All was prepared, and the eighteen dragoons assembled in readiness, no doubt, conducted their astonished victims to that dungeon which they left only to be mangled by the executioner's hand" (Clark ed., pp. 166–168).

In this essay Shelley sketched the full course and spirit of the reform movement of 1816–17 which enlisted him as an enthusiastic partisan. He had traced its beginnings in the famines of the autumn of 1816, had contributed a pamphlet (analyzed in the next chapter) to help organize its energies, and now believed it had been crushed by the extraordinary powers of repression which the government had chosen to exercise. Despotism had for the moment won.

In March 1818 Shelley left England. But his interest in purely English issues did not diminish. As exiles, the Shelleys were, as Mary told Leigh Hunt in 1821, almost ultrapolitical.[16] They came to depend particularly on Thomas Love Peacock to keep them informed on contemporary English politics, and they continually solicited him for news and perspectives. "You will be able now," Shelley commented, "to give me perhaps a closer insight into the politics of the times" (January 23–24, 1819, *Letters*, II, 75). Soon came what Shelley termed "highly inspiring" news. The reform party succeeded in returning all eight members in the City of London election. In Westmoreland, however, where the "self-seller" Wordsworth, according to Peacock's account, had written in favor of the Lowther interests, the opposition candidate, Brougham, had been defeated.[17] Still the ministerial majority had been considerably reduced, a clear gain for the moderate opposition; and Shelley was sufficiently elated by such a favorable turn as to wish for revived health and spirits that he might once more enter into public affairs. Domestic peace is now the principal goal, he felt. If peace could be maintained, the present state of England should be propitious for effecting some remedy — "not to the universal evils of all constituted society — but to the peculiar system of misrule under which those evils have been exasperated now" (to William Godwin, July 25, 1818, *Letters*, II, 22).

Further encouraging reports came from Peacock in December concerning the success of true justice in the Banknote trials. The jury had found the defendants "not guilty" in four capital trials for forgery of bank notes. In February 1819, however, Byron's friend Hobhouse, though he stood in the radical interest and was supported by Burdett, was defeated in a hard-fought contest for the seat at Westminster. Shelley attributed such defeats to Cobbett's work in weakening and disuniting the popular party, "so that the factions who prey upon our country have been able to coalesce to its exclusion" (to Thomas Love Peacock, April 6, 1819, *Letters*, II, 94).

Shelley's views at this period, and for that matter during the rest of his life, may be associated with Byron's. Byron too was sympathetic with the revolutionary ideal of liberty, but he tempered his enthusiasm and may well have influenced Shelley with practical and realistic reservations about human nature. One of the principal mourners of Waterloo, Byron had voted with the Whigs for censure of the Tory role at the Congress of Vienna,[18] where was forged "the impious alliance," as he referred to it later in the preface to *Don Juan*, "which insults the world with the name of 'Holy'!" At the beginning of Canto IX of *Don Juan* he reproached Wellington for having "repair'd Legitimacy's crutch" and crushed the world's hopes at Waterloo, when he might have nobly freed fallen Europe from "the unity of tyrants." "Never had mortal man such opportunity,/ Except Napoleon, or abused it more." Apparently Byron at one time planned to have Don Juan finish his career by playing a role in the French Revolution like that of Anacharsis Cloots, the "friend of the human race."[19] Generally Shelley's comments on the period of reaction resemble Byron's. The two poets influenced each other, confirming their aristocratic radicalism through such sympathy. Like Shelley, Byron had ambitions to return to England, if needed, to be a revolutionary leader, though he conceived of a role well above the "filthy puddle."[20] Byron objected to Hobhouse's radical companions, excepting gentlemen like Sir Francis Burdett, and professed himself a friend to reform but not to reformers like Henry Hunt. He saw the hard-working radicals of the period as very low imitations of the Jacobins who might well be worse than Robespierre and Marat, "could they throttle their way to power." [21] Nevertheless, Byron thought that revolution in England was inevitable.

The year 1818 witnessed abnormal prosperity, attended by speculation and overproduction. With the approach of winter the usual reaction occurred. The market was glutted and prices fell. Manufacturers tried to undersell competitors, largely by cutting wages below the subsistence level and adding to the hours of work. A political crisis even more severe than that of 1816 followed the economic distress. Apparently both the reformers and the establishment had been preparing for the past three years for the inevitable test of strength.

Parliament made no gesture to reform itself, and agitation spread throughout the country in the first half of 1819. In June a series of mass meetings began and continued regularly once a week. Enormous crowds of people, largely from the working classes, demonstrated in favor of parliamentary reform and the repeal of the Corn Laws.

What was Shelley's reaction to this popular movement? Conditioned by fears generated by the course of the French Revolution, his former refrain had been that a revolution begun by the long-oppressed people would be followed by anarchy and eventually despotism. Now his attitude may be said to have changed, for in this crisis he composed a number of political lyrics, popular in style and theme, which represent his feelings about the turbulent condition of England at the time of the Peterloo Massacre. They are simple and vigorous poems, designed for the direct inspiration of the common people in the revolution Shelley thought was approaching. They were not published, however, during his lifetime. In the well-known "Song to the Men of England," the best of the short lyrics, the poet tells the toil-worn laborers that the fruits of their labor are consumed by drones who give nothing in return. The more they work, the more wealth and power they provide for the class which enslaves them. They would do well to use their hard-wrought wealth and superior strength in their own defence. The fragment "What Men Gain Fairly" is particularly significant. What we earn by fair toil rightfully belongs to us; and utility, "Private injustice may be general good," prescribes that we should be able to will such property to our children if we like, even if it means that they "inherit idleness." *

> But he who gains by base and armèd wrong,
> Or guilty fraud, or base compliances,
> May be despoiled; even as a stolen dress
> Is stripped from a convicted thief, and he
> Left in the nakedness of infamy.

The government might justly have charged Shelley with inciting the people to violence, for this is no less than an invitation to class warfare, directed against the paper wealth of the newly rich. Apparently Shelley too now judged, like the radical reformers, that for the moment at least it was visionary to expect the ruling class to initiate reform even though one might continue to urge this course as the best and wisest. Finally, in the "Sonnet: England in 1819," he assessed the state of the nation. Unfeeling, parasitic rulers, a starved and oppressed people, an uncertain army, a "Christless, Godless"

---

* A source for this un-Godwinian sentiment may be found in Mary Wollstonecraft's *Vindication of the Rights of Men*, p. 51: "The only security of property that nature authorizes and reason sanctions is, the right a man has to enjoy the acquisitions which his talents and industry have acquired; and to bequeath them to whom he chooses."

religion, an unrepresentative Parliament, where selfish interests have left "Time's worst statute unrepealed" — these are as the graves of a nation's hopes and from them the "glorious Phantom" of liberty may rise.

The line, "A people starved and stabbed in the untilled field," directly relates Shelley's sonnet to the current crisis. On August 16, 1819, approximately sixty thousand people had gathered in St. Peter's Fields, Manchester, to hear an address by the radical reformer and orator, Henry Hunt, one of Byron's bêtes noires, and to pass the usual resolutions against the unpopular policies of the government. The banners which they carried declared their objects to be "Equal Representation or Death," "Repeal of the Corn Laws," and "Annual Parliaments." These were cited at Hunt's trial as evidence of inflammatory, treasonable intent.[22] The meeting had just begun when one troop of yeomanry cavalry were, after the reading of the Riot Act, ordered to go to the aid of the civil constable in arresting Hunt at the speaker's platform. Shelley, incidentally, praised Hunt for behaving "with great spirit & coolness in the whole affair" (to Thomas Love Peacock, September 21, 1819, *Letters*, II, 120). The yeomanry tried to slash their way through, but the crowd closed in on them. Four troops of hussars were sent to assist the yeomen and to disperse the crowd. In the tumult which followed eleven persons were reported killed, including two women, and several hundred injured.

To Shelley, thinking in terms of his own "West Wind" imagery, these happenings seemed to be "the distant thunders of the terrible storm which is approaching." He waited anxiously to hear "how the Country will express its sense of this bloody murderous oppression of its destroyers" (to Charles Ollier, September 6, 1819, and Thomas Love Peacock, September 9, 1819, *Letters*, II, 117, 119). In the *Examiner* of August 22, 1819, the general attitude of the public toward the tragedy was fully discussed. The article charged that the government had been the first to draw the sword and the first to shed blood systematically.[23] Shelley echoed the comment and pointed up a significant parallel to French history: "The tyrants here, as in the French Revolution, have first shed blood" (to Thomas Love Peacock, September 21, 1819, *Letters*, II, 119).

The authorities were not bowed by the storms of public indignation. The thanks of the Prince Regent were sent to the magistrates and the military at the instigation of Lord Sidmouth, the Home Secretary, who first remarked on hearing of the tragedy that he "trusted the proceedings at Manchester would prove a salutary lesson to modern reformers."[24] In Parliament, Lord Eldon suggested that if the magistrates "had erred at all during the late excitement, their error had been rather on the side of remissness than of due vigour."[25] But the judgment of Sidmouth and Eldon was not the judgment of history. The Oliver affair and the Peterloo Massacre had a decisive effect in arousing the English educated public from a long lethargy of anti-Jacobinism and, it has been claimed, won the English middle class to reform.[26]

The Mask of Anarchy, Shelley's poetic memorial to the Manchester victims, is written in a vigorously plain style suited to common readers rather than to the "esoteric few" capable of comprehending an *Epipsychidion*. Murder, Fraud, and Hypocrisy in the guise of Lords Castlereagh, Eldon, and Sidmouth, pass slowly by in ghastly masquerade, followed by a deathly pale personification of Anarchy, riding a white horse splashed with blood. Anarchy, identified in Shelley's central irony as God, King, and Law, is accompanied by a mighty troop, "Waving each a bloody sword." In London, Anarchy directs his slaves, his "Lawyers and Priests," to seize his Bank (paper money) and Tower (stronghold for political prisoners) while he proceeds to meet "his pensioned Parliament." These were the immediate instruments of oppression by which Shelley conceived that the rulers had brought England to the brink of revolution. But at that moment a "maniac maid," "her name was Hope," fled past and lay down in the street before the horse's hoofs. She was not destroyed, however, for between her and the pageant of Anarchy arose a misty form, small and weak at first, but soon growing into a bright-mailed Shape before whom the forces of Anarchy were suddenly annihilated. It was the Spirit of Liberty and Love.

> And the prostrate multitude
> Looked — and ankle-deep in blood,
> Hope, that maiden most serene,
> Was walking with a quiet mien. (126–129)

Thus did Shelley conceive that the massacre of Peterloo had been a climax of oppression which was to rekindle the light of liberty.* It is proclaimed that another assembly must be called to meet on some wide plain. When men declare that they are free and the tyrants come to cut them down once more, they will not resist. Shelley vividly recreates the scene at Peterloo:

> Let the charged artillery drive,
> Till the dead air seems alive
> With the clash of clanging wheels,
> And the tramp of horses' heels.
>
> Let the fixèd bayonet
> Gleam with sharp desire to wet

---

* *The Mask of Anarchy* is an application to practical politics of the moral doctrines of *Prometheus,* also in the process of composition at this time. One thinks particularly of Demogorgon's parting admonitions to a world freed by love, especially the obscure injunction "to hope till Hope creates / From its own wreck the thing it contemplates."

Its bright point in English blood
Looking keen as one for food.

Let the horsemen's scimitars
Wheel and flash, like sphereless stars
Thirsting to eclipse their burning
In a sea of death and mourning. (311–322)

There remains an English tradition of liberty which will teach
the wisely passive multitude never to return violence or nurse
thoughts of hate and revenge. The contagion of their example
must reduce their slayers to inert shame.

And that slaughter to the Nation
Shall steam up like inspiration,
Eloquent, oracular;
A volcano heard afar. (360–363)

And yet the concluding stanza, a kind of refrain, sounds much
more like a call to arms than to wise passiveness.

Rise like Lions after slumber
In unvanquishable number —
Shake your chains to earth like dew
Which in sleep had fallen on you —
Ye are many — they are few.

In November 1819 it appeared to Shelley that the state was
mustering troops in preparation for bloody civil war. The
people were nearly in a state of insurrection, and the least unpopular noblemen had begun to perceive "the necessity of conducting a spirit which it is no longer possible to oppose" (to
John and Maria Gisborne, *Letters*, II, 149). But he feared

that the rulers would not learn in time to yield to "the spirit of the age." "The great thing to do is to hold the balance between popular impatience and tyrannical obstinacy; to inculcate with fervour both the right of resistance and the duty of forbearance" (to Leigh Hunt, November 14–18, 1819, *Letters*, II, 153). The official response was to pass a series of coercion acts generally known as the Six Acts. The fifth act was particularly designed to prevent the recurrence of such events as Peterloo. It strengthened the restrictions on the right of assembly and placed all meetings more completely under the supervision of the magistrates.

The actions of the more violent reformers at this time seemed to justify the precautions of the government. The Spenceans, feeling it was their patriotic duty "to massacre the government and overturn all existing institutions,"[27] conspired to assassinate the ministry at a cabinet dinner. The slaughter was to be followed by the seizure of sufficient cannon to overawe the populace, the occupation of the Bank, the establishment of a provisional government at the Mansion House, and the firing of London. However, as their plans matured, the Home Office, supplied with the details by another *agent provocateur*, prepared to step in, and finally ambushed the "Cato Street Conspirators." Arthur Thistlewood and four others were executed for treason.[28] Shelley deplored the "Cato Street Conspiracy" as more likely to conspire against reform (to Thomas Love Peacock, March 10, 1820, *Letters*, II, 176). It, in fact, had this effect, for the authorities remembered this lurid affair when they examined the reasonable demands of the constitutional reformers. Weighing English domestic affairs at this time, Shelley judged, on the basis of his limited information, "that a civil war impends from the success of ministers and the exasperation of the poor" (to Thomas Love Peacock, May 2, 1820, *Letters*, II, 193).

However, the tension was broken by the trial of Queen Caroline. When the coronation of George IV was being planned, the King decided that he did not want Caroline, from whom he had been long separated, to be crowned as his Queen; he also wished her name to be struck from the liturgy. The ministers, however, conceived that such proceedings would have the worst possible effect on public opinion, and they recommended that the divorce be abandoned, with the proviso that if the Queen should return to England further measures would have to be adopted. George IV finally yielded to the pressure of his cabinet. But Caroline, who had long been traveling in Mediterranean countries without much regard for decorum, returned to England to insist upon her royal position. The Queen's triumphal re-entry actually played into the King's hands, for after several futile attempts had been made to obtain an amicable settlement, the ministers were obliged to take decisive action. Lord Liverpool brought in a Bill of Pains and Penalties on July 5, 1820. Caroline was charged with "scandalous, disgraceful and vicious conduct," and was accused of having "carried on a licentious, disgraceful, and adulterous intercourse" with one of her retainers. There was a motion to dissolve the marriage and cancel her titles and privileges.[29]

The affair of Queen Caroline engaged the attention of the British public for many months. The Whigs took up her cause as a means of reaping political advantages. They defended her reputation in the trial held in the House of Lords, and they made countercharges of misconduct against the King. They were rewarded by the return of popular favor; for in Queen Caroline the injustice suffered by millions had been personified and made palatable. Leigh Hunt told Shelley, "You may look upon the British public, at present, as constantly occupied in reading trials for adultery." Hunt felt that the scandal would provide "one of the greatest pushes given to declining royalty that the age has seen."[30] Cobbett affirmed that the Queen's cause naturally allied itself with that of the radicals. Both were "complainants."[31] But no such identity of interests was ever apparent to Shelley. He wondered that the English should endure such mountains of cant about a "vulgar cook-maid" called Queen (to John and Maria Gisborne, June 30, 1820, *Letters*, II, 207), though he later came to admire the "generous gullibility" of the English people in making Caroline their heroine in spite of their "prejudices and bigotry" (to Thomas Love Peacock, July 12, 1820, *Letters*, II, 213). Shelley began to nourish slight hopes that the mistake into which the ministers had fallen would precipitate them into ruin: "whoever may be their successors in power, it is impossible that they should exercise it worse" (to Amelia Curran, September 17, 1820, *Letters*, II, 235). Byron, without really crediting the Queen's innocence, entered the fray with spirit, looked up witnesses for Caroline, and sought ways of discrediting those brought against her. He even spoke of returning to cast a vote in the cause.[32]

Shelley's rather feeble partisanship for Caroline's party is reflected in his burlesque drama, *Swellfoot the Tyrant*. In this play, the Arch-Priest Mammon (Lord Liverpool) delivers an oracle, when "dead drunk or inspired," to the effect that Boeotia will have the choice of reform or civil war when a Consort Queen shall hunt a King with hogs (Burke's "swinish" herd). Mammon proposes to entice the Queen Iona into the Temple of Famine (House of Lords), where she shall voluntarily undergo the test of the Green Bag,* which, on whomsoever

---

* On June 7, 1820, Lord Holland stated in the House of Lords, "that a green bag and a secret committee were considered by the public as the prelude to the most monstrous displays of injustice, harshness, and tyranny" (*Hansard*, I, new series, 897). The green bag, Shelley's principal stage property, is the case which contained the evidence accumulated against the Queen.

poured, would transform innocence into guilt. The "swinish multitude" are to be persuaded that the contents of the bag are the true test of guilt or innocence. The governors are represented as Malthusians who rely on famine to restrain the people.

As Purganax (Castlereagh) prepares to empty the contents of the Green Bag on Iona, she suddenly seizes it and pours it over Swellfoot and his court, who, transformed into filthy and ugly animals, rush out of the temple. Some of the piggish oppressed seize loaves when the Image of Famine arises. They become bulls, while others are tripped up by the skulls which litter the altar. The Ionian Minotaur, John Bull, arises and urges Iona to mount him for the chase after the fleeing tyrants, promising not to throw her, at least until she has hunted down her game. Iona leads the swine, now bulls, after their prey, encouraging them with the hope of revenge.

> Give them no law (are they not beasts of blood?)
> But such as they gave you. (II, ii, 127–128)

The closeness of Shelley's action to the events and opinions he had read about is clear enough, but more certain is his assurance that the cause of liberty and moderate reform could make no gain through Caroline.

After the agitations of 1819 and 1820, English commerce revived and the country enjoyed a period of calm. "The noisy farce of 1820 had but masked the failure of the political agitation when the industrial depression had passed away." [33] It is therefore quite understandable that Shelley had little to say about conditions in England during his last few years. His opinions may be thought to reflect and reinforce those of Byron, who commented, "revolutions are not made with rosewater. My taste for revolution is abated, with my other passions." [34]

That neither Byron nor Shelley lost enthusiasm for the cause of ideal liberty is proved, however, by their attention to the revived revolutionary movements of the 1820's. England might achieve reform, but clearly the entrenched despotisms in Europe could yield only to violent revolution.[35]

The outbreak in Spain signaled to Byron the coming of "freedom's second dawn" (*Vision of Judgment*, l. 57), the first breach in the Holy Alliance. An army which the Spanish King Ferdinand had been preparing to dispatch to South America to suppress the rebellion of the colonies had revolted and demanded the restoration of the democratic constitution of 1812. The King had been forced to bow to the will of the in-surgents. Shelley felt that the Spaniards, by their magnificent example, had aroused all Europe from the sleep of reaction, had rekindled the lamps of liberty "within the dome of this dim world" ("Ode to Liberty," l. 227). He chose to greet the proclamation of a constitutional government in Naples in July 1820 as a response to Spain's "thrilling paean" ("Ode to Naples," l. 102). In his enthusiasm, he did not think it un-warranted once more to foresee "a system of future social life before which the existing anarchies of Europe" might be "dis-solved & absorbed" (to Claire Clairmont, February 18, 1821, *Letters*, II, 267). These Mediterranean revolutions are the background to the idea and the development of *The Liberal*.*

According to Mrs. Shelley, the poet thought of the revolu-tionary struggles in Spain and Italy "as decisive of the destinies of the world, probably for centuries to come" (*Hellas* note). The international character of the messianic principles of the Revolution, now reinforced by his long residence in Europe,

---

* Cf. Halévy, II, 82, who stresses the significance of the title. "*Verse and Prose from the South* does not simply mean that the *Liberal* publishes articles written in Italy by Byron and Shelley, but is also intended to convey that the publication is animated by the spirit of the southern revolutions."

promoted once more in Shelley's imagination an expanded cosmopolitan vision of humanity. The revolution revived, this was the theme now of both Byron and Shelley. Byron expressed occasional poetic doubts, as in *Don Juan*, about the trials and struggles to be encountered and would have objected, he said,

> If I had not perceived that revolution
> Alone can save the earth from hell's pollution.
> (VIII, 51–52)

Shelley saw perhaps the greatest gains to be reaped from revived enthusiasm and patriotic ardor which might awaken fallen man to a new sense of his plight and his destiny. The Neapolitans, like the Spaniards, and like the French three decades earlier, were experiencing the "sudden & great impulse" which converts slaves into men and citizens and may ultimately produce a social system which expresses the new enlightenment (to Claire Clairmont, February 18, 1821, *Letters*, II, 266–267).

His principal informant on Italian revolutionary affairs seems to have been Byron, from whom, he told Mary, he obtained many details about politics in an all-night conversation. Byron had, in fact, achieved a good deal more than the role of foreign observer and sympathizer. Through his connections with the Gamba family, he had become involved in local intrigues, revolutionary societies, and arms-collecting. He had offered his services and money to the cause, even though he was more realistically skeptical than Shelley about the potentialities for improvement of the Neapolitan character. He doubted success partly because only the higher and middle orders were interested in the rebellion, while the savage peasantry disdained the cause.[36] He was keenly disappointed, however, when the Neapolitans melted before the Austrian army, and he claimed inside knowledge into the causes of failure, an "atrocious treachery which has replunged Italy into Barbarism." The Neapolitans had betrayed the cause.[37] Shelley too felt deeply the resubjugation of Naples and was especially angry at Tom Moore for calling the rebellion an ignominious failure, a "cruel and ungenerous" attitude to Shelley's mind. Although strongly disappointed, Shelley yet said, "I cling to moral and political hope, like a drowner to a plank" (to Lord Byron, May 4, 1821, *Letters*, II, 291).

The fresh outbreak of revolution in Greece rekindled some of his old ardor. Shelley's optimism was always qualified by his knowledge that slaves could not become freemen overnight, but he was sufficiently encouraged by the news from Greece to compose his dramatic poem, *Hellas*, "at the suggestion of the events of the moment." In its preface he characterized the age of reaction with great bitterness. England gave particular cause for despair, as Shelley thought the English had supported the Turks against the cause of Greek independence. "This is the age of the war of the oppressed against the oppressors, and every one of those ringleaders of the privileged gangs of murderers and swindlers, called Sovereigns, look to each other for aid against the common enemy, and suspend their mutual jealousies in the presence of a mightier fear." In the poem he described through the person of the Turkish sultan Mahmud what he conceived to be the fears of all the reactionary Tyrant-Anarchs of the age, quaking at the spectacle of renascent freedom.

Byron on the revolutionary scene later echoed some of Shelley's opinions about the French Revolution in his estimation of the Greeks. The Greeks, he said, had been slaves for centuries, and "there is no tyrant like a slave." When men exchange the "chains of the prisoner for the freedom of the jailor," violence and disunity are to be expected.[38] He appraised the Greek character and possibilities of success realistically, and expressed a practical man's view of the people he was trying to revolutionize which is actually less distant from Shelley's own ultimate views than it might seem. Byron said: "we must not look always too closely at the men who are to benefit by our exertion in a good cause, or God knows we shall seldom do much good in this world." His statement is compatible with a philosophy of reform which would "neither heed nor see what things they be." One of Shelley's main ideas is that the ardor of the idealist may be so smothered by a detailed examination of human corruption and other practical obstacles that he will accept as inevitable the evils which the visionary imagination can look beyond. Byron believed that liberty would educate the Greeks, taught deceit by their slavery, into the true ways of liberty. He himself seems to have acted with prudence and moderation, dispensing his funds only when he was assured of doing real service, and ignoring the importunities of disorganized factions. As he assured Hobhouse, "it must be *the Cause,* and not individuals or *parties,* that I endeavour to benefit."[39] Shelley would likely have seconded these views, for sanity, practicality, and a sense of the realities of such obstacles to improvement as human inertia and conservative opposition or indifference may be observed in most of his comments on contemporary affairs.

Shelley's last comments on the situation of his own country betray some doubt and despair but also continuing deep concern. It is doubtful that life ever triumphed so completely over him as some have suggested. In the spring of 1821 he wrote to Byron, "Our own country is, perhaps, on the brink of demanding all our sympathies" (May 4, 1821, *Letters,* II, 291). In December 1821 he described the state of the nation to Claire Clairmont. Rebellion did not seem possible in Ireland, for, though the people refused to pay taxes or rents, they were not regularly organized under capable leaders. "In England all bears for the moment the aspect of a sleeping Volcano" (*Letters*, II, 371). Finally, on June 29, 1822, a few days before his death, Shelley summed up his position on life and politics for Horace Smith with a half-joking turn of pessimism.

> England appears to be in a desperate condition, Ireland still worse, & no class of those who subsist on the public labour will be persuaded that *their* claims on it must be diminished. But the government must content itself with less in taxes, the landholder must submit to receive less rent, & the fundholder a diminished interest — or they will all get nothing. . . . I once thought to study these affairs & write or act in them — I am glad that my good genius said *refrain*. I see little public virtue, & I foresee that the contest will be one of blood & gold two elements which however much to my taste in my pockets & my veins, I have an objection to out of them. (*Letters*, II, 442)

That Shelley should seem to end like Volney, a "désillusionné" (as predicted by Peacock, Wolfe ed., p. 359), is not inconsistent with the pessimism running beneath the surface of his intense life, a pessimism which he sloughed off during those brief periods of hope when the possibilities of practical improvement seemed enhanced. Then would his curiously recurring desire to fill some active role in public affairs grow strong. Action, or the possibility of it, always galvanized the Platonic Shelley.

Shelley was an intent observer of the trends of the times. We may find one justification for his strong interest in reform in the temper of his age. Of the three ideals — liberty, equality, and fraternity — which inspired and empowered the French Revolution, fraternity was the most important to him. It necessarily implied the others. Mankind united by the spirit of justice and love was the burden of Shelley's poetic vision, and when he looked to Regency England he could see only oppression, degradation, and selfishness. The educated classes had inherited a climate of opinion hostile to reform. What must be done? Since imagination is the source and power of progress, the imagination of the gifted members of the ruling classes must be awakened to perception of the truth of the poet's vision of society and to sympathy with the poet's love of humanity.

In Shelley's England, when economic distress prompted men to propose reforms, the government turned to repression. Moderate reformers, radical reformers, and fanatical anarchists were all seen as potential revolutionists or Jacobins. The farm laborers and factory workers who expressed their discontent in violence, in the burning of hayricks and the destruction of machinery, became English "sans-culottes." The history of the French Revolution was always in the back of the minds of the ruling class. The rabble, the "swinish multitude," had swept all order and good government out of France when a measure of political power was granted to them. The governors of England in Shelley's time were fundamentally sincere. This was something he was not quite capable of recognizing. They were men who had faith in their venerable Church and State constitution. Much of the troubles in France had been caused, it seemed to them, by insidious attacks on the religious establishment by atheistical philosophers. The natural order of society was the established order, and the established order was guarded and maintained by the constitution of Church and State. If free criticism of either religion or the political system were permitted, England might be reduced to the same anarchy which had desolated France.

Shelley's point of view on men and reform was the resultant of two forces. For one, he was born into the ruling class. His aristocratic Whig background was an important formative influence which no doubt lingered in the slight element of contempt for popular violence and demagoguery which he often expressed. He retained a great respect for the finer qualities of the class to which he consciously belonged. The other force which acted on Shelley was the living religion of humanity which had its greatest expression in the early days of the French Revolution. He was by nature an enthusiast and an idealist. The ideals of the French Revolution gave him his medium. Shelley's early interest in social problems was indeed somewhat rhetorical, but he later studied them in great earnest, and confirmed the wisdom and justice of his radical sympathies by reflection and by practical experience. He understood contemporary issues perfectly well from the point of view of the reformer, and he followed their developments with sober intent, though he had no specialized knowledge of the factors involved, sharing perhaps overmuch the reformer's bias for seeing the present only in the light of the future.

IV

Views on Practical Reform

J. L. Hammond, in his biography of Fox, makes a distinction between English and French speculations on freedom which throws some light on the relation in Shelley's thought between practical reforms and social ideals. Hammond argues that the difference between an English liberal like Fox and radicals in the French revolutionary tradition like Paine was that Fox started from the Whig Revolution of 1688 and Locke's interpretation of it, whereas the radicals started from an abstract individual right, which they regarded as positively outraged, and not merely imperfectly recognized, in the British constitution. "In the one case speculation centered around institutions, in the other around ideas. In the one case the right to demand reform was based on the fact that existing institutions were the instruments of freedom; in the other that existing institutions were the contradiction of freedom."[1] Shelley's speculations on reform were influenced by both the English and the French traditions. He proposed practical measures for improving specific political institutions in the fashion of Whig moderate reformers, and he projected visionary goals for social progress under the influence of the social and political philosophers of the French Revolution.

Practically, Shelley urged, like Leigh Hunt in the pages of the *Examiner*, a union between Burdett reformers and left-wing Whigs against the Tories and the right-wing Whigs in power. What Hunt said in his *Autobiography* about the intentions of the *Examiner* illuminates Shelley's own approach to literature and politics.

> The main objects of the *Examiner* newspaper were to assist in producing Reform in Parliament, liberality of opinion in general (especially freedom from superstition), and a fusion of literary taste into all subjects whatsoever. . . . It disclaimed all knowledge of statistics; and the rest of its politics were rather a sentiment, and a matter of general training, than founded on any particular political reflection. . . . It gradually drew to its perusal many intelligent persons of both sexes, who would, perhaps, never have attended to politics under other circumstances.[2]

Shelley, too, wished to reach these politically unawakened intellectuals. Like Hunt, he maintained the necessity for reformers to subordinate their differences and emphasize their common ends. It was a lesson also taught by the French Revolution.

In December 1816 Shelley and Leigh Hunt became friends, and the moderate program of reform which Hunt advocated in the *Examiner* as the best means of restoring the equilibrium of English society became the basis for Shelley's own considerations on practical reform. Like Hunt, Shelley believed that men's politics are to be made liberal mainly by liberalizing and developing their characters, and literature and the fine arts are the true means to this end. Ceaseless agitation for specific reform policies which too much ignore the difficult and unbending realities of practical politics will achieve little. Men must first perceive the necessity of reform.

The young Shelley had on the whole adopted a doctrinaire

and revolutionary position, and he urged all available auditors "that politics were morals more comprehensively enforced" (to Elizabeth Hitchener, January 7, 1812, *Letters*, I, 223). He learned in Ireland that in particular situations practical concessions must be made. Moreover, his study of the French Revolution unquestionably moderated his views, and he began to understand better the implications of Godwin's theory of gradualism. Godwin was no political radical. He attacked Shelley's proposed Irish associations, and he thought universal suffrage unreasonable and impracticable.

> Truth, however unreserved be the mode of its enunciation, will be sufficiently gradual in its progress. It will be fully comprehended, only by slow degrees, by its most assiduous votaries; and the degrees will be still more temperate, by which it will pervade so considerable a portion of the community, as to render them mature for a change of their common institutions. Again: if conviction of the understanding be the compass which is to direct our proceedings in the general affairs, we shall have many reforms, but no revolutions. (*Political Justice*, I, 244)

Godwin may well have had considerable direct influence in shaping the later Whig cast of Shelley's interest in practical politics. Harriet Shelley testified that Godwin tried in the winter of 1812–13 to persuade Shelley to join the Whigs (to Catherine Nugent, January 16, 1813, *Letters*, I, 350). Godwin wrote to a young disciple in 1820 and reminded him that "the Whigs, as a party in the state, were of the highest value to the public welfare, and constituted the party to which a liberal-minded and enlightened man would adhere."[3] To Caroline Lamb he frankly admitted, "I am in principle a Republican, but in practice a Whig."[4] Perhaps the same distinction would apply to Shelley. Shelley subscribed to the political programs of the moderate reformers, but at the same time he adhered to the abstract principles of the radicals. A philosophy of history mediated.

Ultimately Shelley adopted a political position like that of a group of left-wing Whigs who had begun between 1807 and 1812 to forge a new reform program. This group concentrated its attack on the more glaring political and economic abuses, advocated the disenfranchisement of the "rotten" boroughs, and suggested that some extension of the suffrage and the institution of triennial parliaments would be salutary. As their principal historian has commented, these Whig moderate reformers made expediency rather than abstract universal justice the foundation for their political action. Reform should take place "in parts and piecemeal."[5] Shelley also came to accept a modified version of political expediency. In the essay "On Christianity," he says that Christ, in accommodating his doctrines to the predilections of his audience, was only doing what all successful reformers have done and must do. Hypocrisy is lamentable, "But this practice of entire sincerity towards other men would avail to no good end, if they were incapable of practicing it towards their own minds" (Clark ed., p. 200). Shelley later admitted in "A Philosophical View of Reform": "All political science abounds with limitations and exceptions." Expediency must be our guide when we are dealing with "the difficult and unbending realities of actual life." Government cannot immediately begin to regulate human affairs by those abstract principles which humanity as a whole can only hope to realize in the process of time, but the people can and should be granted as much liberty and political responsibility as they are capable of using intelligently. Institutions must be improved in proportion to man's progress in wisdom and virtue. We may draw inspiration from the great object of our hopes, the perfect society of the poet's vision in which all men are united solely by the bonds of reason and love, but then "it becomes us with patience and resolution to apply ourselves to accommodating our theories to immediate practice" (Clark ed., pp. 251, 254).

In March 1817 Shelley published "A Proposal for Putting Reform to the Vote Throughout the Kingdom." The pamphlet shows that he had not yet arrived at a clear distinction between practice and theory, for he rather uncritically applies French doctrines of abstract right and justice to contemporary political problems. The prerogatives of Parliament, he argues, constitute a sovereignty which is exercised in contempt of the people. Sovereignty should be restored to the people, but it may be that they are so enslaved as to desire the continuation of their degraded position: "perhaps custom is their only God" (Clark ed., p. 159). If this be so, the reformers must retire "until accumulated sufferings shall have produced the effect of reason." But if the majority of the adult population should will that the House of Commons be composed of their representatives, Parliament would be required, not merely petitioned, "to prepare some effectual plan for carrying the general will into effect." To refuse would be presumption. "Parliament would have rebelled against the people then." The use of Rousseau's phrase, "the general will" is significant. For Rousseau, sovereignty was identified with an almost mystical general will. The general will is a Platonic form of society seen as acting ideally within the complex of actual existing societies, which of course limit it practically. "The general will is always in the right, but the judgment which guides it is not always enlightened."[6] The general will may seem to be a debatable and obscure abstraction, easily degenerating into the mere will of the majority. Like Rousseau, Shelley in his essay apparently identified the will of the majority by a sort of mystical equivalence with the general will.

Continuing his argument, Shelley urges the reformers to discover some means of determining the general will on the question of reform. He suggests that the whole of Great Britain and Ireland be divided into equal districts and that commissioners circulate the resolution "That the House of Commons does not represent the will of the People of the British Nation." It should be made clear that their objects are "purely constitutional," that they do not intend to sanction any "revolutionary and disorganizing schemes." Shelley may owe his suggestion to Paine, though in fact Parliament was being flooded by petitions during that very period of distress.* Studying the situation in England as he composed the *Rights of Man*, Paine had suggested, "as to reformation, whenever it comes, it must be from the nation, and not from the government" (I, 442). Shelley combines this proposal with the concept of the general will and suggests the use of the already popular petition as a means of avoiding revolution and educating and expressing public opinion. Petitions, the London Corresponding Society had said during the early days of the Revolution, might not produce reform, but they would keep controversial subjects open for discussion and awaken the people to the value of thinking for themselves (Barruel, IV, 49–50 introd.).

Shelley emphasizes unity. The advocates of reform should settle all the points on which they disagree. "It is trivial to discuss what species of reform shall have place when it yet remains

---

* A reform petition from Horsham was discussed in the House of Commons on March 7, 1817, that is, about a week after Shelley's pamphlet was published. Sir Timothy Shelley took part in the debate concerning the legality of the petition. He testified that the Horsham reform meeting had been orderly. His short speech seems to have been the only one he made in the course of his eighteen years' membership. See my letter in the *Times Literary Supplement*, August 18, 1950.

a question whether there will be any reform or no" ("A Proposal for Putting Reform to the Vote Throughout the Kingdom," Clark ed., p. 161). Shelley was by then a close friend of Leigh Hunt, who had since 1810 stressed in the *Examiner* that the reformers must be one in purpose before any detailed programs could be considered. Hunt has been credited with perceiving before anyone else that, if reform were to be carried without revolution, it must be by an alliance between the moderate reformers among the Whigs and those radicals who were willing to compromise.[7] Shelley sent copies of his pamphlet to such prominent Whigs as Lords Grey, Holland, Brougham, and Grosvenor.

While Shelley thought at this time that annual parliaments should be immediately adopted as a means of political education, to "familiarize men with liberty," he opposed agitation for universal suffrage on the grounds that progress toward "beneficial innovations" should be gradual in order to avoid "anarchy and despotism." It is perhaps difficult to see how he logically could accept the principle of the sovereignty of the general will and still deny complete expression to that will. However, he is no more inconsistent than the French parliamentarians of the generation before, who spoke of both property qualifications and the general will. French doctrines of abstract right, Godwinian gradualism, and practical necessities were not elements which could be readily fused into a consistent program. In this instance Shelley was obviously influenced by his reflections on the causes of the failure of the French Revolution. "The consequences of the immediate extension of the elective franchise to every male adult would be to place power in the hands of men who have been rendered brutal and torpid and ferocious by ages of slavery." Universal suffrage was associated with the Jacobins and Jacobinism by many observers, and Shelley's caution indicates that he shared the fears of a Jacobinical revolution which motivated moderate reformers, men who were for the most part impatient of theory. While enlightened men must agree with Tom Paine that a pure republic is that "system of social order the fittest to produce the happiness and promote the genuine eminence of man," the time is not ripe. Abstract thinkers can construct the most obvious and irresistible plans of perfect polity in their visions, but right reason and "beneficial issue" demand that the present regal and aristocratical forms should not be dismissed "before the public mind through many gradations of improvement shall have arrived at the maturity which can disregard these symbols of its childhood" (Clark ed., pp. 161–162).

The greatest difference between the 1817 pamphlet and the "Philosophical View of Reform," composed in 1819–20, is increased emphasis upon economics. A few weeks before Shelley published his earlier reform tract, Leigh Hunt, then his closest associate, had noted in the *Examiner*: "Finance, as directly operating to a change of system, is, in a political sense, the most interesting progression of the day, and will therefore in future engage a proper share of our attention." [8] The part that financial problems played in creating the background of revolution had been observed and commented upon by students of the French Revolution whose works Shelley studied attentively. However, the fact that no reformer in his time was able to discount the importance of the financial contribution may largely be attributed to the popularizing efforts of William Cobbett, who had asserted in his *Paper Against Gold* and the *Political Register* that the funding system was behind the rotten boroughs and parliamentary corruption and was, in fact, responsible for the obstinate resistance to reform. Shelley's observations on the connections of finance and reform derive from his reading of Cobbett.

According to Cobbett's argument, when the Bank of England

stopped specie payments in 1797, their bank notes soon became worthless paper. He accused the government of failing to limit sufficiently the amount of notes circulated. The resulting inflation forced increases in the national debt. As Cobbett put it, to pay the sinecurists and finance the liberticide wars, the government was forced to continue to float loans. But now they must make larger loans to meet the increase in prices — "thus the increase of paper would continue causing addition upon addition to the quantity of the paper." [9] To pay the interest on new loans, the government merely circulated more paper. The fresh supply of paper further accelerated the depreciation, a continuing process which the people had to underwrite through burdensome taxes. Cobbett felt that if, as some economists suggested, cash payments were resumed, first prices and then wages would dip, hugely increasing the burden of the debt and resulting finally in national bankruptcy, once the interest on the debt could no longer be met from the taxes.

Apparently Shelley was referring to the fulfillment of Cobbett's prophecies when he told Peacock (July 17, 1820) that "Cobbett's euthanasia seems approaching" (*Letters*, II, 212–213). "How Cobbett must laugh at the 'resumption of gold payments.' I long to see him" (to Thomas Love Peacock, March 10, 1820, *Letters*, II, 176–177). Shelley was a constant reader of the *Political Register*, and he recommended *Paper Against Gold* in "Philosophical View of Reform." Even Leigh Hunt acknowledged that Cobbett's "Twopenny Trash" figured high among the principal sources of public enlightenment. He was the "most powerful as well as popular political writer now living." [10] Cobbett was sent a copy of Shelley's 1817 reform pamphlet. From Italy, Shelley repeatedly asked about him: "Mention Cobbett and politics," he wrote to Peacock in April 1818 (*Letters*, II, 4). The two subjects were scarcely separable in his mind.

Hunt's *Examiner* and Cobbett's *Political Register* were two very different newspapers, and their reform programs appealed to two distinct sections of the public. The former disseminated more or less advanced ideas in literature and politics among the educated class, while the *Political Register* was rather the organ of popular instruction, though the power of Cobbett's style attracted readers of all classes. Each has a kind of correspondence to a particular aspect of Shelley's thinking about revolution, for Shelley wished both to educate the rulers to a sense of their responsibilities to society and to educate the people so that they might make intelligent use of any extension of their liberties.

Shelley sketched the historical process of deterioration in the economic system and the resulting development of the reform movement in "An Address to the People on the Death of the Princess Charlotte" and "A Philosophical View of Reform." The Long Parliament, his account begins, had been a great organ of both the people and a truly noble aristocracy. Unfortunately, however, as population increased, a new class came on the scene, "the unrepresented multitude." It had not been understood that the principal business of government was just distribution of the national wealth. The combination of "prosperity and power" had been permitted to introduce, gradually and inevitably, "despotism and misery." Profits had been drawn from the industrious part of society, and paid to the idle and luxurious. Shelley concludes: "the cause of this peculiar misery is the unequal distribution which, under the form of the national debt, has been surreptitiously made of the products of their labor" ("A Philosophical View of Reform," Clark ed., p. 256).

But what had this unjust national debt to do with the cause of political reform? It was, Shelley asserts, and his argument leans heavily on Cobbett, merely a trick employed by the ruling oligarchy in order to add strength to their oppressive government. They had devised this system of public credit "as an instrument of government" (Clark ed., p. 243). The fraudulent increase in paper money had benefited only the fund-holders and financiers, at the expense of the mass of the people. The government, by substituting paper money for gold, has simply "fabricated pieces of paper on which they promise to pay a certain sum." Shelley recommends Cobbett's *Paper Against Gold* for those who wish to understand these practices. Shelley's concern is with the consequences. "I would awaken, from a consideration that the present miseries of our country are nothing necessarily inherent in the stage of civilization at which we have arrived, foresight and hope" (Julian, VII, 338n).

Why do rulers resist even the mildest reform? They are frightened by the example of France, to be sure, but more basic is their excessive selfishness. Reform would cause them to suffer "a diminution of those luxuries and vanities in the idolatry of which they have been trained." But if the utilitarians are right in asserting that government is instituted to secure "the advantage of the greatest number," these special interests must be sacrificed to the general good. Because of the violation of this fundamental law of social preservation the state of the majority of the English people had been so reduced as to admit but three future alternatives: reform, military despotism, or a revolution.* Revolution would mean an almost fruitless struggle between two parties, "one striving after ill-digested systems of democracy, and the other clinging to the outworn abuses of power," while a small group of intelligent liberals waited for that limited portion of social improvement which might have been peaceably negotiated before the struggle. It would be wiser to contend now for a reform in the representation.

The question of reform and the problem of the national debt

---

* The repressions and scandals of 1819 and 1820 made sensible men perceive that "the state of England would soon necessitate a choice between revolution and reform." Albert Venn Dicey, *Lectures on the Relation between Law and Public Opinion in England during the Nineteenth Century* (London, 1926), p. 124.

were linked so closely as to preclude separate consideration. Shelley proposes a plan for settling the debt which, he fails to recognize, could only have been adopted after a radical reform of Parliament if not a revolution. Before we can hope to settle the national debt, he says, we must first define exactly what we mean by the term. "The fact is that the national debt is a debt not contracted by the whole nation towards a portion of it, but a debt contracted by the whole mass of the privileged classes towards one particular portion of those classes" (Clark ed., p. 249). All the property in the nation, including that which is represented by the money lent by the fund-holder, is mortgaged for the amount of the national debt. Since the fund-holder acts in a dual part, "bound to pay a certain portion as debtor whilst he is to receive another certain portion as creditor," the solution is easy. "The property of the rich is mortgaged: to use the language of the law, let the mortgagee foreclose."

In other words, Shelley suggested that all property, including that of the public creditor, be assessed and that a property tax or capital levy be imposed sufficient to pay off the debt. Apparently he thought that this "mere transfer" among persons of "property" would bring "the juggling and complicated system of paper finance" to a sudden end. He had good precedent in the French Revolution for his proposals. In 1789, as reported by Mary Wollstonecraft, Necker recommended a temporary income tax of 25 percent to remedy the ruinous state of the finances. Mirabeau, in a speech Mrs. Wollstonecraft printed, backed the proposal as the only means to avoid national bankruptcy, and suggested that they "immolate without pity these victims," that is, the two thousand notables with wealth sufficient to restore the kingdom. Only a momentary pecuniary sacrifice would be required, however (*View of F. R.*, pp. 373–374, 387). Lacretelle, commenting on the general course of the Revolution, charged that sizable revolutionary taxes were often exacted of the wealthy, "un emprunt forcé, un emprunt progressif sur les riches" (a forced loan, a progressive loan imposed on the rich).[11] It is also possible that Shelley borrowed his notion from David Ricardo who similarly advocated the immediate repayment of the national debt by means of a general assessment on all property. Leigh Hunt had commented on Ricardo's plan in the *Examiner* in terms similar to Shelley's. Hunt thought it a good idea that the means of liquidation should be drawn from those who possessed large capital. "The Debt would be discharged by a part (the richer part) of the community, while the whole (both rich and poor) are at present equally weighed down by the burden." [12] In another such recommendation Hazlitt emphasized the relation of the debt to the war against the French and Napoleonic conceptions of liberty. He said that it was an obligation undertaken by the government on the part of the tax-payers in order to indemnify the wealthy tax-receivers. The capitalists paid for the French wars because the allied armies were protecting their own concepts of property and government. This power of attorney extracted from the masses gave a few men of property an unlimited command over the nation, its resources and productive labor.[13]

Later Shelley moderated his views on the question of settling the debt. Apparently his doctrines were alarming his friends in Italy with money invested in the funds. It became almost an obsession to Byron in 1818 and 1819 to get his money out, motivated both by distrust of the Tory government and worry over what Shelley was saying.[14] The Gisbornes traveled to England to look into their investments. Shelley, thinking in terms of the possibility of a violent revolution, advised John Gisborne that, even if the ministers subdued the popular party for a time, they would have to diminish the interest of the debt once the taxes exceeded the capacity of the people to pay. Should the people be victorious and eliminate the "perpetual inheritance of a double aristocracy," the public creditors would surely suffer, though Shelley felt (and here the French example was to hand once more) they might be partially compensated by the sale of crown and church lands (November 6, 1819, *Letters*, II, 149). Shelley apparently accepted Cobbett's prophecy that a financial collapse would soon overthrow the government, but his fear of the revolutionary anarchy which must accomplish such an event caused him to stress the need for a political reform from above which might forestall such senseless chaos.

The first problem for Shelley, as for every other reformer, was how to persuade Parliament to reform itself when the membership of the House of Commons was for the most part dedicated to and profiting by the perpetuation of the old order. He conceived that this might be done by both direct and indirect means. In a sense Shelley urged parliamentary reform in all of his writings. He was trying to change the climate of opinion which opposed reform. It is important to remember that he intended his poetry to help create a will for reform in the minds of his educated and responsible readers by developing their powers of imagination. The imagination, he felt, was the ultimate source of all social improvement. But Shelley did not overlook the problems and programs of practical reform.

Shelley acknowledges that the House of Commons ought immediately to be nominated by the people. But, on the other hand, it would be unwise to attempt universal suffrage, for we would then face the dangers of "an immature attempt at a republic." Whatever small degree of reform the government chooses to offer should be accepted, even if it amounted only to the disenfranchisement of the rotten boroughs. But it will then be important to follow up the opening and demand more and more with firmness and moderation, "so that the people may become habituated [to] exercising the functions of sovereignty, in proportion as they acquire the possession of it." Shelley's notion of moderate reform is "a suffrage whose qualification should be the possession of a certain small property, and triennial parliaments" (Clark ed., pp. 254–256).

Should Parliament refuse to grant the limited reform outlined, he was prepared to advocate "universal suffrage and equal representation." But would this be of any avail when the authorities were ready to shoot and hew down the unresisting multitude? Let us meet this difficulty by considering other related questions, said Shelley. The people will not long continue to endure passively the worst oppressions of a confederation of tyrants who have conspired their way to power. Evidently a struggle will be necessary. Were the majority enlightened, united, and enthusiastic, the struggle would be brief and mild. But when a people has been long enslaved they need intelligent and enlightened leaders. Here the philosophic patriot and reformer will find his true role. "He will endeavor to rally round one standard the divided friends of liberty and make them forget the subordinate objects with regard to which they differ by appealing to that respecting which they are all agreed" (Clark ed., p. 257).

The people should be taught political truth. They should exercise their right of assembly, and, if they are again attacked as at Manchester, they ought not to resist. It was not that Shelley thought active resistance was never justifiable, but that he was more concerned with the question of utility: "temperance and courage would produce greater advantages than the most decisive victory." The leaders should try every possible means to create a consciousness of oppression in the people. The general will must come to life. The right to impose taxes should be formally contested. The House of Commons should be flooded with petitions. The poets and philosophers should be enlisted to demonstrate the "inevitable connection between national prosperity and freedom." When finally the will of the people has been firmly convinced that reform is necessary and has expressed its firm intention to have reform, it is to be hoped, Shelley concluded, that the oppressors, however reluctantly, will concede some limited portion of the rights of the people. The people must then be exhorted to pause and digest this morsel before demanding more.

But if the oppressors would rather start a civil war than resign any portion of their usurped authority, the people of England would be obliged to exercise their famous right of resistance, "acknowledged by the most approved writers on the English constitution," that is, by Whig writers. Mary Wollstonecraft also had said that revolutionary violence must purge the world when the upper orders are so degenerate that no remedy less than the horrors of civil strife can cure the ills of society. The time can come when the reformer must place the needs of oppressed humanity before what Mrs. Wollstonecraft called the aristocratic virtue of charity (*View of F. R.*, pp. 70–71). Civil war may be the last resort.

Once the people have won their cause, by whatever means, and have "assumed the control of public affairs according to constitutional rules," they must commence the great task of "accommodating all that can be preserved of ancient forms with the improvements of the knowledge of a more enlightened age" (Clark ed., p. 260). Shelley had absorbed some of Burke's and Godwin's faith in the necessity of preserving the historical continuity of progress, that salutary and uninterrupted progress which political truth and social improvement bring (*Political Justice*, I, 274–275).

Shelley's writings in the cause of moderate reform were

directed to the governing classes of England. They, he felt, were responsible for the stubborn opposition to suggested alterations in the country's institutions. He recognized that the government could not immediately begin to regulate society by abstract principles, but it could at least remove the restraints on progress and allow enlightened opinion freely to determine social changes. Enlightened opinion in the first instance was identical, Shelley believed, with the opinion of the cultivated section of the governing class, the group whom the poet would invest with the will to lead rather than to govern the people. It was their duty to teach the people and to grant them as much political responsibility as they were progressively capable of exercising. As enlightened opinion became more and more closely identified with the opinion of the general public, so would the people be granted an increasingly greater share in the government. Shelley was a moderate reformer because he believed in a government of poets and philosophers. If and when all men became poets and philosophers, government as we know it would no longer be needed to mitigate the evil effects of men's vices.

Shelley's speculations on practical reform were influenced by the programs of the moderate reformers who based their proposals on property and the radicals who urged universal suffrage. The moderate reformers were interested in practical measures for securing the more effective representation of property. Shelley, too, was willing to adopt the expedient of basing intermediate reforms on property because he felt that men with property were likely to be more intelligent than farm laborers or factory workers. If the rulers would not grant a limited reform, however, he was ready to stand with the radicals and demand universal suffrage. His chief concern was to keep the principle of liberty and of resistance to oppression alive.

Shelley was a poet who visualized the perfected society of

the future and shadowed forth the ideal conditions of its attainment; but he was also a practical reformer who busied himself with the minute details of effecting some limited reform in the institutions of England. Immediate reforms measure and express present progress. Nothing is more idle than "to reject a limited benefit because we cannot without great sacrifices obtain an unlimited one" ("A Philosophical View of Reform," Clark ed., p. 256). We can conceive what man might be, but we know what he is now. We draw inspiration from the great object of our hopes, but we press forward toward what we regard as perfect by accommodating our theories to the limits of our present imperfections. Shelley's program of practical reform is ultimately based on abstract ideals, but the realization of those ideals is projected into the future.

V

Program of Associations

Besides trying to work out a program for practical reform in keeping with his social vision, Shelley developed another scheme for gradually bridging the gap between the existent and the ideal society. This was the plan for philanthropic associations, early proposed by the poet and frequently mentioned in his later writings. It was another inheritance from the French Revolution and its philosophical background. Shelley's analysis of the values of these intermediating associations indicates that his social and political views are more practical and institutional than Godwin's and confirms the impression that he was considerably closer to the mainstream of revolutionary thought and action than the more anarchistic Godwin ever was.

In "A Defence of Poetry" Shelley spoke of man in society as almost a separate being from "natural" man, possessed as a "social being" with a distinct set of emotions and expressions from which spring the social sympathies (Clark ed., p. 278). As a political doctrine this concept has a kinship to Tom Paine's distinction between society and government. According to Paine, society is always a blessing, since it naturally expresses our needs as social beings, while government is at best a necessary evil, which he defines in Christian terminology as the product of original sin. Society is of Eden. "Government, like

dress, is the badge of lost innocence; the palaces of kings are
built upon the ruins of the bowers of paradise." The formula
comes close to serving as a motto for the age of revolution.
Either eliminate government and let society by itself, as the
free-traders urged, supply the wants of men, or make government as nearly like society in the absence of hereditary and
illogical restraints as possible. The doctrine of man's natural
goodness when released from institutional bondage lies behind
such views. The right kind of government will be "nothing
more than a national association acting on the principles of
society," which permits men's social propensities to create a
close bond through their natural identification of interests
(Paine, I, 4–5, 358–359, 361). What more natural then than
for an ardent disciple of Paine to promote a scheme of associations designed ultimately and almost insensibly to replace the
old and bad restrictive governments. They will simply fall
away from disuse as the looser forms of associational government gradually conduct liberated man to the classless society.

The association idea had a considerable history behind it.
Frenchmen had been discussing revolutionary ideas long before
the Revolution in such organizations as "literary societies, smok-
ing clubs, Masonic Lodges, where the remaking of human society was an accepted goal."[1] The older societies had long
provided discipline in abstract thought. Citizens were initiated
young and trained thoroughly. In Adolphus' biographical
sketches Shelley would have found much information on the
work of revolutionary indoctrination which went on in such
societies. In the article on Mirabeau, Adolphus described the
work of German revolutionaries called the Illuminati, whom
he saw as joining with the Encyclopedists in the work of sup-
planting priests and kings by a "system of cosmopolitism" and
government by experts. He charged Mirabeau with importing
Illuminist doctrines into French freemasonry and planning to

create an association which would expand into a world federation by training and placing young and ardent disciples.[2]

The plan for a world revolutionary government had been worked out by the German Illuminati between 1776 and 1785. They were led by a former professor and Jesuit named Adam or Spartacus Weishaupt, who, using Masonic ceremonial and Jesuit doctrines of blind obedience to the leader, proposed to reform the world by sending select missionary heroes to organize revolutions. "Give me only six such men, and I will engage to change the whole face of the universe" (Barruel, IV, 106). Weishaupt's program was described in l'Abbé Barruel's book on the background of Jacobinism, which is the central source for Shelley's concept of associations. Barruel gave very full documentary evidence, letters, reports, and essays, which the young Shelley found useful in ways which would have shocked the compiler.

Shelley, as Hogg noted, read Barruel's four volumes again and again. Hogg apparently was fascinated by the book, too, for in his *Memoirs of Prince Alexy Haimatoff* he describes his hero's initiation into the Illuminati at a German university. The nature and purposes of the society were explained to Prince Alexy by a venerable eleutherarch. The society was dedicated to liberty, but it required careful discipline of its members. There were oaths and ceremonies as well as soul-steeling experiments. Prince Alexy began his novitiate, underwent three months' confinement without books designed to strengthen and condense his thought, and was introduced to the special language based on philosophical principles which the communicants employed; Alexy balked, however, when he learned that he must accept the Jesuit principle of absolute obedience to his master's will.[3] Shelley's criticism of this section of his friend's novel suggests that he may have discussed plans for a fuller development of Illuminati principles with

Hogg. "The adventure of the Eleutheri, although the sketch of a profounder subject, is introduced and concluded with unintelligible abruptness" (Clark ed., p. 305). The objection would fit the description of Shelley in Peacock's *Nightmare Abbey* as a "transcendental eleutherarch."

Weishaupt conceived of his associations as maturing into invisible governments within existing societies, able to take over the country in times of crisis and coerce the laggards and reactionaries into submission. He stressed, as Shelley did later, the necessity of unity and mutual support. As Weishaupt said, "men would triumph even over heaven were they but united." Their associations could be forged into "the most perfect model of government" to base the society of the future on. In Barruel's ironic description, they proposed to create a "famous association which, by perpetually perfecting its laws and governments, at length taught mankind to cast off every law and every government" (Barruel, III, 55, 347).

The French Revolution had been dominated by the idea of associations. The Jacobin club had itself been the product of a long heritage of associational thought. The Jacobin philosophy was strongly indebted to Rousseau's doctrine of the general will, developed in terms of an ideal society which, like Holy Church, could do no wrong — a perfect contract society endowed with the general will. Through the network of Jacobin societies which finally emerged, the sovereign people were provided with theoretical control over the government. Justification for the excesses of the terror was ultimately the righteous wrath of the divine people, acting as "la volonté présente et agissante du dieu" (the active and immediate will of God) in purging the evil backsliders and moderates.[4] Thus, in the idea of association of like-minded patriots, the Jacobins discovered an effective expression of the idea behind Rousseau's doctrine of the general will. Their affiliated clubs became the effective government in France, the means by which the general will objectified its thoughts in the drama of the National Assembly. Liberty, equality, and fraternity were converted, Brinton comments, into powerful emotional symbols which formed the Jacobins into one body of worshipers of the general will enshrined in their activities.[5]

Whether their philosophy was directly influenced by Illuminist principles or not, the Jacobins did perfect the concept of an effectively unified association of patriots serving and expressing the general will. By the time the true weaknesses of the National Assembly as a governing body were revealed in the many conflicts of authority, the Jacobin clubs, by then far removed from the rudimentary political organization of the old *sociétés de pensée* and similar associations, had become the only strong national organization. Beginning as discussion groups where the ideas and programs of the Enlightenment were debated, the Jacobin organizations soon began to take over governmental functions. Finally they created an "essential form of group action which turned mere talk and speculation into revolutionary political work."[6]

However Shelley might disclaim violence, decry secrecy, and protest against pressures to uniformity, he was undoubtedly aware of the real history of earlier associations and hoped that some such powers might be recovered, however modified or qualified by the bitter results of past experience. One of his sources, Adolphus, traced in some detail the rise to power of the Jacobins from a discussion club to the *de facto* government of France. He explained the work of their committees of correspondence. He showed the Jacobins extending and strengthening their influence through a network of affiliated societies. The most popular and influential journalists were Jacobins.[7] They really governed the country while remaining ostensibly a discussion society of the type Shelley was later to praise and promote. Much of their power was due to their unity. Through their system of affiliation they were able to bring the pressure of their united clubs to bear on the Assembly by repeated petitioning, both national and frequent, expressing the so-called general will in the same manner that Shelley was later to propose in his 1817 pamphlet. Their procedures likely influenced the London Correspondence Society's views on the value of petitioning. They were described for Shelley in Barruel's book. While petitions might not produce reforms, they would keep the subject open for discussion and awaken the public mind so that eventually the lethargic general will could enforce its demands on a dilatory Parliament (Barruel, IV, 49–50).

There were comparable societies in Ireland and England during the period of the French clubs. An account of their ideas and activities was available to Shelley through a fifty-page essay appended to Barruel's work by his translator. It was a time, in fact, when discussion and correspondence societies flourished in Britain as never before. At first mostly discussion societies without strong political coloring, they gradually grew in size and influence, developing regional committees and propagandizing through pamphlets and public meetings. The Irish associations posed the greatest threat to English security during the French wars. It is appropriate that it was in Ireland where Shelley's full-scale proposal for associations was first launched. The Irish rebels had been in league with the French. The announced goals of the Irish Brotherhood, later the United Irishmen, were to "make the light of philanthropy converge" (Shelley's associations were to be called philanthropical associations), and to battle for the rights of man in Ireland. The plan was to organize a Central Society or Lodge from which lodges in smaller towns would radiate. The account in Barruel's book claimed that all the societies in Ireland, England, and France were closely linked by correspondence and a common program. Enlightenment was to spread from town to village and village to town "until the whole nation be sufficiently enlightened and united in the same cause." Provision was made for the breaking up of larger bodies into units of ten with representatives to be elected to councils (Barruel, IV, 3, 29–31, 33). In general the outline of program and procedures strongly resembles the analysis of effective associations and their organization presented in Shelley's works.

Shelley wrote one complete essay on the organization and philosophy of associations, the enthusiastic and entertaining though immature pamphlet published in Ireland in 1812 as part of his program of quietly revolutionizing that part of the kingdom. While he never outlined a program of associations in detail again, his many later references to the idea show that he never gave it up. In his first letter to Leigh Hunt, suggesting a mutual protection group modeled on Illuminism as a means of aiding men like Hunt who face expensive prosecutions for speaking truth, Shelley urged that such an association would fight political corruption by strengthening efforts of reformers against "the coalition of the enemies of liberty" (March 2, 1811, *Letters*, I, 54). Years later from Italy he offered a nearly identical suggestion in his essay-letter (November 3, 1819) on the case of Richard Carlile. Sympathizers with Carlile and his cause should create an asylum for the oppressed in "the frank & spirited union of the advocates for Liberty." However much reformers may disagree in theory — and this is Shelley's constant theme and the foundation for his continuing insistence on the value of associations — they ought to reconcile their practical differences to present a united front against conservative resistance to all change (to Leigh Hunt, November 3, 1819, *Letters*, II, 148). It may also be noted in this context that when Shelley's visionary aspirations for ideal societies were darkened by doubt and despair, he tended to project ideal escape worlds where the poet, the poet and a maiden, or the poet and like-minded Platonists, lovers, and intellectuals might retreat from the corrupt and heedless world to realize their hopes microcosmically and show lagging society what might be done. This theme of retreat to some isolated paradise, a reflection of the earlier idea of philanthropical associations, is expressed in many poems, but most significantly in *The Revolt of Islam, Prometheus Unbound,* and *Epipsychidion.*

Shelley's groups were to be, in the first instance, associations for discussion, governed by the "spirit of sobriety, regularity, and thought" ("An Address to the Irish," Clark ed., p. 54). His "associated philanthropists" were to be, however, both theoretical and practical leaders. They would debate proper measures and the ways of getting necessary legislation enacted. They would criticize existing regimes, marshal the energies of a moribund general will by diffusing knowledge and virtue, consider means of improving the system of national education, and debate publicly appropriate moral and political topics.

Shelley planned to organize and integrate his associations by dividing the country into equal districts. Each local association, animated by a cadre of "Friends of Liberty," would consider and debate reform resolutions. The arrangement reflects Weishaupt's procedures in extending Illuminism as well as the processes of affiliation and correspondence through which the Jacobins extended and consolidated their power. The procedure in the meetings was to be "purely constitutional," not "revolutionary and disorganizing." Assuring Godwin of his nonrevolutionary intentions, Shelley promised to eliminate the *"unnatural unanimity"* of the Jacobins by providing for the free secession of minorities. Associations might proliferate into twenty different societies, "each coinciding generically, tho

differing specifically" (February 24, 1812, *Letters*, I, 259).
One might recall the process of club-making during the French
Revolution which saw a proliferation of societies, Girondists
separating themselves from Jacobins, then being themselves
rent by factions, while the Jacobins in turn divided into En-
ragés, Cordeliers, and Jacobins. It is clear that Shelley intended
to avoid the dangers of revolution while correcting the errors
which had made the French Revolution fail. He wanted to
steer a course with his societies between revolution and the
trifling expediencies of "temporizing reform" ("An Address to
the Irish," Clark ed., p. 59). His associations were to promote
moral and individual reform. The gradually enlarging associations might also endow their members with a larger sense of
the ideally united human community. Thus morality and politics might be unified. Failure to regard politics as an extension
of morality, subject to the same principles and practices, was,
he felt, a central cause of the failure of the French Revolution.
Robespierre had unfortunately tried to bridge the gap with the
guillotine.

The French Revolution had been preceded by a brilliant intellectual movement, but the development had been too one-
sided. The French people "had not been fitted for the possession
of freedom by any moral movement preceding the Revolution." [8]
The necessary moral reinforcement might well be provided,
Shelley believed, by his associations, miniature societies which
would provide stimulation and training for the richer moral
sympathies. Philanthropic associations, as he conceived their
workings, might realize microcosmically now the ideal future
society which would ultimately result from continuing progress.

Shelley's associations were then conceived by the poet as
embryo utopias, reflecting in their organization and their activities the nature of the new world around the corner when
rational and imaginative men compose society. In the immediate

sense they were to work for the specific reforms needed in existing governments, but the long-range view dominated his outlook. Each association would help better the condition of man by being a "society of peace and of love" dedicated to the true "religion of philanthropy." The associations in a sense bridged the gap between practical present reforms and the goal toward which men of good will were to press. They reveal something more in the way of political realism in Shelley than Godwin's systems show without sacrificing the vision. In his comments on the associations one may see, rather more clearly and definitely than in the great social visions of his poetry, the specific outlines of a society at once real and ideal, the kind of society which man can freely create when he begins to will his visions into this world. The long poems shadow forth the golden age, the goal of striving humanity; the prose describes what may be attained now if the enlightened members of the community will but act.

In the world as it is now, the associations could also groom the enlightened leaders required to advance the cause of philanthropy and give them the experience of working together. The weaknesses of logic, character, and understanding of human nature revealed in the writings of the philosophes were carried over to the revolution created by their abstract ideas. One important function of Shelley's philanthropic associations was to correct this weakness by selecting the potential leaders of the new era of orderly change and giving them a broader schooling in humanity than Voltaire, Rousseau, Helvétius, or Condorcet — the men he names — had experienced or conceived ("Proposals for an Association of Philanthropists," Clark ed., p. 61). Thus a second cause, in Shelley's estimation at the time of his proposals, for the failure of the French Revolution, was the inherent weaknesses of a leadership nourished on thinly abstract matter which soon hardened, under the pressures of the times, into dogmas that spilt blood.

The disunity, lack of vigor, and tendency to generality of its leaders were frequently singled out by observers as destructive to the French Revolution. Adolphus attributed the fall of the Brissotin philosophical moderates to their lack of unity in the face of the desperate and active unity of the Jacobins. Perhaps, he suggested, enlightened intellectuals were less capable of subordinating their differences. They tended to idolize themselves as sages of antiquity, but in trying to demonstrate that "the world was made for the wise" they got too wrapped up in metaphysical speculations about theoretical perfection and neglected the culture of the heart, which remained "cold, malignant, and selfish." [9] The Jacobins who succeeded them were acutely described by Riouffe as mainly dedicated men of philosophic and legislative good faith who were led to extremes of ferocity and barbarism by their vanity, inadequate knowledge of human nature, and inability to penetrate the atmosphere of systematic illusions which their activities and abstract discussions generated.[10] Shelley studied these grim pictures of well-meaning but one-sided intellectuals whose excessively abstract and legalistic outlook led them to preach fanatically their sectarian dogmas and to kill by principle. As a result of his awareness, he tried to enrich his own idealism and to sketch a new society which would be governed by the imagination rather than by mere reasoners. His philosophers, poets, and politicians would learn in the sympathetic bonds of the new associations how to live and feel together as well as think together. Once a truly representative government had been achieved by these united reformers, then variety and individuality would enjoy fuller scope.

Shelley, therefore, intended to correct with his new conception of the principles of association the central weaknesses in the philosophy of revolution. He studied the causes of failure of the French Revolution and proposed specific programs to strengthen the new efforts. There must prevail "a certain degree of coalition among the sincere Friends of Reform," especially when the issue was not which reform program or measure should be supported but whether any change at all could be effected against the widely prevailing reactionary spirit of the times ("A Proposal for Putting Reform to the Vote Throughout the Kingdom," Clark ed., p. 161).

A central issue in discussions of associations was the question of secrecy. Secret associations with arcane rituals were, to Godwin, an abomination, and he felt that such secrecy had much to do with the failure of the Revolution. Shelley asserted that his associations were certainly not to be secret. "Concealment implies falsehood." The good cause courts publicity, never submits to the false principle that the end should justify the means ("Proposals for an Association of Philanthropists," Clark ed., p. 64). Shelley may, however, have been rather less adamant against secrecy than his mentor. To Elizabeth Hitchener he confided that his first Irish essay was "*secretly* intended" as a preliminary thrust against Catholicism (January 26, 1812, *Letters*, I, 239). Certainly his sources stressed the role of secrecy in mounting the revolution. Voltaire's watchword of *Écrasez l'infâme*, borrowed by Shelley for the motto to *Queen Mab*, was described by Barruel as the rallying cry for a concerted and concealed attack on all religious and political institutions. "Strike and conceal your hand," said Voltaire in a letter to D'Alembert. He advised his correspondent that the true method was association in a powerful "secret academy." "Let the philosophes unite in a brotherhood, like the Free-Masons, let them assemble and support each other; let them be faithful to the association" (Barruel, I, 116–117). Since the tyrants and imposters are strongly united, the friends of truth must follow their example.

Other sources similarly emphasized the necessity of secrecy.

According to Adolphus, Condorcet, whom Shelley admired, was an active member of corrupted freemasonry in a lodge called *Le Contrat Social*, "which meditated the destruction of religion and government, under pretense of forwarding the reign of philosophy and freedom."[11] Certainly Condorcet defended secrecy in his *Historical Sketch* as the only means of expressing, nourishing, and extending truth in times of persecution and forced conformity.[12] The Irish societies of the early period had also stressed secrecy as a means to survive. Some modified acceptance of the need for secrecy is perhaps involved in the doctrine of progressive expediency which Shelley ultimately developed. Philosophers must often screen their motives and purposes to secure desirable ends, the poet acknowledged in the "Essay on Christianity." Perhaps high truths must always be veiled in myth. Men must be gradually led by their unacknowledged legislators into the experience of the true forms regulating ideal moral and political behavior.

A most complete defence of secret associations was offered by Weishaupt, whose program, as described by the Abbé Barruel, featured a union of reformers and agitators in secret associations to provide the "natural" antidote to despotism. These new societies would give their members a sense of liberation from political bondage. They would almost insensibly learn the power of unity; as their strength grew, the bonds of church and state would be progressively and quietly weakened before this new and more intimate allegiance. Thus, an invisible government would arise within society, ready to triumph even over heaven; for only disunity continues to subject man to the yoke. Because of the present strength of the despots, the associations must disguise their purposes. As Weishaupt proclaimed, "in secrecy our strength principally lies." The repressive powers of existing governments and their readiness as "slaves to ancient forms" to suppress all criticism and opposition made secrecy necessary to the diffusion and discussion of new truths (Barruel, III, 160, 178–179, 212–213, 345).

Actually the strictures of Godwin and Shelley against secrecy of association were in keeping with the official views of the older revolutionary societies. The Jacobins as they developed power and influence through their efficient system of affiliation continued to advocate freedom of discussion and absence of secrecy. This was the fashionable philosophy, though in practice the Club operated more coercively in creating public opinion by a flood of petitions, by control of the press, and by drilling their membership through party whips and caucuses designed to suppress the conflict of views.[18]

Though Shelley's convictions on the subject might under similar stress of action and the exercise of authority have become more flexible, he consistently disapproved of secrecy in associations because of the tendency to produce violence and unnatural unanimity. Later, he worked out carefully reasoned objections against secrecy in the course of an analysis of the failure of premature revolution. In "A Philosophical View of Reform," he emphasized once more the need for the "divided friends of liberty" to be united in "open confederations." Secret associations tended to cause a premature developing of the national will by encouraging theoretical patriots to unite abstractly their political views. Associations would be less prone to thoughtless consolidation of views and forces if kept open to criticism from a variety of outside opinions (Clark ed., p. 257).

Shelley got no encouragement in his practical interests and programs from Godwin. Godwin feared revolution and promoted peaceful and philosophic progress which, he felt, would be distorted by any form of political organization or association. Men are best converted to the cause of the future a few at a time. Godwin had seen the Corresponding Society at work and had as a result become skeptical of any form of political association. In general, when they outlasted some specific occasion which might call them into temporary activity, associations, Godwin accused, foster a fallacious uniformity of opinion which made mind quiescent and stationary. Declamation, petty cabal, and the tumult of party spirit too often accompanied the proceedings. He was willing, as he said in *Political Justice*, to countenance associations which were brought into being by some particular crisis, for example, to protect a man being unjustly attacked by tyrants, but these associations should be disbanded quickly before the natural process of degeneration of good purposes began (I, 299).

Godwin reserved a chapter of his treatise to the analysis of associations. He does not give any overt historical commentary on those of the age but confines himself to the general arguments for and against associations. The contemporary implications are sufficiently clear. He outlines their presumed advantages for organizing and expressing public opinion as well as for rapidly diffusing political information to the public. Godwin says, however, that institutions are already sufficiently sensitive to public opinion, and that the tendency in associations to create an atmosphere of contention and to give excessive power to demagogic individuals severely diminishes their practical utility. In other words, his numerous objections to associations are founded on their failure to do precisely what Shelley had in mind for them to do, that is, produce a lively unity and effective leadership. They tend rather, says Godwin, to engender counterassociations with all the "uproar of revolution." Either the free play of individual opinion and spirited inquiry, the only real sources of truth, are too much subordinated to the official views of a group, or the compulsion to align one's views with the prevailing sentiments through a sympathetic participation will weaken the influence of reason. Each man feels a pressure "to identify his creed with that of his neighbor." Thus, associations tend to check the progress of truth or make its workings "unnatural and mischievous." Truth grows only in "sequestered privacy" under conditions of "tranquil interchange" between two people. Conversation, reading, and independent thought — these alone produce the variety essential to true progress and the creation of the necessary clusters of great minds, not the "insatiate gulf of noisy assemblies" where unscrupulous and turbulent characters coerce the community and develop systems as inimical to true philosophic growth as any organized government (*Political Justice*, I, 285–287).

These lessons were confirmed directly by Godwin in an early letter to Shelley. "Discussion, reading, enquiry, perpetual communication: these are my favourite methods for the improvement of mankind." For Shelley's benefit, he described his own experience at political dinners in the 1790's with the distortions of political insights caused by the "artifices of organization." [14] He warned that Shelley might be preparing baths of blood for the people with his pamphlets in Ireland.

Shelley, however, insisted that his associations were strictly compatible with the principles of *Political Justice*. They were designed primarily to foster the "eager activity of philanthropists," and whatever unanimity they might create was to be founded strictly on reason, with provisions made for the philosophical secession of dissentients. Unity of purpose and general direction would be protected; but the "refinement of secessions" would eliminate "fictitious unanimity," and the absence of secrecy would make "violent innovation" impossible. Shelley assured Godwin that his own experience with Irish political dinners had corroborated Godwin's charges against such gatherings, but he felt that his associations, which he said had actually been suggested by reading Godwin, would really create an atmosphere for the "confidential discussions" which the older philosopher recommended. They could perhaps establish "familiar parties for discussion," not so much of immediate grievances and solutions, but of the larger questions involved in the "progress of human perfectibility" (March 8 and 18, 1812, *Letters*, I, 267–268, 276). Godwin had, however, he acknowledged, made him less sure that his associations could "festinate" progress.

While it may seem surprising that Shelley should have refurbished ideas and programs which had in the past aroused violent opposition and had been credited with the worst destruction of the Revolution, his basic position seems well-balanced. In general, he worked to invest the cause of moderate revolution and enlightened patriotism with some of the same fervor and effective unity which animated the single-minded partisans of the past, while adding the richness and variousness of thought and activity characteristic of a wider and deeper philosophy.

Furthermore, Shelley's association schemes reveal a more realistic and practical spirit in his approach to reform than Godwin's. He could acknowledge the value of the other's criticism of the dangers of unreasoned unity without divorcing himself from revolution. His views are closer to revolutionary practice than Godwin's. The French Revolution was an even greater stimulant or influence to his political thought and activity than his reading of Godwin, though he tried to learn moderation and foresight from both. He re-experienced and communicated freshly the old fervor and visionary hopes of the earlier period, tempered by the knowledge earned through partial failure and general loss of hope. Philanthropical associations could yet function as living models of what man might be, while training men in the responsibilities of citizenship in the new world and grooming the natural leaders and inspirers of men. Shelley blended principles and practice in his proposals, tried to look toward immediate and ultimate reforms at once, and sought to avoid the dangers of collective opinion and action which Godwin and the Revolution pointed out.

In associations the seeds of the future could be nurtured, man's last, best hopes kept alive in an age of near total eclipse. Shelley never forsook this idea of a unity of men of good will, and his practical efforts to help substantiate the idea place him in the line of later nineteenth- and twentieth-century socialist thought, which extended and strengthened the concept of unity and power by association. Shelley, the Avelings said, perceived clearly the nature of later social development as a contest between the possessing and producing classes; the theories and solutions he presented place him among modern rather than among Utopian socialists.[15] His ideas of association are not ultimately compatible with the rigidity of Marxist thought on collective thought and action, but he does realize the function and importance of associations and even appreciates the usefulness of the kind of pressure toward change that such groups can produce. Shelley gave greater stress, however — and this separates him from subsequent socialist thought — to the role of the revolutionary heroes: the poets and prophets who create the revolution in the minds of men.

VI

Revolutionary Ritual and Revolutionary Lyric

In his long revolutionary poems Shelley describes his new religion of humanity, and he borrows from the rituals of the French Revolution in developing this creed. His interest in ritual further distinguishes his outlook from Godwin's, but it does link him closely to the mystical and emotional elements prominent in the French fetes. At the beginning of the Princess Charlotte essay in 1817, he particularly discussed the value of public rituals. He proposed that there be national mourning "for those who have benefited the state," as, for example, Milton, Rousseau, and Voltaire. Presumably Shelley had read in his sources the accounts of the reburying of Rousseau and Voltaire in the Pantheon. It was tremendously important, he said, to conduct large public rituals for such occasions and for other calamities too. The whole world should have mourned when the French Republic failed. He then defined his basic theory of ritual. "This helps to maintain that connection between one man and another, and all men considered as a whole, which is the bond of social life" ("An Address to the People on the Death of the Princess Charlotte," Clark ed., p. 164). As a poet Shelley found revolutionary ritual congenial. His poems may be partly interpreted as rituals designed to help bring about the ends they celebrate though they are also of course rational and imaginative constructions which may be profitably considered in quite different ways.

The French Revolution was not simply a revolution in the name of reason. It formulated its own myths, its forms or ideals, which were conceived to act on the new masses rather like divinities. It was not a godless revolution. Robespierre was to react against the libertinism of the period in the name of the new Rousseauistic faith which had belief in God and immortality as its minimum tenets. Gods there were of another kind also, the great semianimated, half-deified new abstractions of *liberté* and *patrie*. Ritual worship of *la patrie* became, in fact, an enforced dogma in many ways akin to Catholicism, though espoused by worshipers who found the rites and beliefs of the older church unacceptable. It was a great epoch of faith, supported and enriched by spectacle, which appealed both to the senses and the rational souls of its believers. The creed was the declaration of the Rights of Man, called by Rabaut St. Étienne, one of Shelley's sources, "la théologie sociale" of man. One might think that such religious formulas and practices would make the Revolution unpalatable to Shelley. On the contrary, there is a good deal of theological language and ritual in his poetry, especially the "hymns" and the revolutionary epics in which he revives the old cause with new religious fervor. Shelley's religion did lack dogma, and he parts from revolutionary practice in this sense.

The new revolutionary religion had the sacred dogmas of "Liberté et sainte égalité," a form of worship adapted from Catholic ceremonial which was elaborated in connection with civic fetes, a body of saints, heroes, and martyrs like the "holy Marat," and an energy sustained by the "mystical faith in humanity" and the "ultimate regeneration of the human race." In this new secular religion of *civisme*, the extension of rational knowledge was substituted for grace as a means of salvation, and the ideal of the general progress of the race was felt to be a sufficient ideal, a brightly beaconing future becoming a kind of deity whom men can help bring into power by contributing to a development whose direction is already clear. "Without a new heaven to replace the old, a new way of salvation, of attaining perfection, the religion of humanity would appeal in vain to the common run of men." [1]

That Shelley was aware of these tendencies and these convictions may be inferred from his enthusiasm for the program of the Illuminati, as described by Barruel. Spartacus Weishaupt had also proclaimed the need for a new morality and a new worship. "Let reason at length be the religion of men." Barruel connected this sentiment directly with the altars, the worship services, and festivals of reason of the French Revolution (III, 200). The Jacobin club promoted the new religion most extensively and in the most modern way. As a new religious sect, according to the author of *Mémoires d'un détenu*, they created their own sacerdotal formulas and intricate ritual. [2] As disciples of Rousseau rather than the dry reasoners of the main line of Enlightenment thought, they distrusted mere intellect and favored a culture of the heart which would use rituals to make citizens "feel the mystic identity of the general will," and to make the principal revolutionary abstractions real to the senses. In the work of creating "a visible Revolution as a substitute for the visible Church," they endowed the early events of the Revolution with symbolic values which were honored at the great festivals by citizens sympathizing publicly in mass assemblies. [3] They increased men's emotional awareness of their corporate identity with their cults, altars, trees of liberty, party symbols. Churches were called "temples de la Raison." [4] At their meetings they convened before busts of their heroes like Marat and framed copies of the Declaration of Rights. Formulas, sermons, oaths — all served to complete and reinforce the ritual and emotional bonds. Missionaries were sent out to the unenlightened in other provinces and countries to raise zeal for Jacobinical causes by oratory. One recalls Shelley's similar mission of liberation to Ireland. These procedures culminated in the great fetes which Robespierre initiated. This same religious zeal, M. Cochin claimed, created and justified later the most odious excesses of the Terror, when the wrath of God and the righteous wrath of Jacobin terrorists purging man of antique evils were as one.[5]

Writing to Peacock, July 12, 1820, Shelley said that he anticipated some "rough festivals at the apotheosis of the Debt" (*Letters*, II, 213). The comment reflects knowledge of the great fetes ordained by the Jacobins to bring the people into the unity of Rousseau's general will. Shelley not only knew of the revolutionary fetes, but he also created similar ritual panoramas in his poetry, in *The Revolt of Islam* most notably. The revolutionary festivals were designed to create an imaginative sympathy of the citizens for the cause of liberty, equality, and fraternity. Spectacle was the means selected to stimulate the imagination. Abstract ideas were personified in the ritual and dance before thousands of spectators. Torches of knowledge were kindled all over France by pretty women disguised as Goddesses of Reason. Liberty trees were planted as the people danced about them in the spirit of renewed innocence and joy for a reborn humanity. Thus were the revolutionary abstractions imprinted on the popular mind, Truth presented in visible form.

The fetes, in their revolutionary sense, may be traced back to Rousseau's *Letter to D'Alembert*, where he discussed the value of conducting public rituals — open-air performances were best — in which spectators may participate and thereby learn to think and feel as one.[6] The Jacobins apparently related Rousseau's doctrine of the general will to his notions of the value of public rituals and festivals, which were intended to unite the individual and the social will. The general will is reflected by, implicated in, or perhaps, at least to the eyes of faith, really present in actual societies, like the divine presence in the wine and wafer of the Mass. The general will like the will of God in Christian theology is always true and unerring, though the individual simply as an individual cannot truly comprehend or obey it.[7] The general will was to be discovered in the decisions of the clubs and then accepted by society as the new divinities of liberty and *la patrie* were progressively socialized, secularized, and humanized. The fetes were a principal agent in effecting this development toward a new unity.

These attempts to substitute a secular religion of humanity for Christianity, reflected in Shelley's own hymns and pageants for humanist revolutionaries, began with the first celebration of the Fall of the Bastille, July 14, 1790, and were a principal feature of the whole era. Napoleon too made effective use of such public rituals. In a comprehensive scholarly account of their function in the Revolution, M. Tiersot credited the fetes with being a strong force in bringing the people together physically, intellectually, and emotionally. The symbolic representations which they featured both captured the intelligence and touched the heart. The citizens of the whole nation came together spontaneously, and a collective sentiment was created and strengthened. Thought and feeling were made one, particularly when the music, the chanting voices, and the abstract lyrics brought about a new extension of meaning in experience. Through such means citizens could reach toward and really feel that they had attained some unknown and almost inaccessible ideal and power — "la prière dont l'expression imprécise est dans tous les coeurs" (the prayer whose obscure expression is in every human heart).[8]

Shelley had available to him a good many specific descriptions of the fetes. Helen Maria Williams mentioned their value in arousing great and general feelings which would enable the untutored masses to enter into noble or exalted sentiments, heroical actions, or the spirit of generous sacrifice. She felt that the patriotic energy which the festive rituals produced had helped create the courage and successful fighting of the French revolutionary armies.[9] Mary Wollstonecraft testified in her work on the Revolution to the strength of such patriotic and humanitarian sentiment. Contagious enthusiasm accomplished more than military knowledge could have effected in weeks, a "resolution, more powerful than all the engines and batteries in the world." When united citizens turned to resist the invading tyrants, they created the power to succeed from "a common interest resembling an electrical sympathy" (*View of F. R.*, pp. 58, 114, 169, 193, 201, 264).

These were words well calculated to fire the enthusiasm, even of a second-generation revolutionary like Shelley, often disheartened by the decline of hope and the grip of reaction. What might be done! This was to become his theme. Yet Mrs. Wollstonecraft, like Godwin, criticized such devices as fetes and associations for resorting to mysterious appeals to the imagination, a faculty which betrays men into irrational follies by supporting "the enthusiasm of the moment." "Mystery alone gives full play to the imagination, men pursuing with ardor objects indistinctly seen or understood" (*View of F. R.*, pp. 425, 468). Shelley, with a more exalted view of the imagination and a faith in the prophetic and visionary elements of a poetry which has clear kinship in nature and function with such rituals, would not have fully shared either Mrs. Wollstonecraft's or Godwin's reservations. The fetes, garlands, and altars, which in France lent dramatic energy "to the conviction of truth and justice" and seemed to observers like Hazlitt a judgment on French superficiality and sensuality,[10] reappeared in Shelley's revolutionary poetry in the service of a richer, more comprehensive faculty of knowledge than Godwin's discursive reason. He did not accept Mrs. Wollstonecraft's dictum that the imagination inhibits and obscures the intellect, for like any artist he had come to regard his creative powers as semidivine, as bringing him into living contact with truths known in no other way.

The two revolutionary spectacles which apparently influenced Shelley most particularly, the first great fete of the federation (the first Bastille Day) and Robespierre's fete of the Supreme Being, were described in his major sources with especial fullness. Both Adolphus and Rabaut St. Étienne wrote accounts of the great pageantry of the earlier fete. Four hundred thousand citizens turned out as one to complete the necessary building in the days before and then witnessed the great procession led by Lafayette, followed by a Mass and the swearing of oaths by the King and people.[11] Before the great altar "de la patrie," "Tous jurèrent aussi de vivre libres ou de mourir." [12]

Adolphus also described the Festival of Reason held at Notre Dame in November 1793, the inspiration of Hébert and the most spectacular attempt to dramatize the substitution of the new secular religion of humanity for Christianity. It was but the working out, said Barruel, of the prophecies of the hierophants of Illuminism for a public leader to pronounce, "France recognizes no other worship but that of reason" (Barruel, IV, 413). The ceremonies were very like Shelley's rituals in book V of *The Revolt of Islam*, after the temporary victory of the cause of the nearly bloodless revolution. Women standing before the old Christian altar in Notre Dame saluted the flame of human reason. Then an actress representing Liberty and holding a pike in her hand likewise bowed, as a hymn to liberty by Marie Joseph Chénier and Gossec was sung.[13]

Déscend ô Liberté, fille de la Nature:
Le peuple a reconquis son pouvoir immortel:
Sur les pompeux débris de l'antique imposture,
Ses mains relèvent ton autel.*

Women were often used in other fetes as symbols of reason in ways very similar to Shelley's use of Cythna in *The Revolt*. At this particular feast of reason, the whole convention was present, according to Adolphus, offering vows and adoration to the new deity in the great cathedral, now converted into a temple of philosophy.[14] Thus, Barruel judged, the atheistic revolutionaries had accommodated their seditious and blasphemous doctrines to the natural propensity of the pious French people to worship (III, 381).

As Robespierre's political strength and influence grew, he apparently became restive, as a disciple of Rousseau's more impassioned religious ideas and feelings, over the atheism of the fetes of reason. He tried to discredit the cult of reason in favor of a worship of a supreme being who guards oppressed innocence and punishes crime. In a speech preparing his colegislators and constituents for his feast of the Supreme Being, Robespierre proclaimed, in the spirit of the Savoyard Vicar, that nature was the priest of the Supreme Being, that the universe was his temple, and that high-republican virtue was the appropriate mode of worship. The fetes, he said, witnessed "la joie d'un grand peuple rassemblé sous ses yeux pour resserrer les doux noeuds de la fraternité universelle, et pour lui présenter l'hommage des coeurs sensibles et purs,"† and he emphasized their

---

* "Descend O Liberty, daughter of Nature: / The common people have reconquered their immortal power: / Upon the pompous wreckage of the ancient imposture, / Their hands lift up thy altar once more."

† "the joy of a great people joined together under His eyes in order to tighten the gentle bonds of universal brotherhood, and to present to Him the homage of pure and sensitive hearts."

importance as a means of arousing enthusiasm for liberty and love of country, of creating respect for laws, heroes, benefactors of humanity, and of commemorating the sacred events of the holy Revolution — especially when all these highly appropriate rituals were conducted in a spirit of dedication to the Supreme Being.[15] Thus the Theophilanthropic phase of the Revolution was initiated, and the blood purges, to remove the civically unvirtuous, were accelerated.

At the feast of the Supreme Being, in Paris on June 8, 1794, there was considerable pageantry. Robespierre set fire to a cardboard figure with ass's ears, symbolizing atheism, and a somewhat smoke-stained form symbolizing wisdom and philosophy was revealed. Adolphus, extracting his comment from a Helen Maria Williams letter, further mentioned a sermon by Robespierre, the offering of prayers, and the mass swearing of an oath of fidelity to liberty by an immense chorus of some five hundred thousand Parisians[16] "tous frappés de la même emotion" (all struck with the same emotion). One judgment of the scene was that "l'âme du peuple entier s'exhala en s'unissant en un chant collectif et universel" (the soul of the entire populace breathed forth in unison a collective and universal hymn).[17] The possibilities of creating a strong sense of social sympathies and lofty religious feelings by uniting the agencies of poetry, music, and religious ritual had been demonstrated. The celebrated symbolic spectacle marked the culmination of eighteenth-century enthusiasm for the semideities or daemons of liberty, justice, truth, and humanity. Emotionally charged projections of nature and the new cosmical science had been added to the mixture. As Condorcet suggested, according to Adolphus, the French Revolution had become a religion, and Robespierre the high-priest of a sect within it.[18]

It is such a compound of religion, humanitarianism and social radicalism that Shelley inherits. His kinship to these forms and feelings of the new religion of humanity is closer than his relation to the thought of Godwin. Godwin carried on the work of the rationalists in the Enlightenment, the main tradition of Voltaire, Diderot, D'Holbach, and Condorcet. Shelley accepted their abstractions but expanded his vision with the more enthusiastic doctrines of Rousseau and his followers in this later stage of the Revolution. Godwin helped furnish Shelley with the critical perspective to avoid the abuses and irrational excesses of the Messianic revolutionaries, but the disciple went far beyond the master in his views of man's needs and limitations and his definition of the faculties which may bring him to ultimate fulfillment of his destiny.

The rituals of a society draw their life and value from the sense of an underlying metaphysical unity which ideally arouses and shapes the larger sympathies of both the actors and spectators of the rituals. The rituals may describe and adumbrate an as yet unrealized social meaning or content. Shelley has such a social content as a central theme for his poetry. Integrated in his imagination was the framework of a new world of forms. The audience which shared his experience might discover special sustenance and inspiration in his poetry. His poems will manifest a latent social and spiritual unity and arouse the emotions of hope and love which help produce the reality. Thus, men in society may acquire, ritually and emotionally at least, this sense of oneness. To suggest this unity is to make an important beginning in the task of bringing the ritual forms and the real society together.

In *The Revolt of Islam*, Shelley's enlightened rebels celebrated "a sacred Festival / A rite to attest the equality of all / Who live" after the fall of the tyrant. An altar of federation, as on the first Bastille Day, was erected, and hymns with revolutionary content (like Shelley's own "Hymn to Intellectual Beauty" presumably) were sung by female choirs as the offi-

ciating priestess conducted the new rites succeeding the abolition of "Faith, an obscene worm" (canto V). The "divine
Equality" is likened to the coming breath of spring which
renews and awakens the sleeping world as the mind clasps
the barren globe in its "bright embrace" (canto V, stanza 3
of ode). Thus the mystic action of a creed awakens the mind
through the sympathies generated by a large mass of celebrants
united in admiration of a semidivine idea. The revolutionary
poem, like the ritual objects or dances of other forms of worship,
resembles the visionary goal of aspiring reform, expresses it,
and thus becomes a source of power capable of releasing or
creating "mana."

Godwin had said, "Men are weak at present, because they
have always been told they are weak, and must not be trusted
with themselves" (*Political Justice*, II, 409). Like Godwin,
Shelley wanted to teach men that they might become better if
they so willed, since the faculties and the abilities were in them.
But he was not contented merely with reason and philosophic
anarchism. Unlike Godwin and Mary Wollstonecraft he did
not limit himself merely to rational argument. The idea of a
collective sentiment aroused by poems and rituals and directed
toward nearly inaccessible forms of power, beauty, and energy
was to become a central source of reforming afflatus for Shelley
in his renewed religion of revolution.

Poetry unites ritual and myth, the primitive and the civilized, the rhythmic dance and the philosophic abstraction. In
the revolutionary poem, the new world is acted out and thus
established as contingently real, as a permanent possibility.
When celebrated in the poetic visions of the poet-prophets,
that world is given power to operate directly on the imagination
of its beholders and to set the will to unite vision and reality
to work.

The special function of revolutionary ritual and poetry was

to invoke and give objective existence to the great humanistic personifications — Liberty, Equality, Fraternity. Abstractions were to be made alive and visible to the susceptible people. The new deities whose worship was celebrated at the fetes were summoned to grace the renewed worshipers with their holy energies. Through the rituals which celebrated the presence of these new deities, men acquired strength for their mystical faith in humanity and the golden age to come. In order to strengthen this religious bond among men the French Committee of Public Safety had asked the poets to turn their attention to dramatizing the main events of the Revolution, to publicize the heroism of the soldiers of liberty, and to compose patriotic hymns and republican dramas.[19] The goal was, as Mackintosh put it, to eliminate the old master-slave psychology and to carry "the spirit of equality and freedom into the feelings, the manners, the most familiar intercourse of men." [20]

One could emphasize the process of gradual rational development necessary to accomplish the ultimate saturation of men by these principles, and such was the way of Godwin, or one could emphasize the need for conversion through sympathetic and often rapid communication with the new gods. Shelley really accepted both views. As a poet he worked to give motive power to the abstract ideals whose cause he served. To make abstractions real, cogent, and effective became a central goal for him as a poet-prophet and "unacknowledged legislator." Thus, the abstract character of much of his poetry, a subject for complaint by some readers and critics, may be evaluated in a different light when one realizes how much emotional and rational human content Shelley was attempting to endow the abstractions with. His practice was in keeping with that of poets like Chénier in the revolutionary period whose poems are described by Tiersot as celebrating simple abstract ideas and attempting to obtain the character of generality essential to success in revolutionary hymns.

During the Revolution the poets had been enlisted by the Committee of Public Safety, by a decree of 27 Floréal II, to celebrate appropriately the heroic achievements of the liberated people in order to inspire further patriotic and humanitarian sacrifices. Revolutionary hymns like those of Chénier gave lyric expression to the simple abstract ideas of the kind which the Revolution was dedicated to propagate.[21] To enrich such intentions as these, Shelley later contributed the notion of the language and harmony of high poetry as a medium and an instrument for conveying inexhaustible meaning in a progressive revelation which continually developed new relations ("A Defence of Poetry," Clark ed., p. 291). Moreover, like the other Romantics he worked to discard the mechanical faculty psychology inherited from Enlightenment and Revolutionary associationists and to discover a new theory of poetry which would explain his own experience and demonstrate the importance of the organizing imagination to a knowledge which draws from both thought and feeling.

If such is the highest knowledge, then one's conception of the true revolution must be altered to agree with it. So Shelley in "A Defence of Poetry" urged that social reasoners and mechanists, that is, philosophes who were credited with creating the French Revolution, yield the palm to the poets. The rationalists had pushed their efforts to transform society by the guide of limited insights too dangerously far. When they neglected "those first principles which belong to the imagination," they succeeded only in further exasperating the differences which divided men into hostile camps and produced the threat of alternate "anarchy and despotism." The cure is to recognize and establish the pre-eminence of the inventive and creative faculty, so far superior to "application of analytical reasoning" to social aberrations. In great poetry men may see as in a "prismatic and many-sided mirror" the nobler selves latent in their present distorted identities. By collecting what is best in man, the forms of art lend strength and beauty to man's efforts to be reborn. Especially in the drama does the "connection of poetry and social good" become most obvious, as the drama combines many more poetic modes than the others (Clark ed., pp. 292–293, 285), Shelley's own lyric dramas seem to be animated by this conviction.

Prometheus gave "man speech, and speech created thought, / Which is the measure of the universe" (II, iv, 73–74). The language of poetry is man's most comprehensive language. Shelley, unlike Byron, was convinced that his own age had created poetry of startling power, capable of sensing and directing the spirit of new life and change circulating in the dizzying abysses of thought. Byron said, "That this is the age of the decline of English poetry will be doubted by few who have calmly considered the subject." [22] Shelley, taught by other masters, and more aware than Byron of the true value of poets like Wordsworth and Coleridge, trumpeted a new age of gold hid from all but the poets in the shadows of unfolding time.

Social institutions help create poets when these institutions are governed by the spirit and life of poetry, and poets discover the institutions which truly reflect the world of imaginative forms. The social forms or institutions which shape, regulate, and may unfortunately restrict human development must be made expressive of the richest insights of the poet-authors of moral and intellectual revolutions. These insights in turn will deepen in response to the newly intense and comprehensive social forms, forms which will at best both measure and direct the progress of humanity in its ceaseless and dynamic growth. The power of intense communication among men increases as the poetic impulse revives. Whether they serve the revolutionary gods consciously or not — as Wordsworth, Coleridge, and Southey certainly did not — Shelley saw revelations in contemporary poets of the potential order of humanity which they could not help apprehending though they might as men resist the changes and innovations that kindled their glowing imagery and impassioned idealism. "The most unfailing herald, companion, and follower of the awakening of a great people to work a beneficial change in opinion or institution, is Poetry" ("A Defence of Poetry," Clark ed., p. 297). Mary Wollstonecraft had said: "Perhaps the most improving exercise of the mind, confining the argument to the enlargement of the understanding, is the restless enquiries that hover on the boundary, or stretch over the dark abyss of uncertainty." [23] Her words suggest the kind of program for investigating the shadows of futurity which Shelley's poetry of revolutionary idealism carries out.

The poet as man can scarcely comprehend the power and significance of the currents of meaning stored in his images and ideas, for he draws inspiration from the transient visitations of that immortal god of the imagination who redeems this sublunar world from decay. Poets are spirits of "the most refined organization" who can "colour all that they combine with the evanescent hues of this ethereal world," yet their poetry is not under the control of their "active powers." The spirit of an age of revolution creates responses in these "hierophants of an unapprehended inspiration," though they may have renounced revolution for nationalist conservatism.

The poet has an advantage over other artists in immediacy and impact because he speaks the language of the people. It is his task, however, to restore the inert energies of language by investing his poems with revolutionary content and purging away the mammon of everyday use. Thus man, pre-eminently "an imaginative being" whose "own mind is his law" ("A Treatise on Morals," Clark ed., p. 186), is trained by the myth-making imagination of poets to comprehend the universal relatedness of all things and ideas. Poets lift the veils blurring the forms of the ideal revolution and instruct the will of man how to enact the vision.

The poet-reformer reopens communication between the latent forms of the beautiful world within the mind of man and the existing social forms whose errors and departures presently inhibit the flow of inspiration. Then the "Planetary music heard in trance" (*Epipsychidion*, l. 86) by the impassioned poet may exercise more effectively its shaping power. Implied in such views is the notion of a pre-established harmony between the inner and outer worlds. The forms of the perfected world which reside in the mind of man have their obscure objective counterpart outside the mind. The poet must accept this "psycho-natural parallelism" [24] in order to support faith in the effort to bring the world into unconscious "sympathy with hopes and fears it heeded not" ("To a Skylark"). The new world lies ready to be born when the enlarged and active moral imagination senses the "seldom-heard mysterious sound" which the spinning world "enkindles" ("With a Guitar, to Jane"). What the poet saw, Godwin said, was "beauty and harmony and life, accompanied with a silent eloquence which spoke to his soul. The universe was to him a living scene, animated by a mysterious power, whose operations he contemplated with admiration and reverence." [25] Shelley often echoed this passage.

The poem reflects the essential forms of nature and human experience because the poet has cultivated a "wise passiveness" which enables him to perceive the dim forms of beauty in society and nature. Other symbol systems may tend to distort, inhibit, or paralyze human responses because of the tendency to fix and dogmatize implicit in most descriptions, but poetry presents ideas and attitudes in novel contexts of image and experience. It continually reshapes our perspectives so that they may in progressively more adequate ways mirror the elusive forms of our destiny. The poet is the natural enemy of dogma.

The imagination as the instrument of awareness of the "shadows of futurity" continually breaks up the old patterns of knowledge and experience and freshly synthesizes the vital forms caught in its activity. The poet re-creates the world in a new light and then combines his creations "by a master-spirit's law." Moved by an intense apprehension of the nature of his own mind's workings, he brings nature to life, or endows it with the life of mind, "Wakening a sort of thought in sense" (*Peter Bell the Third*, ll. 303–312). The poet has a "passion for re-forming the world," but he does not, as a poet, present reasoned doctrines for the "direct enforcement of reform." Rather he projects fresh myths of the new man by creating "beautiful idealisms of moral excellence" which will help prepare the mind of man to love, hope, and endure.

There is to be sure a continual tension between older patterns or orders and fresh experience. The poet tries to maintain this tension or balance. He does not reject the past, for the forms were implicit there too, but he continually re-apprehends them and provides them with fresh energy so that they may fuel progressive improvements. Current social forms have a built-in tendency to harden into dogmas; therefore, the poet, who feels within himself the power to "shake the Anarch Custom's reign, / And charm the minds of men to Truth's own sway," renews the imagination and reopens the flow from outer sources of energy to the answering inner changes and continual adjustments of men. Men unfortunately accumulate knowledge rather than assimilating it to their moral and imaginative natures. The poetic impulse shaping knowledge into feeling may dwindle. "We want the creative faculty to imagine that which we know; we want the generous impulse to act that which we imagine; we want the poetry of life." It is only when man is "passionately and morally involved" in the truth he knows that it becomes effective.[26]

A poetry of the ideal revolution, with the abstract dimensions of life, which reflects the eternal forms toward which change directs, is the prescription offered by Shelley to the sickness of the imagination and will he described. His kind of poetry was designed to make the forms penetrate into the moral imagination, for his "curious and metaphysical anatomy of human passion and perception," while it does luxuriate in abstract ideas, does not present those ideas blandly and undramatically, but clings, as Mrs. Shelley noted, "to the subtler inner spirit" (Hutchinson ed., p. x) rather than the outward and ceremonial forms of the revolutionary abstractions.

To be governed by the imagination is to be always a revolutionary, for the imagination, like Shelley's West Wind, continually destroys to re-create. It works organically, not mechanically. Both man and society are living things which grow and change. The institutions which give the organism the stability necessary to measured growth must express the poetry of life and the times rather than distort and thwart development by acting as rigid landmarks of a decayed past. Revolutions in the mind and in society are required to destroy selfishness, dogma, and convention and replace them with new and living forms of truth and beauty, forms which should not themselves be worshiped lest they in turn repress growth. The ideal revolution should be a bloodless, continuing process, inspired by love of man and marked by a balance of institutions and man's development. The poet's role in this continuing revolution is to "awaken the feelings, so that the reader should see the beauty of true virtue" and be inspired to look for a nobler moral and political creed than now governs society. Poets should not didactically enforce specific creeds and dogmas, but present images, as Shelley did, of the true revolutionary hero in his development and self-expression, images of the "growth and progress of individual mind aspiring after excellence" and loving mankind. Thus may "public hope" be awakened and directed (*The Revolt of Islam*, preface). How easily men might become better, Godwin had said, if they so will. They should be made aware of their abilities and the purposes which their faculties indicate.

Poetry or imagination thus becomes a central agent in reform. Though we are bound by time and the defects and obscurities of our perceptions, which keep our apprehension limited and partial, the world of forms remains as a stable truth.

> For love, and beauty, and delight,
> There is no death nor change: their might
> Exceeds our organs, which endure
> No light, being themselves obscure.
>
> (*The Sensitive Plant*)

So also the ideal society is true, whether realized in experience or not. The imagination is, to Shelley, the active organ of morality and poetry; poetry and morality have the same source in the imagination. The sympathetic imagination responds to the possible perfection in all men, and men are united by this common awareness as they are progressively governed by the imagination. In part Shelley, like Morris and Ruskin later, would bring about the new world by making everyone an artist or poet. When men produce the poetry of life, the world of economic units, of producers and consumers, is on the wane.

Active poets, or men at once most sensitive to harmony and best able to produce it, bring the arts into conspiracy with morality and knowledge to interpenetrate life and society with beauty and truth. They make men greater by habitually elevating their minds to magnificent conceptions. Imagination, Mrs. Wollstonecraft said in a passage likely influential on Shelley, produces "all those fine sympathies that lead to rapture, rendering men social by expanding their hearts." [27] One judges that a thing is good when he beholds its goodness in images and experiences of sufficient intensity and conviction. Once men can agree that a thing is good, "the object is more than half accomplished" (Paine, I, 450–451). The power and the will to good may be united. The poet of the ideal revolution, "considering either the moral or the material universe as a whole" (to William Godwin, December 11, 1817, *Letters*, I, 577), must teach this lesson, not simply by bold dramatization of semipersonified abstractions but by training readers in the apprehension of the "minute and remote distinctions of feelings" inside the abstract forms which give them their power. For Shelley, aesthetics and ethics are inseparable, since "perception of the beautiful underlies all human sympathy." [28]

By arousing and nourishing the passions of hope and love, poetry contributes centrally to the creation of the new world of the imagination. This highest faculty of knowledge is identified Socratically with the loftiest virtue in a nearly classic theory of imitation by Shelley in the "Defence of Poetry." The writer embodies the "ideal perfection of his age in human character." His readers escape from their ordinary, earthbound selves into the enlarged knowledge and sympathies of the revolutionary hero and heroine. The movement is from admiration to imitation to identification with the presented beauty and nobility and charity of a Laon or a Cythna. So, in the preface to *Revolt*, Shelley expressed the hope that his dramatization of the "lofty passions" of his characters would arouse a "generous impulse" in his readers, "an ardent thirst for excellence." Rather than reasoned doctrines, men need this ideal poetry which awakens and enlarges the mind, makes them receptive to new combinations of thought and feeling, tears away the veil of familiarity from the hidden beauty in man and nature. Morality, Shelley said in the "Defence," means love, a sympathetic identification with the beauty in thought, action, and personality which the lyric dramatist may project. This power of love is produced by the imagination, the specifically moral, strongly willed, and creative sympathy which projects us into the situation of other beings. One may say that imagination is thus the source of all moral good, all progress of civilization. Poetry awakens, directs, and enlarges the domain of the imagination with new thoughts and feelings that further kindle the enthusiasm for ideal good and beauty (Clark ed., pp. 282–283).

Thus, the natural Platonist in Shelley broke with the nature poetry and natural religion of Wordsworth to proclaim the "power of poetry to create a golden world surpassing nature." [29] Humanity is schooled into Utopia through the education of the heart and intellect which expands our social sympathies. So practical a revolutionist as Spartacus Weishaupt had similarly urged his Illuminati: "Above all, stimulate them to the love of the object. Let them view it as grand, important, and congenial to their interests and favourable passions. Paint in strong colours the miseries of the world; tell them what men are, and what they might be" (Barruel, III, 111).

The poet, made ardent by his vision of the possible, must busy himself, however, with the actual by applying the insights of holy imagination to practical and contemporary problems. He must fuse metaphysics and politics. His vision must give courage and direction to his political faith rather than provide a substitute for action. His poetry has the power of making "harmony" become "love" ("The Woodman and the Nightingale," l. 38). The poet must help reveal the hidden splendors in man so that all men may enjoy the union of beauty and liberty known now by a few artists.

The imagination is both the source of revolutionary energy

and the fulfillment of the perfect revolution. Its enemy is the social corruption which at present destroys sensitivity to its high pleasures. The imagination and the poetry which it creates are the "light of life," affording whatever beauty and truth a corrupt age can behold. This light may flicker in periods of dogma and destruction, yet it continues to illumine the way to a brighter future, whose seeds lie latent in the present debris. These potential forms of the future are beheld by the poet-prophet: "For he not only beholds intensely the present as it is and discovers those laws according to which present things ought to be ordered but he beholds the future in the present, and his thoughts are the germs of the flower and the fruit of latest time" ("A Defence of Poetry," Clark ed., p. 279). Undoubtedly this text is central to the comprehension of Shelley's conception of the role of the poet as revolutionist. Poets are the authors of revolution in opinion. They generate the thoughts which measure infinity and bring form to chaos. They penetrate to the permanent analogy of things beneath the veil where the forms of perfection which compose the oneness of the new world reside. They create the revolution in the mind of Promethean man who needs then but will it into existence.

The long poems in which Shelley presented the motives, the program, and the progress of the ideal revolution reflect his study of the actual revolution. They may be regarded as ritual enactments of the successful revolution they foresee. They focus on the achievements and character of individual heroes and heroines. They measure the social and personal evils which fetter the mind and weigh down the will to good. But two of Shelley's lyric poems, "Mont Blanc" and the "Ode to the West Wind," reflect the tensions the poet experienced in creating the new myth of revolution.

The "West Wind" poem measures the accumulation of

elemental energy in nature and man which the poets capable of directing the course of revolution may convey and express. As a record of energy, power, and hope, the poem might well be thought to restore ideal enthusiasm to its receptive auditors: it communicates with Shelley's special fervor the strength of the cause, defines the workings of the ideas it celebrates; demonstrates the feelings arising from such opposites as hope and despair, love and hate, destruction and creation held by the poet; and quickens our own pulses as we respond to the poet's visions and hopes. "Mont Blanc," on the other hand, marvels at the uncaptured and uncontrolled turbulence which resists the efforts of the shaping and subduing imagination. It examines that in man and nature which precedes and nearly eludes the value-making process but is a source of value. "Mont Blanc" is largely about destruction, the "West Wind" about both destruction and creation.

"Ode to the West Wind" is, among other things, a poem about the necessity of revolution once the energies that are to be discharged or expressed in the organisms of man or society have come into being. There must be death and destruction designed "to quicken a new birth" and preserve what is best and most deserving to endure. Its imagery of "congregated might" does convey, as Bloom suggests, something of the "pent-up fierceness that is precipitated out in popular rebellions." [30] But this strain is balanced by imagery of active grace and beauty "moving everywhere." The poet invokes and channels the strength and beauty which he senses so that he may transform it into poems capable of reviving "unawakened earth" to an awareness of the truths it has discarded in despair. His poems are microcosmic revolutions which help "quicken" the unborn worlds whose outlines they reflect and describe. If the successful revolution must be first made in the mind of man, then the poem which strives in prayer with the power that makes and unmakes revolutions and the poem which limns the form of the ideal revolution must seem the central instruments for bringing that revolution into being.

The movement of the poem is designed to convey the breath, power, and wildness of the wind, but form and direction and climax are imposed upon those energies just as the revolution itself must evoke and control the energies of destruction and creation in man. The three movements of accumulating, liberating, and reordering, which the poet describes as produced by the "unseen presence," are presumably the movements of successful social reform. This general design is carefully articulated in the poem.

"Mont Blanc," like "Ode to the West Wind," explores and tries to tap a natural source of power and energy. Unlike "West Wind," it expresses a strong sense of failure, an inability to create the necessary rapprochement between man and nature, the *I* and *Thou* relation that Professor Bloom expounds so profitably in his study of Shelley's myth-making poems. "Mont Blanc" describes intense perceptions and the state of feeling created by such perceptions. Shelley seems to commit himself in this poem, perhaps more than in any other he wrote, to skeptical exploration of possible attitudes toward experience.

The central image of the poem is the cold white mountain, aloof and inaccessible — below it a process of violence and destruction. The main focus seems to be on the effort of the imagination, the synthesizing and transmuting power, to create value from the "fast influencings" of a "vast river" of sensation. As he gazes into the dizzy ravine, the poet feels that he is musing as in some sublime and mysterious trance upon his own "separate phantasy." His imagination seeks an underlying principle of unity and power adequate to account for the phenomena. The imagination is not nurtured by close observation and analysis of the qualities and quantities of things, but seeks

"Forms more real than living man" in the "aereal kisses / Of Shapes that haunt thought's wildernesses" (*Prometheus Unbound*, I, 740–751). (As presumably the ideal revolution is more real than existing unrevolutionized societies.) Coleridge, in his "Hymn Before Sun-Rise in the Vale of Chamouni," says he gazed upon Mont Blanc until it vanished from conscious thought though "still present to the bodily sense." But the "most awful Form" was blending all the while with his thought within a "mighty vision," and the joyful poet, united in the imagination with the beauty and power about him, raised a hymn to God: "Earth, with her thousand voices, praises God!" Shelley says, rather like Coleridge, that from the "unremitting interchange" of mind in a passive trance with the clear universe of things arose "One legion of wild thoughts," but he remains detached and doubtful about a significance behind the rhythm of his experience.

Myth seems to fail the spirit in this "still, snowy and serene" world of storms, geologic ruin, and natural cruelty or indifference. The poem confines itself to describing the state of alert passiveness in which one seeks to understand and channel the "wilderness" world of ample but not clearly and wisely directed force and energy. The scene reminds one somewhat of Shelley's strictures on Napoleon, the model of tremendous human power but deficient in charitable wisdom. The strength — "the secret Strength of things" — is there. It doesn't have man's specific good or ill in mind, but it is power and it can be tapped "to repeal / Large Codes of fraud and woe" by unacknowledged legislators who see the same power in both man and nature, a power which may destroy, as in precipitate revolutions, or may become the inexhaustible fuel for wise and steady growth when the "adverting" minds of those who can "Interpret, or make felt, or deeply feel" so convert it.

In the final section Shelley sets the detached calm of the

towering peak, an image which suggests an analogy to that calm of contemplation in the mind's "still cave," against the devastation of its slopes and the turbulence of its currents. Similarly, perhaps, the mind is thought of as a principle of stability which lends meaning and definition to the torrent of impressions. The snows descend on the mountain, though "none beholds them there." Winds silently heap the snow, and the "voiceless lightning" broods over the snow in these solitudes. Shelley is apparently impressed with a sense of the processes of nature as independent of the human percipient. He asserts that the source of power governs not only the material universe, but also the human mind.

> The secret Strength of things
> Which governs thought, and to the infinite dome
> Of Heaven is as a law, inhabits thee!

Behind the forces of nature carving out the valley of the Arve there is a constancy of law, a power for change expressed in a symbol of eternity's "white radiance."

Professor Kapstein argues[31] that the last three lines of the poem constitute an anticlimax which contradicts the climax of lines 139–141 by saying that not external Necessity but the mind of man creates our knowledge and makes the reality of the universe.

> And what were thou, and earth, and stars, and sea,
> If to the human mind's imaginings
> Silence and solitude were vacancy?

Shelley, however, has emphasized that the processes of nature — "clear," "everlasting" — go on independent of man's knowing mind. The course of his speculation may be to ask how any of this could be changed even if man should imagine that nothing exists but as it is perceived? The external world does indeed exist for us only as we perceive it, but the imagination's sense of the unfathomable and elusive cause of experience convinces us that it must also exist independent of our perception. The mind, as Shelley described its work in the opening section of the poem, is passive in perception — it cannot create its sensations; yet it can select from them according to its own structure in order to build up the unified world of conceptual experience. Mind can do this because it is governed by laws, probably the same laws that regulate the external universe. However, the laws of nature are in a very real sense laws of mind, for they are known, concatenated, and comprehended only by mind. Necessity or Power acts in both mind and the external world, but mind as the value-seeking, judgment-making, myth-creating process of the universe is somehow superior to the impersonal processes of nature. It is part of the operation of Necessity that it excite the mind to discovery of the presence and power of Necessity in the universe, but the mind by reflection upon the data of sense comes to the assignment of meaning and so creates knowledge.

"Mont Blanc" and "Ode to the West Wind" reveal the poet lyrically, searching his images and feelings for foundations of hope, describing in miniature the quality of revolution, and outlining the path the idea of revolution follows from the imagination of the beholder of its forms to the larger sensing of their relevance and their chances of realization.

VII

Queen Mab

Shelley's long poems all describe successful or partly successful revolutions. They are lyrical, dramatic, philosophical. They describe more largely the process of ideal revolutions, the characters who lead and support them, the failures and the evils met, the difficulties overcome, and the final resolutions in worlds larger yet than the revolutionary scene.

The poet's first full-scale description of the new revolution in *Queen Mab* is more negative and critical than constructive. Here the young poet sets out to destroy the old order, to find convincing arguments for the necessity of this destruction, and to leave the building of the new world of hope largely up to the sure and steady operations of Necessity, the mother-goddess who directs blindly working wills toward the happy earth of the future. Kings, priests, and capitalists must make way for the liberated poets and priestesses who feel the new order to come on their pulses and respond readily to the larger rhythms of progressive change currently impeded by corrupt men and laggard institutions. As a violent and vigorous attack on the older order, *Queen Mab* became the one work by Shelley to have considerable practical influence, not on the enlightened leaders but on the proletariat, now just beginning to emerge as a political and social force in England.[1]

Queen Mab makes an excellent introduction to Shelley's mature poetic radicalism, for it presents his basic images, motives, and ideas in clear and partly reasoned terms. The work does not fully describe either a practical or an ideal revolution; that is the job of *The Revolt of Islam*. The identity of the enemy — kings, priests, and capitalists — is announced. The vision of a new golden age is leavened neither by practical considerations nor by an awareness of man's limits or his often large indifference to social developments. It is the work of the Messianic missionary to Ireland and disciple of Voltaire, who labored to liberate suffering humanity by pamphlets, glass bottles, embankment projects, impassioned speeches, and now a furious long poem.

An early, sympathetic reader of *Queen Mab*, impressed by the sense of gleaming infinite space, a vast stage of radiant immensity and rolling spheres, which the poet created at the beginning of the poem, might have been surprised by the abstract revolutionary broadsides which comprise most of the work. Shelley has adapted Pope's contrast between the magnificent harmony of the macrocosm and the incredible spectacle of human folly to the purposes of political radicalism. Within the perspective of cosmological order and unity, it baffles the imagination to behold human errancy and human indifference to the revolutionary idea. From the scientists and agnostics of eighteenth-century Enlightenment thought Shelley produced the notion of an uncreated world of living matter governed by law. As Professor Peyre said, the idea of Necessity satisfied a profound need in Shelley for a stable and immutable element in the universe, and he embraced it "avec l'exaltation d'un croyant."[2] This world of necessity is described by Queen Mab, the symbol of the prophetic imagination. What she apprehends and conveys is, in objective and scientific terms, a world of law, where all links in the "great chain of nature" (II, 108) bespeak unity and harmony. It is a "machine" whose every spring functions according to "irresistible law" (VI, 163).

> No atom of this turbulence fulfils
> A vague and unnecessitated task,
> Or acts but as it must and ought to act.
>   (VI, 171–173)

Like Lucretius, Shelley described the orderly movement of atoms in space with an almost religious spirit of veneration for so noble and constant an order. Like the Stoics he referred to a compound of soul and matter whose operations are characterized by harmony and reason. Shelley, in fact, seems to focus on the element of value in all such semireligious metaphysical systems. There is a regulative and impersonal principle which progressively enforces its wise commands on our submissive wills. One may of course see the nature of things in terms both of law and of value, separate perspectives perhaps but not really inconsistent. At least it is clear that some notion of an underlying metaphysical unity of man and nature was basic to Shelley's ultimate statement in the poem of faith in linked moral and natural progress.

All nature is of the same stuff as man. There is some congregative or assimilative principle at work in man and nature which Shelley describes in *Queen Mab* as a central and eternal spirit, a stable form or activating organism, which lies within the process of change, destruction and reforming. In mechanistic terms this spirit or abiding form is called Necessity, which the poet endows with value by calling it "mother of the world." It is described primarily, however, as an impersonal, active, allsufficing, unvarying force which controls every atom of the restless world. Even tyrants are the necessary products of Necessity's laws. It is a doctrine which Shelley claimed must destroy religion because it reveals that "in no case could any event have happened otherwise than it did happen."

Like most reformers and enthusiasts, the poet begins by assuming the most complete determinism but spiritualizes the world so deeply that mystery, wonder, and perhaps inconsistency are added. Such paradoxical acceptance of both determinism and the need for active reform seems a curious but characteristic feature of the thought of revolutionaries. However the opponents may rage, the predestined goal will follow, whatever name may be assigned to the guiding and insuring power: "God for the Calvinist, nature and reason for the Jacobin, dialectical or scientific materialism for the Marxist." [3] However unpromising the present circumstances may seem, the hopes of the rebel can create out of the wrecks of those hopes because he acquires power from his perception of an inevitable logic behind history. Brinton's comments on the psychology of the ardent revolutionist who is passionately anxious to assist in the creation of Time's sure goal suggest Shelley's own belief in himself as a chosen instrument and trumpeter of the new prophecy and revelation in the "Ode to the West Wind." "Rigid determinists are also usually ardent proselyters, presumably on the grounds that they are instruments of the inevitable, the means through which the inevitable realizes itself." [4]

In this scene of "Nature's unchanging harmony" (II, 257), every sentient monad is perfectly governed as "passive instruments" (VI, 214) of Necessity. Something, however, eludes the eye, for though all nature bespeaks order and harmony, though nothing "acts but as it must and ought to act" (VI, 172), man, who it might seem is as "natural" as anyone, is somehow an outcast and an impediment to the workings of the machine. He fabricates a state of things which a reformer must call intolerably evil.

Shelley's characteristic wavering between labeling man as a passive creature of circumstance and insisting that he actively will the good creates considerable confusion. Like all subjects of natural law, man fulfills passively and unconsciously the will of nature. Clearly, however, something went wrong somewhere. This very passivity of "man's weak will" (VI, 201) seems to have caused much of the trouble. It made him easy prey for rather less passive kings, priests, and capitalists. Man's "submissive abjectness" has "destroyed Nature's suggestions." The force of nature or necessity appears to be, like Hume's principles of association, a gentle force that commonly prevails. It does not speak loudly, but its "silent eloquence" does speak insistently and may be heard when experience teaches men to listen.

Difficulties or inconsistencies in his philosophical position do not seem to engage Shelley's attention at this stage, possibly because it is action rather than theory that is called for. There is nothing either moderate or philosophical about the attacks on the tyrants and priests who take advantage of man's wanderings from Necessity. The suffering which misrule and priestcraft bring is real enough. The revolution needs a prominent target. If the evil is simply to be located in the fallen and corrupt nature of man, there is no incentive for change. One must be convinced and convince others that the situation is rectifiable, that the reforms needed are obvious, and that there is something in the course of nature which favors his efforts. The doctrine of Necessity becomes, like the doctrine of Providence, a way of explaining history. Necessity operates progressively. Order, beauty, energy, mystery in nature, and the appearance in life of a few noble and generous men assure us that one day "the unbounded frame" which the spirit of nature pervades

Will be without a flaw
Marring its perfect symmetry. (III, 239–240)

The "flaw" is the creation of the past, the special inertia of history which permits abuses to accumulate. Hired killers immolate women and children to the inebriate rage of the god of war and selfishness. When the "sulphurous smoke" clears away, nothing is left but the ravaged wasteland of the battlefield. Shelley grew up during an age of nearly continuous war from 1793 to 1815. It was for him a peculiarly destructive war because he saw it as a device of tyrants for weakening the energies generated by the French Revolution, the one great attempt in his time to liberate men from the domination of the past. War will go out with the kings and priests and statesmen who "blast the human flower" as it begins to grow. Men make mistakes and sometimes in their ignorance forge the chains which eventually doom them to "abjectness and bondage" (IV, 138). There are men in existence suffering from a blight of vice, madness, or discord who take advantage of the immaturity of mankind to confirm their misery. But men can learn from their mistakes when taught to heed the orderly and impersonal laws revealed by Necessity's workings "Of pain or pleasure, sympathy or hate, / That variegate the eternal universe" (IV, 149–150). By then, however, the system that scourges humanity has consolidated itself and is not easily blasted from its entrenched positions.

Shelley's doctrine of necessity permits no reference to original sin, natural depravity, or real human inadequacy to explain the present plight. Ignorance and immaturity, tinctured with vice and reinforced by law and custom, make man the monster he appears to be. He might be otherwise. He might cooperate with Necessity in the work of redemption. Instead, he is bound by the woes of his parentage and his environment before he comes into the world.

> Let priest-led slaves cease to proclaim that man
> Inherits vice and misery, when Force
> And Falsehood hang even o'er the cradled babe,
> Stifling with rudest grasp all natural good.
>   (IV, 117–120)

As a result of his subjection to custom and tyranny, man had acquired a psychological burden of hopelessness and self-contempt to throw off.

Shelley devoted special attention to the history of the errors of religious institution, since basically, like other prophets of the Enlightenment, he was a propagandist for a new religion of humanity. In Barruel he had studied the program of Voltaire and his fellow conspirators to "Écrasez l'infâme." He found a motto. Attack and destroy was described as the burden of some forty volumes of Voltaire's work. The Voltairean policy was to "strike and conceal your hand" (Barruel, I, 27, 40, 159). Shelley strikes without much effort to conceal.

> Religion! but for thee, prolific fiend,
> Who peoplest earth with demons, Hell with men,
> And Heaven with slaves!   (VI, 69–71)

In *Queen Mab* the attack on religion is relentless and central to the poem. Shelley provides a sketch of the processes by which men in the "untutored infancy" of the race created a demonic God, the "prototype of human misrule." However, it was organized religion as a prop of tyranny and the tendency of religious doctrine to harden into blind dogma that he really attacked. Later, as his rhetorical radicalism diminished in fervor and his political vision penetrated deeper, it was this paralysis of orthodoxy that mainly concerned him. Outmoded ideas of order are clutched desperately by profiteers who believe in nothing except maintaining their power over enslaved humanity. First men have kings, then a god in the age of the kings, and finally, the true god of men in a commercial age, Gold — a god who unites the three tyrannies. The result of the perverted worship of this latest deity is war and human bondage.

Drawing much of his matter from Enlightenment thought, Shelley developed this theme of social injustice in *Queen Mab*. Cities and the larger culture they make possible help men to acquire the "urbanity of improved reason," but when unnatural extensions of the principle of the division of labor render mind inactive, the good which industrial progress might bring is lost. Men are turned into machines for the pursuit of wealth (*View of F. R.*, pp. 518–519).

> The harmony and happiness of man
> Yields to the wealth of nations.   (V, 79–80)

Gold has its uses. Commercial development is integral to social and civic progress. Without it there cannot be a nobler Athens born from the debris of the past. But when gold becomes a "living god" (V, 62), enabling rich men to subject the poor to daily "fruitless toil," fed only by the "rhetoric of tyranny," an important balance between industrial development and wider prosperity, between production and distribution, is lost.

Though statesmen may boast of wealth, "There is no real wealth but the labour of man." Of the fruits of this labor all must share equally. Great cities, centers where flock "Strangers, and ships, and merchandise" (II, 200–201) to bless man with good things, are not condemned. But the mean lust for gold

and fame has produced the modern city where, in a Wordsworthian image, Shelley sees

> . . . every slave now dragging through the filth
> Of some corrupted city his sad life,
> Pining with famine, swoln with luxury,
> Blunting the keenness of his spiritual sense
> With narrow schemings and unworthy cares.
>
> (V, 159–163)

Such is the world without the moral imagination, where, as
Shelley noted years later in the "Defence," the extremes of
luxury and want have been exasperated, where man, "having
enslaved the elements, remains himself a slave" (Clark ed., p.
293). Since it is not really human nature, however, but kings
and priests who are responsible for the situation, one may still
have faith in the ability of men to unite vision and reality.
Great men have emerged and will continue to emerge as
beacons of hope and liberty, men whose virtues anticipate
what all may become in that glorious future when "life's
smallest chord," including man's, is finally "Strung to unchanging unison" (IV, 91–92).

The nature of the new hero is outlined by Shelley in *Queen
Mab*. In the world of the present, where the destructive work
of kings, priests, and capitalists continues unchecked, the characteristic hero is really the Wandering Jew, whom Shelley
develops as a symbol of the negative and defiant force in man.
He is an outcast and an emblem of suffering humanity, whose
will has remained proof against all the onslaughts of a demonic
God. He developed the virtues of endurance which outlasted
a history of misrule. Like Satan in *Paradise Lost*, he "learned
to prefer / Hell's freedom to the servitude of Heaven." His
"stubborn and unalterable will" (*Queen Mab*, VII, 194–195)

never submitted to despair though he witnessed and suffered from the crimes and miseries inflicted in the name of Christianity. The Wandering Jew represents what man has been. His career reveals how the vital spark was kept alive through centuries of oppression.

The dawn of a new age of revolution has revealed the power to create a golden world in the intellect and will of man.

> Nature, impartial in munificence,
> Has gifted man with all-subduing will.
> Matter, with all its transitory shapes,
> Lies subjected and plastic at his feet,
> That, weak from bondage, tremble as they tread.
>
> (V, 132–136)

The hero and sage, lately present in every human being, can unite a "cloudless brain, / Untainted passion, elevated will" to govern a world of thought and desire (V, 154–158). Love is law, "Unchecked by dull and selfish chastity" (VIII, 84). In the new world, the reason and passion of man will no longer be in conflict, for the spirit of sweet human love will govern with a larger and ampler grasp to dispel the old "unenjoying sensualism" which once corrupted lives and brought love itself to the public mart to be bought and sold.

Happy, liberated men and women will resume the steady pace of progress which necessity decrees but which was so long impeded and delayed by inert dogmas and institutions. Human happiness and human science will gain strength from each other as matter yields new secrets to flexible, searching, and powerful minds alert to opportunities for creating new benefactions for humanity. The new heaven on earth may be realized when man's will is guided by well-founded hopes, known only in the visions of an occasional liberated genius.

The intellect passively accumulated insights until truth could bear with its full weight on the blindly-working will. The gathered rays of thought, "diffused throughout all space and time," converged on the goal of a "Happy Earth! reality of Heaven!" (IX, 5, 1). Now Nature waits for man's will to begin to operate so that she may lay bare her secrets and lend her "force to the omnipotence of mind" (VIII, 236). When power and will are one, truly the new kingdom of humanity is realized.

The doctrine of progress Shelley outlined in *Queen Mab* betrays little sense of history. Progress is something about to begin. The past is dominated by the tyrants, warriors, and priests who created a bloody barbarous scene where an occasional moment of glory in the midst of universal ruin revealed more clearly the "moral desert" where human lives were wasted. The past serves primarily as a warning of what to avoid in the future. Godwin's admonitions about the value of older institutions in their time are disregarded. Shelley's real ardor of the imagination is devoted in *Queen Mab* to the visions of a glorious future, the prize of man's renovating will. Generations pass, but finally—and the process of the intervening ages is described with the "West Wind" images of leaves, frost, compost, "germs of promise," and lovely new growths—the long-anticipated world of virtue, delight, and love appears.

Both man and nature bloom in "a perfect identity between the moral and physical improvement of the human species." Man attains mastery over his mind, but he also subdues matter with help from natural law as the obliquity of the earth diminishes. A note asserts the strong presumption that the progress toward perpendicularity of the poles is "not merely an oscillation" (Hutchinson ed., p. 808). Deserts, bleak polar wastes, and lonely oceans disappear; the lions lie down with the lambs; eternal spring arrives. Behind the pastoral vision probably lies the old psychophysical parallelism of seventeenth-century rationalism. Let man achieve moral rectitude and nature will follow, for nature and man move by parallel sets of laws. God who gave us an unhealthy climate to correspond with our moral degeneration will in that day restore fertility to the earth, draw up the waters from seas studded with "bright garden-isles" (VIII, 101), and lengthen and brighten human and animal life.⁵ Shelley says Necessity, but the difference is minimal and nominal. Man gets his strings in tune with the "planetary spheres" and becomes once more a microcosm reflecting the glorious macrocosm of love, law, and life. Such are the visions which "Renew and strengthen all thy failing hopes" (VIII, 52).

The demographic pressures foretold by Malthus never arrive in this world where love inspires ever-burgeoning life. Enriched earth keeps well ahead and bountifully supports all living things, now united in the bonds of peace and equality, a unity enforced by the gentle rule of enlightened custom.

> The fertile bosom of the earth gives suck
> To myriads, who still grow beneath her care,
> Rewarding her with their pure perfectness:
> (VIII, 109–111)

Queen Mab is strong in vision and abstract logic, deficient in fact. It is a vision less concerned with practical ways, means, and present possibilities than with arming the imagination and will. We begin with imagery of order, law, and connection in the macrocosm. Then we glance at the microcosmic outcast man and show how he might echo the larger harmonies, perhaps only individually at first then hopefully and finally in perfected societies. At last the macrocosm is itself reconquered to receive the stamp of man's values. The deforming powers of tyranny will be no more as the mind of man generates thoughts "that rise / In time-destroying infiniteness" (VIII, 205–206) to defeat all the older evils. But it is to be no easy overnight journey, the parting words enjoin. It can happen only gradually — mind and nature transforming reciprocally — as man, defining and reflecting each step of progress on his mind (VIII, 142–146), moves under the aegis of enlarged and moving hope. Much work and aspiring struggle lie ahead in the "pathless wilderness" which waits to be subdued by "man's reclaiming hand" (IX, 144–145).

Queen Mab is largely poetry of statement. The organization is logical and chronological rather than narrative or dramatic. There are generalized scenes of carnage and confusion and cosmic imagery of orderly spheres in a Copernican universe, but there is no really vital mythic structure to the poem, consisting, as it does, of a series of visions offered by the "Queen of Spells." In this setting the evils described are seen as transitory and remediable, though on the other hand the poem never departs for long from its focus on ruin and human viciousness. Disorder, faith, tyranny, and selfishness are attacked directly in abstract denunciations and indirectly by inculcating a sense of the beauty and harmony in all that is not man. How easily it seems Paradise on earth might be attained if men would properly direct the will. There it lies all about us and within us. Yet the evils that outcast man fabricated in the youth of time continue to ravage his restless being relentlessly. How is man to end their rule? Beyond the suggestion that some few eminent in virtue and knowledge will rise to reveal the true path and to teach cooperation with the implied will of nature, *Queen Mab* does not answer the basic questions and doubts.

VIII

The Problem of Evil

Shelley in *Queen Mab* does not offer, it must be acknowledged, any very satisfactory explanation of the origin and nature of evil. He had other purposes. The immediate targets were large and obvious. Enough philosophy was required to support the campaign. The poem does not, however, represent all his thinking on the problem, even in his early writings, and he later measured the adversary in progressively more subtle descriptions.

Shelley's early writings reflect the Enlightenment contrast between unspoilt Nature and outcast man. He did tend to regard Nature with a religious reverence, and he did see political institutions mechanically as departures from the ideal. If man could shed his ignorance and superstition, the ills of capitalism, priestcraft, and tyranny could not long endure. The praise of "natural" simplicity and self-dependence suggests a degree of acceptance of the ideals of primitivism and natural innocence. Primitivist doctrines are reflected in Shelley's juvenile vegetarian tracts. In "The Vindication of Natural Diet" he claimed that "no mere reform of legislation" can effect any real good while the "furious passions and evil propensities" fostered by our carnivorous habits continue unabated (Clark ed., p. 85). Against the notion of human depravity, Shelley argued that it is extreme social inequality which corrupts man ("An Address to the Irish," Clark ed., p. 52). Though he did, therefore, assume something akin to Rousseau's much misunderstood notion of man's original goodness, as a liberal and a believer in progress Shelley did not share Rousseau's conviction that knowledge and civilization have worked the corruption. In fact, Shelley said, Rousseau's description of the noble savage, like Christ's injunction to be as the birds and the lilies, is merely an effective and dramatic way of teaching nobler views of human nature and destiny. Nothing could exceed the misery and squalor of savages in a primitive state. Equality, justice, and knowledge are the associated fruits of higher civilization ("Essay on Christianity," Clark ed., pp. 210, 212).

The main problem of "human science," as Shelley stated it in "The Vindication of Natural Diet" is to reconcile the "advantages of intellect and civilization" with the "liberty and pure pleasures of natural life" (Clark ed., p. 83). Original sin is rejected for the belief that the present obvious taints in our nature are "the result of unnatural political institutions" (to Elizabeth Hitchener, January 2, 1812, *Letters*, I, 216). The view of radical empiricism that character is a product of circumstance, particularly early circumstance, was adopted by Shelley. Frankenstein's monster, he said in his review of Mary's book, was a being formed by his first impressions as "affectionate and full of moral sensibility," but men turned him into a misanthrope by treating him as an "abortion and anomaly." When the uncommon circumstances of his existence "became developed in action, his original goodness was gradually turned into inextinguishable misanthropy and revenge" (Clark ed., p. 308). Thus also for all men. The villain is not society in itself nor civilization nor the advancing knowledge which graces both. It is the corrupted and distorting institutions which have not kept up with the general progress of civilization. These defective forms blight men from birth. The question-begging nature of the indictment was not at first realized by Shelley.

On the other hand, as early as 1811, we find the poet writing, "High powers appear but to present opportunities for occasioning superior misery" (to Elizabeth Hitchener, November 8, 1811, *Letters*, I, 168). To the same correspondent in the same year he commented at greater length: "You say that equality is unattainable, so will I observe is perfection; yet they both symbolize in their nature, they both demand that an unremitting tendency towards themselves should be made, & the nearer Society approaches towards this point the happier will it be" (July 25, 1811, *Letters*, I, 125). To Hogg, Shelley confided his doubts about the possibility of a "satisfactory general reform" because of the seemingly hopeless corruption of the masses (May 9, 1811, *Letters*, I, 81). These remarks come from a period when Shelley was supposedly so dazzled by the certainty of Utopia that he lost sight of the real obstacles. Early and late he presented his love as a desolation masked, his hope as a veil concealing despair. The French Revolution demonstrated how social movements, incontestably good in intention and favorable in early development, ultimately may produce evils of bloodlust and anarchy which seem worse than the despotism they overthrew. Power and will rarely operate under the aegis of wisdom. Energy produces ruin.

Shelley had no single consistent answer to the problem of evil, as one might expect given the nature of the problem, the many possible ways of looking at it, and the multiplicity of varieties, kinds, expressions of evil in man and society. When the metaphysical impulse was strong in him, his sense of the reality of the evils confronted by radical reformers may very well have tended to dwindle. There is nothing surprising about that. One's view of the surface is directly affected by the depth of his basic penetrations. Social problems must seem remote to the astronomer while he is charting the heavens. One can, of course, hold both radical and Platonic views of evil. The natural Platonist is bound at least at times to associate evil with the imperfect world of matter and becoming, change or mutability. When one lives in a world of changeless ideas outside the imperfect world of matter and becoming, violence and wrong must often seem as a dream beside the reality of "steadfast truth" (*The Revolt of Islam*, IX, 20). So regarded, the evil principle must seem less malignant than frustrating, a clog of mutability which opposes its inertia to the soaring and aspiring spirit.

It is possible that Shelley's interest in the manifold problems of this world grew less vital as he later came to emphasize cyclic views and Platonic goals. In *Adonais,* the poet beyond and above the world of becoming seems to prefer the passionless, quiescent existence of contemplative wisdom to the unceasing struggles of the will guided by undying but wearying hopes. The desire for release from the struggle often became strong in the later Shelley, though the urge to reform the world never died and indeed sometimes acquired strength from the Platonic distancing. After all, the effect of the Revolution had been to generate the belief that a match might be made between form and matter, between the heavenly city of the philosophers and its earthly reflections. The principles of good wait to be brought to light and freed from the fettering and obscuring mechanism of ordinary life, once man's will is put in harmony with nature. In short, while Shelley did tend toward mystical solutions of the problem of evil in his later works and did see evil at times as an inevitable expression of a world of space and time, no more than Plato did he desert his passion for reform.

In the terms of environmentalist psychology, evil within is a result of exposure to evil outside. Men become what they behold, and they may feed on ugliness and poison as well as beauty and truth. But men also act; evil passions can create their objects as well as good ones, can worship the evil principle enshrined in self and immolate victims to it. There is a degenerative as well as a progressive tendency loose in the world. Shelley did not completely share, at least not for long, Godwin's simpler faith in the omnipotence of truth and the belief that the cure for vice, or erratic miscalculation of consequences, is the knowledge and experience gained in the "simple process of rational progress." He upheld the banners of Love and Hope, but in a world dimmed by their opposites.

Evil may, then, be created by distorted perceptions and perverted will. Thus, the ordinary sources of energy and matter for progress may serve the wrong cause, provide poison rather than nourishment. "Evil minds / Change good to their own nature." The vicious passions and inadequate ideas which result from distorted perception may work actively within us to change our seeing and our being. "Whilst I behold such execrable shapes, / Methinks I grow like what I contemplate." As the Furies say, the evil can exult in their deformity, may obtain form and reality from their victims (*Prometheus Unbound*, I, 380–381, 449–450, 465–472). All passions create their objects, not merely the good ones, and when men are united in a "brotherhood of ill" (*The Revolt of Islam*, X, 6) they have a strength, like that of united philanthropists in associations, which can grow in power and sway. Evil is not merely external, temporary, and feeble. It is seen in *Prometheus Unbound* at least as viciously inward and united with basest impulses, dread thoughts, and foul desires which astonish our bright ideal self as they crawl through our veins like our very blood.

If there is, as Utopian visionaries of the Enlightenment seemed to think, analogy or correspondence between the moral and natural worlds, if nature and man are directed by parallel sets of laws, then man, who restores Paradise by projecting his inner illumination out onto nature, may also create an Inferno of disease, storms, and ugliness which reflects his moral degeneration. The path of progress may seem clear but not easy to follow, as long as the distorting mind transforms all things into its own misshapen forms. The evil stain "Heaven with obscene imagery / Of their own likeness" ("Sonnet: Political Greatness"). Like Purganax's gadfly with his "convex eyes," they see "fair things in many hideous shapes" (*Swellfoot the Tyrant*, I, i, 160–162).

Moral evil certainly exerts a morbid fascination over man. Cenci planned to make Beatrice will her own complete degradation by reducing her insensibly to his own malevolent element (*The Cenci*, IV, i, 10–12, 85–86). Though he might well do otherwise, man's infected will permits evil to exist. Perhaps evil is as real as good, and certainly it sometimes seems to have more energy and endurance. Otherwise how could Napoleon, "child of a fierce hour," wreak such destruction of the world's hopes in his quest for blind power (*Triumph of Life*, ll. 215–229). If the lessons of the French Revolution are to be attended to, men have latent capacities for violence and carnage as well as for benevolence and humanity.

On the whole, what appears to be an evil taint in man is regarded by Shelley as "the result of unnatural political institutions." Civic disorder is perpetuated by the incomplete minds, the selfish prejudices, the blind faith in dogma and authority of men nurtured by such forms. The poet did not necessarily minimize the obstacles to millenarian hopes because he chose to concentrate on nourishing the revolutionary dream with visionary poetry. The cultural and institutional environment remained for Shelley to the last the strongest influence on the character of the individual, and he always stressed the necessity of uprooting the poisonous forms blighting growth: "The system of society as it exists at present must be overthrown from the foundations with all its superstructure of maxims & of forms before we shall find anything but disappointment in our intercourse with any but a few select spirits" (to Leigh Hunt, May 1, 1820, *Letters*, II, 191). Hence, though the poet did not espouse the shallower brands of primitivism and deny ultimate responsibility for evil to man, he did stress the special corrupting work of the selfish kings, priests, and capitalists who use war and ruin to stifle the "natural good" in man. Like Godwin and Paine he traced the major moral evils and calamities to social, economic, and political institutions. The generous affections are kindled in society but often blunted and dwarfed by the action of government, which makes enemies out of men and starts wars to hold its powers.

The excesses of the people during the Revolution were traced by Paine to the evil influence of past despotism: "They learn it from the governments they live under" (I, 266–267). For that matter, the Revolution might have flourished and developed peacefully all over Europe, Paine felt, since men everywhere greeted its arrival with enthusiasm and natural friendship, had not governments inspired a spirit of jealousy and ferocity for fear of losing their sway. The system must be changed. Individual moral reform cannot advance very rapidly or extensively while political institutions mold men according to the dead images of the past. Shelley fundamentally wavered perhaps between two approaches, stressing individual reform as a poet, institutional reform as a practical thinker. The thesis that institutions shape men was essential to faith in the efficacy of revolution, while interpretations of the failure of the actual Revolution tended to focus on weaknesses in the human actors. One must believe in both the value and necessity of rebellion. He must have clear notions of what must be uprooted and what new social forms would be useful. To place all the blame on human nature does not inspire revolution.

Godwin and Paine emphasized the evils of government considerably more than did French thinkers. Godwin especially felt that all laws and institutions inhibit beneficial change, and he rejected the faith of men like Helvétius and D'Holbach in the good to be achieved through the wise laws of a benevolent despotism. He wished to dethrone all forms of "implicit faith" because of their natural tendency to reduce the infinitely various qualities and aspirations of men to some dull norm. "Law tends, no less than creeds, catechisms, and tests, to fix the human mind in a stagnant condition, and to substitute a principle of permanence, in the room of that unceasing progress which is the only salubrious element of mind" (*Political Justice*, II, 403, 411).

Shelley particularly scored the ill-effects of religious establishment, which "augments in so vivid a degree the evils resulting from the system before us" (to Elizabeth Hitchener, July 25, 1811, *Letters*, I, 125). Man has a fatal facility for creating Jupiters to subdue his freely ranging imagination. Partly the trouble lay in the human unwillingness to accept uncertainty or the imaginative poise of creative doubt. Shelley said that he preferred the Greek account of the origin of evil, for the Greeks saw God as limited by the reluctant and stubborn nature of the material available to his molding hand and thus forced to accept the "nearest arrangement possible to the perfect archetype existing in his contemplation." Christianity, on the other hand, tried to reconcile omnipotence, benevolence, and equity in its account of a world where good and evil were obviously and inextricably mingled; as a result, the Christian thinkers had to invent a Devil to account for the inherent contradictions of the creed ("Essay on the Devil and Devils," Clark ed., p. 266). The requirement of implicit faith was the way chosen to avoid the difficulty, but it was the way also to restrict individuality and true progress. Authority creates slaves; authority supporting error and contradiction causes a stagnation of public opinion as soon as the lies and distortions fixed by dogma are "fenced about and frozen over by forms and superstitions" ("A System of Government by Juries," Clark ed., p. 263).

When the flexible, synthesizing imagination discards the outworn forms of past perception, the lesser faculties and lesser minds seize upon these separated deities and set them on thrones from which they govern men. They become oppressors and destroyers who impose limits on that imagination which had once freely created them. Dead deities, like dead metaphors, give no life to their users, though they may represent advances both formal and spiritual over the past. "An established religion turns to deathlike apathy the sublimest ebullitions of most exalted genius and the spirit-stirring truths of a mind inflamed with the desire to benefiting mankind." Such, Shelley felt, had been the fate of Christ's profound insights into truth ("Essay on Christianity," Clark ed., p. 213). Repressive political systems had similar effects. The most benevolent of tyrannies still imposes principles of self-distrust and blind submission to authority.

In societies governed by despotic institutions the evil concepts too readily assume attractive masks like those described in the *Mask of Anarchy*. Murder, Fraud, Hypocrisy, and Anarchy find respectable disguises as God and Law to befuddle and bedazzle the people. Tyrants urge men to fear God, for a religion of fearful submission breeds the "jealous hate of man" on which the tyrant may found his throne (*The Revolt of Islam*, I, 34–35). The mind closes to vision. Such is the psychology of Reaction. When the expansive energies generated by love and hope retract, then the minions of priestcraft and tyranny can begin to nourish the narrowing, self-centered passions of fear, hate, and revenge. These passions the principles of tradition and authority soon enforce over shrunken imaginations. Thus, the French Revolution had foundered after a brief dawning when men began to attack one another.

The outmoded forms of the past, fixed in the repressive creeds and dogmas which fetter the imagination, continue to weigh down the aspiring spirit of man and lime his wings with the poison of hopelessness and self-contempt, "the dark idolatry of self" which brings hate and fear. The true virtues of free men are "Love, Hope, and Self-esteem" ("Hymn to Intellectual Beauty," l. 37), and the first two are largely the creation of the third. The central principle of true revolutionary action, Mary Wollstonecraft had said, is "Respect thyself" (*View of F. R.*, p. 18). In a mind blunted and blighted by the long-term effects of tyrannical authority, however, the search for self-knowledge may reveal evils within the self which seem deep-dyed and lasting. This evil apparently within must be recognized without permitting it to disarm the hopes which inspire revolutionary action. Shelley probed the workings of self-contempt both in the more pessimistic vein of *Alastor* and *The Cenci* and the hopeful one of *Prometheus Unbound*. Beatrice Cenci became, for him, a tragic character by her partial capitulation to the spirit of revenge, retaliation, and atonement. By murdering her father, she illustrated microcosmically the power of evil over good. It was the French Revolution in miniature.

While Shelley's views of the obstacles to progress seem balanced and penetrating, one may, nevertheless, perhaps because of his emphasis on millenary hopes, still find himself wondering how real evil was to him. Is his view adequately summed up in Mrs. Shelley's note to *Prometheus Unbound*, "Shelley believed that mankind had only to will that there should be no evil, and there would be none"? There is something rather casual about that "only." It scarcely seems to do justice to the poet's measuring of the abyss between man and what he might be. He may lack the tragic vision of the power of evil, evil overcome only with difficulty through the cooperation of heroic energy and intelligence with some poised and mysterious grace. His position is neither superficial nor static, however. As he matured, he recognized a need to place the realization of human hopes in some less abstract and interstellar form.

According to Shelley's later view, as Professor Barnard has put it, the great problem of political justice and human happiness is "not primarily to give men knowledge of what is right and good, but to arouse in them the will to do that right and act that good which they already know."[1] It has also been said that Shelley differs from Plato and from Godwin in allowing for "a separable will, capable of corruption and in need of stimulation by the imagination."[2] Perhaps human perversity rather than human ignorance keeps man in the pit. The position is not far, Mary Shelley noted, from Christianity. It is rather far from Godwin's implicit Platonic faith in human reason, the belief that man does the good that he conceives. Shelley's view reflects a greater comprehension of the force of the irrational, what has been called the "unwilling dross that resists imaginative redemption."[3] Also Shelley suggested a need for some external force to complement the inward regeneration, partly to inspire it, no doubt, perhaps to reflect it, and create the sense of a living relationship. This force may be interpreted with a considerable reference to a kind of skeptical humanism much at odds with religious dogmatism and thus with the element of credulity in both Christianity and Godwinism.

According to Malthus, the disciple of realism against the Utopian visionaries, Godwin's "gorgeous palaces" of happiness and immortality, his "solemn temples" of truth and virtue, would dissolve "like the baseless fabric of a vision" when confronted with real life and the genuine situation of man on earth.[4] Malthus demonstrated the workings of the deeper-seated causes of evil resulting from the laws of nature which make the effects of human institution seem light and superficial in comparison. Because his findings seemed to justify the conservative reaction against revolutionary changes, the *Essay on Population* was frequently cited to prove the folly of tinkering with traditional forms which had stood the test of time. Are there evils ineradicable by institutional change? Obviously there are, except to Dr. Pangloss. The difference lies in the comparative weight placed on the ills produced by bad institutions. The advocates of revolutionary change regarded them as much more sweeping and pronounced than Johnson, Burke, or Malthus. It must be demonstrated that the evils wrought by unjust institutions, themselves perhaps the results of vicious and desolating passions, are remediable, may even be eliminated as disinterested benevolence comes to prevail. A perfectly rational or imaginative society might well find the right checks or controls for eliminating the dangers Malthus predicted. To regard misery, poverty, disease, and war, like Malthus, as regrettable but necessary checks on population increase alienates the propertied classes from reform and leaves mitigable evils untouched.

Perhaps revolutions are dubious ways to improve man. One may well pause before precipitating society into the horrors of bloody strife and anarchy. But, because humanity is ultimately more important than mere order and peace, one must decide at last to root out the "deleterious plants, which poison the better half of human happiness," even though the confusion of revolution may draw "into action the worst as well as the best of men" (*View of F. R.*, pp. 70–71, 128). Shelley did not underrate the power of evil, nor think it easily overcome. There are men who cannot be won over — "Ye cannot change, since ye are old and gray" (*The Revolt of Islam*, XI, 15, 18, 21). In "Lines Written Among the Euganean Hills" the poet lamented the contrast between natural beauty and human depravity and faced the sobering realization that "love or reason" cannot alter "The despot's rage, the slave's revenge."

One must learn to behold evil in its citadel in the human mind without shrinking and without being poisoned by such contemplation lest hope, love, and self-respect be converted into their opposites. With such awareness of the weight of evil, Shelley ultimately did not consider the question of reform, revolution, and progress in a superficial light. He saw progress realistically as a struggle in which the good never quite wins, although society may occasionally achieve the kind of uneasy stability which befits an organism continually renewing itself. Revolutions succeed only when preceded by growth in civilization. They fail when men close their minds, reject even limited reforms, and live lives prescribed by faith, dogma, and self-contempt.

IX

The Doctrine of the Hero

The Shelleyan hero is a poet and a revolutionary who shows in his own character and ideals what might be and leads others to realize the same potential forms in their own lives and in society. This hero is celebrated in all of Shelley's long poems. To Shelley man was pre-eminently "an imaginative being" whose "own mind is his law" ("A Treatise on Morals," Clark ed., p. 186). He recorded in poems like *Queen Mab, The Revolt of Islam,* and *Prometheus Unbound,* with varying degrees of abstractness and subtlety, the life and works of heroes of imagination.

A number of questions about the roles of exceptional men were raised by the Revolution. Were great men produced by the Revolution or did they create it? Were the circumstances of the times conducive to true nobility or were openings merely provided for talented but unscrupulous men capable of taking advantage of anarchy? Do great men disturb the orderly development of democratic institutions? Or are they the main instruments of progress, the media through which the higher truths of social and individual destiny come to the masses? Shelley seems to have felt that the poverty of moral imagination in France's leaders was a central cause of the fall of the Revolution, and he tried to work out a new concept of a revolutionary hero which would remedy this weakness.

He may have found some useful suggestions in the comments by Mme. de Staël. There must be a general concurrence of forces to achieve great and lasting results, she said, but there are eras "when the course of national feeling is dependent on a single man." Though real national superiority depends on good political institutions, it is important to keep merit before men's eyes, and for this purpose great examples of heroic character and the presence of a real aristocracy are important. The danger in revolutions is that equality may replace liberty as an ideal, with a resulting ascendancy of the debased lower orders. Mme. de Staël despised both Jacobins and Napoleon, and she made the point, especially significant to Shelley's theories, that a single intelligent opponent of the way things were going, not to mention five or ten, might have helped stop the process of creating "a political fabric defenceless against faction." "One man alone might perhaps have been able to arrest the fatal impulse." [1]

That the powerful and wise might exercise great influence, might make their visions prevail and change if not reform the world seemed clear enough from the effects of men with great strength and limited vision. Shelley's sources certainly stressed the value of a gifted leader and gave hope that much might indeed be done. Godwin said, "Nor is it possible to say how much good one man sufficiently rigid in his adherence to truth would effect. One such man, with genius, information, and energy, might redeem a nation from vice" (*Political Justice*, III, 292). According to Mary Wollstonecraft, who was skeptical about the enduring utility of heroes and more concerned with citizens, "great men seem to start up, as great revolutions occur, at proper intervals, to restore order, and to blow aside the clouds that thicken over the face of truth; but let more reason and virtue prevail in society, and these strong winds would not be necessary." [2]

An age in need of a hero found Napoleon — an encouraging revelation of human power and energy in one sense — a warning against heroes in another. His career must have seemed to confirm for Shelley the early judgment he made of men: "High powers appear but to present opportunities for occasioning superior misery" (to Elizabeth Hitchener, February 24, 1812, *Letters*, I, 168). Many of Shelley's sources on the Revolution carried the story on through the career of Napoleon, and he also read some books specifically about the Emperor. Of the second class were Labaume's *Narrative of the Campaign in Russia*, which Shelley, perhaps prompted by Mme. Boinville, whose husband perished in the campaign, read in 1815, and the *Manuscrit venu de St. Hélène*, read by both Shelley and Mary in June 1817. Labaume, a Captain of Engineers during the war, gives a highly personal and circumstantial account of the entire campaign. While critical of Napoleon as an ambitious tyrant, he gives due credit to the General's skill, imagination, and presence. The ultimate judgment that Labaume offers of Napoleon's career resembles those recorded by both Shelley and Byron: "The being never existed who possessed ampler means for promoting the happiness of mankind." He finds it difficult to decide whether Napoleon was more guilty for the crimes he committed or his failure to do the good he might have done.[3]

The *Manuscrit venu de St. Hélène* purports to be a review by Napoleon of his trials, decisions, victories, and defeats, though actually a hoax accomplished by J. Fréderic Lullin de Chateauvieux. Napoleon is presented as proclaiming the greatness of his deeds and aims, though acknowledging the mistakes which circumstances forced him into. He had saved the Revolution by giving it a lawful character. He had seen that the revolutionary spirit contained the true strength of the times and made use of it to change the world by conquest and legislation.[4]

The book, though rather short and trifling, is entertaining because of its air of imparting confidential information and general scope and boldness. There is little in it that would influence Shelley, however.

Lacretelle, writing during the Empire, not unnaturally hails Napoleon as the necessary man of destiny whose glory, fortune, and ability finally brought order and energy to France's causes. The stages in his rise to power are analyzed. Lacretelle pictures France as fatigued by anarchy, financial collapses, civil war, and brigandage. Each faction desired power for itself and vengeance against its antagonists. The nation was ready to make sacrifices, no longer for liberty and equality, however, but for glory and order. Hence the drama of 18 Brumaire and Napoleon's success in dispersing the militant assembly. "Telle fut la dernière journée de la révolution française" (Such was the last day of the French Revolution).[5]

In terms that Shelley would have accepted, Lady Morgan commented acutely on the mixture of faculties and motives in Napoleon, "one of the many enemies, whom power had armed against the liberties of mankind." His brilliance placed his faults in deeper shadow. By first dazzling then despotically governing the nation, he marred the progress of the great continuing revolution which, through time and experience, might have produced "a wise and beneficent government, belonging to the genius and spirit of the age out of which it arose, and favourable alike to liberty, illumination, and happiness."[6] According to Godwin, such tragedies must occur when men of "high passions and lofty design" are set to act in a corrupted world. Their passions take a wrong turn and produce abortions of greatness. While maintaining Platonically the unity of virtue and knowledge on the highest level of strength and nobility, Godwin acknowledged that a distempered environment creates a disproportion between the creative energy of the heroes and

their opportunities for action and often produces the characteristic and painful errors and vanities of these great ones (*Political Justice*, I, 324–326). Godwin wrote thus prophetically
before Napoleon's rise, and he probably influenced Shelley's
own description of the imbalance in man, the sad disparity
between power and will:

> The good want power, but to weep barren tears.
> The powerful goodness want: worse need for them.
> The wise want love; and those who love want wisdom;
> And all best things are thus confused to ill.
> (*Prometheus Unbound*, I, 625–628)

Napoleon did demonstrate what man might attain in the
limited sense of power and ambition. Could one but supply
the missing elements of universal sympathy and the will directed
to good what could limit the progress of humanity? As M. Cestre
sums up [7] this view, "si un seul homme peut être puissant pour
le mal, il n'est pas moins puissant pour le bien." * Shelley found
a similarly sustaining hope. He tried to account for the phe-
nomenon of Napoleon and to devise correctives for the tragic
excesses and imbalances which the career of the Emperor
suggested.

Both Shelley and Mary studied the psychology of tyranny.
Mary's novel *Castruccio* contains a detailed analysis of how a
promising and ambitious youth may be corrupted by circumstance into tyranny. Shelley described the hero of Mary's novel
as a "little Napoleon," who brought on his medieval Italian
duchy "all the passions and the errors of his antitype" (to
Charles Ollier, September 25, 1821, *Letters*, II, 353). Castruccio, in Mary's account, was a virtuous and guileless young

---

* "if one man alone can be such a power for evil, he could be no less
a power for the good."

man of great ability who gradually learned duplicity and savagery from the Italian princes and courts. Because no purer passion was allowed to take root, ambition became his ruling motive. His heart was hardened by the life of a soldier. As he overcame successive obstacles, he became more indifferent to bloodshed. Finally he subscribed wholeheartedly to the contemporary creed of fraud and secret murder as the means of satisfying his passion to rule. The complete tyrant emerged, with cruelty and suspicion as the central elements of his character. The book reflects the fascination of the Shelley circle with the career of Napoleon.[8]

Byron's attitude toward Napoleon was considerably more varied and complex than Shelley's. In the "Ode to Napoleon," he identified Napoleon and Prometheus in a way which reminds one of Blake's description of the degeneration of Orc's fresh energy, insight, and passion into the binding forms and dogmas of Urizen. The comparison to Prometheus may well have influenced Shelley. Byron felt a strong kinship with Napoleon, had his coach modeled on Napoleon's, visited the field of Waterloo in the spirit of regret for the "melancholy defeat," and expressed a sense of desolation at the time of Napoleon's death as he urged Moore to write on the subject. "His overthrow, from the beginning, was a blow on the head to me. Since that period, we have been the slaves of fools."[9] Byron himself rebelled in the name of freedom, but unlike Shelley he did not take the trouble to develop a new faith which would make freedom meaningful. He wrote, said Dowden, a Napoleonic poetry of revolt which asserted "the supremacy of the individual will."[10]

Residence in a Europe controlled by the principles of conservatism and legitimacy created in both Byron and Shelley a sense of the significance of the mixture of great and mean in Napoleon. His career was instructive. Had he been moderate and sympathetic to men's best hopes, the energy which this "modern Mars" (*Don Juan*, X, 58) used to crush empires might have liberated fallen Europe (*Childe Harold*, III, 36–38, 42). As it was, "Nor man nor fiend hath fallen so far" ("Ode to Napoleon"). Shelley's subsequent references to Napoleon reflect the greater depth of his general views as well as the later experience of reaction. In an 1815 sonnet entitled "Feelings of a Republican on the Fall of Bonaparte," he said that, while he had hated Napoleon for trampling hopes for Liberty which he might have revived, the return to rule by Custom and Faith taught him that there were worse enemies to Freedom than Napoleon's "Force or Fraud." In 1821, on hearing of the death of the Emperor, the poet expressed wonder that the world could recover from the flaming out of a spirit of such energy. Earth is represented as replying that Napoleon was, as many before him, a "fierce spirit," and a "torrent of ruin," on whom the eternal guilt must be fixed of having caused man's best hope to flee "from his glory" ("Lines Written on Hearing the News of the Death of Napoleon"). The great "Ode to Liberty," Shelley's response to the revolutionary movements of the 1820's, described Napoleon as the "Anarch" of the "bewildered powers" of the spirit of Liberty. Shelley never idealized him, like the French poets who created the Napoleon legend, though his imagination was stirred by the spectacle of his grandeur and his fall.

What Napoleon's career might signify to the hopes of men of vision and good will was expressed most poignantly in Shelley's final allusion to him in *The Triumph of Life*, where he described the Emperor as the "child of a fierce hour" who destroyed the hopes of the world in his blind quest for power. The French leader seems to have haunted his imagination until his death. For Napoleon—and Shelley's judgment epitomized his whole gospel of hope—illustrated by his achievements the great strength which is in man, even though the failure to reconcile "power and will" continues to postpone the arrival of Prometheus' triumphant hour. Napoleon himself, alive on his lonely Atlantic rock until 1820, like Shelley's own Prometheus chained to the Caucasus, worked, it has been claimed, to create a legend of himself as the "new Prometheus" who had been the savior of the Revolution and the chief apostle of the movement for peace and world government.[11]

Shelley criticized the mass-man conception of modern industrialized society which views men as economic units, workers, consumers. Not collective man but the uniqueness of each individual must be stressed, he felt, in the new revolutionary political science. Society cannot develop real vitality if it ignores the qualities of contrast and variety in individual men. Each has his "peculiar frame," important individual differences which enlightened morality and politics must study seriously rather than continuing to found social theories on the trivial similarities ("A Treatise on Morals," Clark ed., p. 192). Richness of character and intellect, receptiveness to fresh experience, flexibility in adjusting to men and ideas — these are the qualities to prize. Their presence distinguishes the revolutionary hero.

Such views do not perhaps seem compatible with an associationist and institutional emphasis. Nevertheless, Shelley's psychology, particularly his emphasis on the mind's passivity to experience, was inherited from British empiricism and the related materialistic sensationism of the philosophes. Locke's rejection of innate ideas seemed to make education and environment the masters of the new world. The most hopeful felt that society might be radically reformed in a generation. If man is, as D'Holbach claimed, "un instrument passif entre les mains de la necessité," [12] then wise legislation or a benevolent despot may create a Utopia. People are more nearly equal, said Godwin, than is generally assumed, for the supposedly essential individual differences "originate in the opinions they form, and the circumstances by which they are controled." Men are created by "the empire of impression" (*Political Justice*, I, 40).

Shelley often echoed the notion that men are passively molded by circumstance. As late as the preface to *Prometheus Unbound* he stressed the dependence of exceptional men on a favorable environment. Multiply the number of Athenian republics, he suggested, and you multiply the number of Athenian philosophers and poets. Productive circumstances in society may change, but the "mass of capabilities remains at every period materially the same." This thesis does not differ essentially from the one argued in 1811 to Elizabeth Hitchener, when Shelley baldly stated that Locke's elimination of innate ideas demonstrated that natural inequalities are the results of circumstance (August 19, 1811, *Letters*, I, 136). These views were never quite deserted by Shelley, could not be of course if he were to continue to maintain faith in the efficacy of reform. He told Hunt in 1820 that a man's honesty was determined by his situation rather than his character (May 1, 1820, *Letters*, II, 191).

The emphasis on environment and the belief in the passively receptive nature of the mind were important grounds for revolutionary hope. For some thinkers the mere accumulation and extension of right knowledge seemed enough. Shelley's distinction, however, between mere knowledge and the perception through the imagination of the right use of it involves a rather more subtle notion of human psychology, potentiality, and possibilities of abortive development. Moreover, it may be presumed that his study of the failure of the French Revolution to realize the hopes it raised must have helped qualify this acceptance of the more extreme environmentalist positions. The Revolution seemed to demonstrate to him the necessity of attending to the ways of developing true heroes who would have insights and complexities not attained by mass-men.

Revolutionary philosophers generally had proclaimed the inalienable rights of man and described men as the passive creations of laws or societies. Trying to reconcile these views, Paine said that man can't make circumstances, but he "always has it in his power to improve them when they occur" (I, 301). Shelley echoed him at the beginning of his Irish association pamphlet: "Man cannot make occasions, but he may seize those that offer." In Godwin's thought the inconsistencies seem especially obvious. He describes man at times as a kind of robot through whom forces operate: "Man is in reality a passive, and not an active being" (*Political Justice*, I, 389). Nevertheless, Godwin assumed that man is fundamentally rational and perfectible. Man must be something more, then, than an infinitely malleable and morally indifferent substance which the wise legislator of the French school may shape in his program of enforced felicity.

Shelley may be thought to have emphasized Godwin's individualism but without really discarding the older faith in the right revolutionary environment. He tried to work out a theory of mind which would satisfactorily account for both the active and the passive elements of experience. We are passive to much of our experience. Locke had said that mind is passive in receiving simple ideas, active in forming complex ones. Berkeley stressed the activity of mind. Our ideas are passive and inert, but the spirit or mind is a simple, undivided active being that we know through our ability to make and unmake ideas. Berkeley stressed more than Locke the selective, structuring operations which the active mind conducts in perception. The perceiving subject conveys into the perceived object much of its own nature. Since Berkeley does not label all such operations and substances as fictions of the imagination, he may ultimately have influenced Shelley even more than Hume did. The poet believed in the imagination, rather than discrediting skeptically the results of its operations.

An acceptance of something like Berkeley's subjective idealism is scarcely compatible with any fervid belief in the power of a material environment to produce real change. Subjective idealism does not seem to support the doctrine of natural equality or supply faith in reform. Shelley's *Hellas* may reflect the ambiguities which result from a compound of Berkeley and revolutionary faith. On the whole, it is difficult to avoid the conclusion that Shelley's ultimate positions on the relation between mind and nature are confusing and contradictory.* We have the fact, however, of Shelley's continuing interest in the ideal world of reform and change, and the sense that this served as both a stimulus to the reforming interests and a retreat when despair mounted.

There may be some solution to the dilemma in the concept of development. Shelley mainly associated the terms "passive" and "unconscious" with unformed or primitive minds, infants or savages, who are dependent on sensation. In general, sensation does come first, and Shelley emphasized passivity in this sense, though he also, like Berkeley and Kant, spoke of the "combinations which the intellect makes of sensations according to its own laws" ("A Treatise on Morals," Clark ed., pp. 182, 188). There is also a higher passivity, it seems, which is

---

* Albert Guerard suggests that there is a basic contradiction in Shelley's thought coming from his use of both the Promethean myth glorifying individualism and impulse and his favorite image of the Aeolian lyre. "Romantic naturalism gives us at once the Promethean monster of will and the gently passive organic harp, in which is imaged the last extinction of consciousness, reason, and will." "Prometheus and the Aeolian Lyre," *Yale Review*, XXXIII (1944), 486.

attained by the disciplined mystical imagination when knowing its proper objects, a knowledge without any shaping or constructive or otherwise distorting operations of the "meddling" intellect. This is the knowledge attained by "hierophants of an unapprehended inspiration" ("A Defence of Poetry," Clark ed., p. 297). But in between there must obviously be activity of the mind under the aegis of the synthesizing imagination. Presumably at some point in growth there is a shift to such activity as the developing mind selects and structures its experience. The creative, shaping, plastic power within us is nurtured.*

Presumably the process of forming all minds, at least in the earlier stages, consists of presenting appropriate forms and circumstances which are passively received. If the forms are right, the first impressions will be good ones and the foundations of the individual and the society sound. Our mind and character are passively developed by the world of impressions, though even then, since we do have a nature and specific organs of perception there must be some doubt about the respective roles of perceived and perceiver. Shelley, however, wished to stress the unique, the individual elements, rather than the merely collective movements which shape economic and political men. The sameness of mass-men was not an attractive concept to him. He did emphasize, more than his environmentalist mentors, therefore, the creative elements of variety and novelty in society which are brought into being by the individual activity of the hero. He was aware of the interplay between per-

---

* Ralph Houston, on the other hand, claimed that Hume, Shelley, and J. S. Mill were all committed to "the idea that the human mind is fundamentally a passive instrument functioning automatically by means of the Principles of Association of Ideas and Impressions (Emotions)." Imagination in this scheme was no more than the "power to sustain a permanent state of feeling." "Shelley and the Principle of Association," *Essays in Criticism*, III (January 1953), 54, 56.

sonality and the collective life. Perhaps he would have accepted Hegel's notion that the greatness of a historical personality stems from the identification of the passionate energy of his will with the unconscious ferment in the collective life which he helps bring to realization. Men are shaped by their age, but they in turn help form the true genius of the time. "Shakespeare and Lord Bacon and the great writers of the age of Elizabeth and James the 1st were at once the effects of the new spirit in men's minds and the causes of its more complete development" ("A Philosophical View of Reform," Clark ed., p. 231).

Shelley's view of perception seems to comprehend two kinds or degrees of passiveness: that of mass character, largely and generally subject to the institutions and prevailing climate of opinion of the age; and the keenly sensitive passiveness of the artist to his nearly ineffable sources of inspiration. The reformer who wishes to transform institutions into the machinery of education and progress must attend particularly to the first. The second kind of passiveness is of importance primarily when one considers the extraordinary individuality and richness of the experience of a few specially gifted men. The spirit of their unique genius expresses "the uncommunicated lightning of their own mind." Their experience differs qualitatively from that of mass-men, but the nature and significance of that experience impels them to active creation and practical political activity in behalf of the latent forms they view in the political lives of all men and all societies. They are the oracles of the truths known to the prophetic mind when it confronts Demogorgon. Possibly Shelley's awareness of human uniqueness and qualitative differences ought to have qualified his social and moral determinism rather more than it did.

In any event, in his poetry Shelley projects the hero of human will and imagination, the exceptional man who alone sees, rebels, and leads others in rebellion. The hero liberates his imagination from the evil which is our element because he has greater powers of feeling and vision. His imagination prophetically figures forth the goals and the means for other men — if they are capable of responding to the will to be reborn from within.

Probably there are no essential contradictions or inconsistencies in Shelley's reflections on the active and passive aspects of human knowledge and activity. Men are both active and passive, in both good and bad senses. Poets are passive before their inspiration, active in their efforts to compose from their vision the elements of a new man and a new society. The distinction is developed in "The Essay on Christianity": "Our most imperial and stupendous qualities — those on which the majesty and the power of humanity is erected — are, relatively to the inferior portion of its mechanism, indeed active and imperial; but they are the passive slaves of some higher and more omnipresent Power" (Clark ed., p. 202). Men generally help to form the institutions and the environments which shape them. The doctrine of progress, moreover, as Shelley develops it, tends to reconcile the apparent opposites. Progress or the true revolution occurs only as the number of enlightened substantially increases, as the forms apprehended by the liberators are communicated more widely and more vigorously.

Because the doctrine of the passivity of man contained political dangers, as conceived by rigorous utilitarians and environmentalists, and because molding masses is a tricky, doubtful business, it was important to stress improvement through the imagination, man's most subtle, flexible, and sensitive register of impressions. Imagination is the individuating power, the strength in the bonds between men, the power of entering sympathetically into the lives of our kind. Some observers believed that the French Revolution failed because it was conducted by mere men of reason, cold analyzers who lacked the humanity which would have prevented the slaughter of inno-cents. Lacretelle claimed, for example, that Robespierre's power derived from the fact that he was a man with a single idea, a single passion, and a single will, who never felt the affections that move other men.[13]

No mere chilly rational progress is envisioned by Shelley. His doctrine of the heroine, the beloved counterpart, shadow, other self, and ideal support of the hero extends and enriches his concept of true progress. The true society will not provide, like the former revolutionaries, a meager satisfaction for the mere reason through the service of abstract forms and purely intellectual enlightenment. Man by enslaving woman, said Mary Wollstonecraft, delays the dawn of true liberty. When morality is corrupted by the domestic experience of a master-slave relationship, it is unlikely that the state can rid itself of the corruption caused by inequality. "Make women rational creatures and free citizens, and they will quickly become good wives and mothers." [14] Thus, in Shelley's long poems it is the woman, who in *Queen Mab* is taught the truths known to prophetic imagination, who as Cythna supports and extends the doctrines of Laon in *The Revolt of Islam*, who finally as Asia in *Prometheus Unbound* penetrates to the ultimate truth as an agent of human redemption. Men and women are transcen-dently equal in Shelley's visioned society, and evil falls before their united beings.

For Shelley, as his wife commented in her note to *Rosalind and Helen*, love is "the essence of our being," and all the woes of men and society may be said to arise from the selfishness and insensibility which thwart love. The collapse of the Revo-lution had been charged by many contemporary commentators to the emotions of hate and revenge which its course gen-erated. There was the viciousness of such men as Marat, Hé-bert, and Carrier and the judicial murders of political enemies.

The observers that Shelley consulted on the Revolution were unanimous in the judgment that factional hatred was a principal cause for the failure. It was the prevailing spirit, Dr. Moore declared.[15] Edwards traced the murders, rapes, and tortures in the West Indies to the violent partisanship and spirit of reprisal fostered by the Revolution. Each successive faction hated the group that preceded it. Revenge was the law. When the planters captured the savages, they punished them according to an inhuman "system of revenge and retaliation."[16] Lacretelle singled out the occasional moments of peace, enthusiasm, and mutual sympathy during the Revolution as exceptional digressions from the spirit of universal hatred. The Jacobins launched a campaign of hate. The spirit of hatred empowered every impulse of the warring factions. "Les complots de la révolution ont tous été formés par la haine; mais c'est la peur qui les a décidés." * Hate and Fear were Shelley's twin Satanic deities.[17] The Directory fell because it too was governed by hate.

The rational and doctrinaire character of the Revolution, and particularly of such leaders as Robespierre, seemed in itself sufficient reason for its failure. Arid syllogisms could contribute nothing to the development of the inward sympathies important to a deeper culture of humanity. Rational progress is not enough for man. He is more than a creature of reason. As Shelley suggested in the dedication of *The Revolt of Islam,* his studies in the thought of the Enlightenment gave him a sense of power and political hope, but he needed the love which Mary brought to complete his preparation for his life's work. "True knowledge leads to love" of the potential form of an expanded and enriched humanity buried in the life of each individual (Clark ed., p. 341).

Reason is a solitary spirit, akin to self-love and passion for

---

* "The plots of the Revolution have all been formed out of hatred; but it is fear which determined their course."

personal salvation. Man aspires to a nobler expansion of his whole nature culminating in a complete communion with a being like himself. Even Platonic contemplation of the beauty and mystery of the universe is not enough, as *Alastor* ambiguously records. The beauty and grace of woman both symbolize and satisfy these eternal longings. She links our world of shadows to the world of forms. The loftiest social sympathies derive energy and direction from this new humanism of love. Thus, Shelley translated the Platonic idea of an intermediary daemon into an idealization of the relationship of the sexes similar to that suggested by Dante and Italian Platonism. The power for true enlightenment which the Revolution lacked could be supplied by the love of the new revolutionary hero and heroine.

Good material for the doctrine of love and the idea of the new woman was available in the history of the Revolution. Louvet's *Memoirs* celebrated the love and the inspiration of his Lodoiska and probably influenced Shelley's account of Laon and Cythna in *The Revolt of Islam*. The poet read of the courage and influence of other great heroines of the Revolution, especially Charlotte Corday and Mme. Roland. Helen Maria Williams, a victim of the Terror and a friend of Mary Wollstonecraft, paid tribute in one section of her *Sketches* to the women of the Revolution, the martyrdom of some, their heroic pleas for the lives of captives, and their ministrations to the suffering. Women, she commented, have a natural inclination to admire what is great and generous, and on them falls the task of educating the youth of the new republic in the duties of enlightened citizenship.[18] Camille Desmoulins, softened by the love of his young wife, finally attacked the outrages against humanity he had once supported; but he was soon guillotined with his wife, regretting "d'avoir trop souvent appelé la vengeance, et trop tard l'humanité" (having too often summoned vengeance and too late humanity).[19] Condorcet, a very strong influence on Shelley, firmly rejected the idea that men and women are unequal. He advised that they be educated for new and important roles in genuine moral and intellectual progress, with special attention to the part which enlightened family relations might play.[20]

Of external influences, however, it was his knowledge of the relationship between William Godwin and Mary Wollstonecraft that affected Shelley's outlook most strongly. Godwin himself acknowledged that his own deficiency in the "intuitive perception of intellectual beauty" was more than compensated for by Mary's strength of imagination.[21] Mary's thesis, already briefly indicated, was that women as well as men were entitled to liberty and equality: "when man, governed by reasonable laws, enjoys his natural freedom, let him despise woman, if she do not share it with him." The powerful influence which the sexes exercise on each other is debasing where women are but bond-slaves to man's appetites and leisure moments, ennobling in the true marriages which produce charity, virtue, and a simplicity of affection. Since women are men's first teachers, presenting their first impressions of the world, as well as their wives and companions, "the most salutary effects tending to improve mankind might be expected from a REVOLUTION in female manners." The love of the sexes could become a part of and help kindle the "glowing flame of universal love." One wonders, however, what Shelley's reaction might have been to her strictures on the dangerous pictures of love which men of genius, heated by voluptuous imagination, draw of shadowy reveries from vapid realities. They describe their sensuality under the veil of sentiment, the lady comments. Such men are "ever panting after unattainable perfection" and fleeting dreams.[22]

With Keats and Coleridge, Shelley saw all passions as essentially creative, especially this passion of love which introduces men to a new life in a diviner world. This love so regenerates perception that all things are endowed with beauty. The mind of a beautiful woman, like that of a true poet, is a mirror in which all shapes are transfigured, and in our communion with such a glorious being who stains the atmosphere with the radiance of love, we behold the true forms of that active power of Beauty which "penetrates and clasps and fills the world" (*Epipsychidion*, ll. 30–32, 90–103).

Love kindles hope, the "winged child" of Justice and Truth (*The Revolt of Islam*, II, 13). Shelley developed a complex and comprehensive doctrine of hope. Love and Hope are the twin deities of his personal and public worlds, and they are closely dependent on each other. The age of Revolution created large public hopes which were still alive for Shelley, who took fire from his readings in eighteenth-century philosophy, where the revolution had been created in the minds of men well before the task of translating ideas into experience was attempted. As Hazlitt said, "The French Revolution was the only match that ever took place between philosophy and experience."[23] "The revolutions of America and France have thrown a beam of light over the world," Tom Paine proclaimed (I, 320). Once rent, the veil of despotism cannot be repaired. The knowledge that men accumulate cannot be unthought. The clock cannot be turned back, though temporary defeats may have to be endured. This was the hope and faith of revolutionaries. Other revolutions must follow. The partial success of the French Revolution seemed to Godwin to create an example which other nations might emulate and improve upon. In the first edition of *Political Justice* he asserted that incessant effort and vigilant propagation of the truth might well give hope for "an early and a favourable event" (*Political Justice*, III, 290). The passage was later omitted and the need for gradual and individual improvement stressed, but it does bear witness to the general belief that it was a great period of renewal of hope. The intoxication of new hopes, which Wordsworth testified to in the *Prelude*, can be found in the reactions of most liberal observers of the time. When the great events of the Revolution dramatized the seeming success of the cause, "un mouvement général d'espérance anima la nation toute entière."[24]

Later commentators, in whom the revolutionary impulses remained active, felt that the great early days of the Revolution continued to animate the minds of men though the "springtime of hope and glow of exultation" had passed. Hazlitt said: "it is perhaps enough for great actions to *have been* . . . and thus to stir the mind in after-ages with mingled awe, admiration, and regret."[25] Sir T. Charles Morgan, reviewing in 1817 the practical achievements of the Revolution, noted that in France, even after the Bourbon reaction, the remaining forms of justice created by the Revolution could produce a revival. He felt that, once the spirit of the age had weakened the Bourbon dynasty, France's judicial rights could be restored to what they had been "during the first pure moments of the revolution of 1789." As a scientist and physician, Sir Charles also saw causes for encouragement which might have influenced Shelley's program for progress as outlined in act IV of *Prometheus Unbound.* "The invigorating stimulation, which accompanied the revolution, has given a vast increase of energy to scientific pursuit."[26]

Among Shelley's teachers, the grounds for hope were rigorously analyzed by Condorcet and Godwin. Condorcet said that Locke's theory of knowledge supported belief in perfectibility and eliminated the possibility of real relapses to old ignorant prejudices. The new enlightened theories of mind, the application of true scientific method, the open lines of communication among men of learning, the increasing number of informed citizens since the invention of printing — these were the grounds of future progress, already so far advanced "qu'on puisse redouter de les voir jamais retomber dans l'oubli" (that one need not fear such hopes can ever fall back into oblivion again).[27]

Godwin emphasized the ease with which men would improve once they are taught their abilities and their destinies. "Men are weak at present, because they have always been told they are weak, and must not be trusted with themselves" (*Political Justice*, II, 409). Whatever excellence men of genius can conceive, can ultimately be attained. Shelley's view of the mind was more complex than that held by the empirical and associationist philosophers of the eighteenth century, but he retained the hopes for man which those theories helped create even though he learned of the difficulties of fulfilling such hopes.

Hope at least keeps one's sense of the power of evil and the weight of reaction from becoming intolerable. As a very young man, Shelley told Elizabeth Hitchener that he felt that it was no crime for those who live in the shadow of mortality to solace themselves with high hopes; "Mine are always rather visionary" (January 26, 1812, *Letters*, I, 239). About this time, Southey, who had been having long talks with Shelley, was writing in an essay: "Hope is the leaven without which the mind becomes inert, and tends only to corruption."[28] Also, as Condorcet had noted and perhaps Shelley observed, it is dangerous to look at man as he is, corrupted by prejudices, factious passions, and social customs. Liberals must think of man as he might be, ought to be, and perhaps can be.[29] Even fear, as Byron commented in his journal, has something pleasurable about it as a stimulus to hope: "*what Hope* is there without a deep leaven of *Fear.*" Hope is the most delightful of sensations. There is no meaningful future without hope. "In all human affairs, it is Hope — Hope — Hope." [30] Byron may be echoing Shelley's customary refrain. Twice in letters, in 1816 and in 1819, he cited Coleridge on the "solemn duty" of Hope; the 1816 letter quoted him as saying, "Hope is a most awful duty, the nurse of all other virtues" (to Lord Byron, September 8, 1816, *Letters*, I, 504). In both personal and political life hope is essential as "a worship to the spirit of good within, which requires before it sends that inspiration forth, which impresses its likeness upon all that it creates, devoted & disinterested homage" (to Maria Gisborne, October 13 or 14, 1819, *Letters*, II, 125). Thus are our passions, our joys and hopes essentially creative. The comment is contemporaneous with the passage on hope at the end of *Prometheus Unbound*.

Of the workings of this passion of hope Shelley shaped a doctrine which is fundamental to his visionary politics. He was insistent on the need for optimism. The poet Lionel in *Rosalind and Helen*, as he looked despairingly through the gloomy crowds from his "dreary tower," found his soul sustained by a "winged Hope" and nearly reborn in a vision of "What poets know and prophesy" (ll. 798–800, 859, 889). The good spirit which Manichean belief sees as eventually triumphant, a belief which makes life tolerable in an evil world of oppression and change, is, said Shelley, "a personification of the principle of hope" ("Essay on the Devil and Devils," Clark ed., p. 265). Our attitudes toward reality contribute to the creation of that reality. Love and ambition empower lovers and ambitious men to achievements not available to the unmotivated, Godwin had said. Desire doubles the activity of the mind as it struggles to attain a goal which is actually within human compass but not to be reached by passive yearning. Grounds for our hopes there must be, but they remain forever out of our grasp, if we do not convince ourselves that they are possible and struggle to achieve them. Men are made greater, Godwin felt, when their minds are "habitually elevated to magnificent conceptions" (*Political Justice*, I, 318, 320, 322).

Shelley's best-known pronouncement on Hope, as well as his most obscure, occurs at the end of *Prometheus Unbound*: "To love, and bear; to hope till Hope creates / From its own wreck the thing it contemplates." This paradoxical statement sums up Shelley's doctrine of hope. Hope like our other passions creates its objects. The Revolution was in a sense the wreck of Hope in its failure; but the sense of possibilities that it dramatized, the energies for change that it generated, the greatness of man that was glimpsed, cannot die or be lost from the memory of man. Tragedy produces strength. The institutions which the Revolution created still leave an imprint on the imperfect forms of society. As once the cross so now the guillotine symbolizes the power of hope to create itself out of the wrecks of hope. Hope realizes itself by steadily contemplating its object and gradually transforming itself into the new apocalyptic identity built on the ruins of the old.

The Hero knows the forms of a perfected world. Like knows like. He becomes the intermediary through whom we too know the forms. The visions of "love, beauty, and truth" we seek to realize are contained in the mind of man, and our dreams of a new earth could be achieved if our acts could match our knowledge and desires ("Julian and Maddalo"). Whatsoever the mind conceives under the guidance of reason, as Spinoza said, or imagination, as the romantics said, it conceives under the form of eternity, and we may, under the control of such conceptions so collapse time that we contemplate and desire the good which is conceived as future as if it were present.[31]

An "unusually intense and vivid apprehension of life" may also accomplish, as love often does, a sense of the merging of the separate identities of men as "modifications of the one mind"

("Essay on Life," Clark ed., p. 174). A political equivalent and expression of such feelings is Rousseau's doctrine of the general will, that mystical identification of individual wills in the corporate identity of the ideal state which always is and acts as one and can do no wrong. It should be our study to make this perfectly functioning general will actual in our individual will and our social institutions. When this "eternal now" arrives, the spirits of the renewed mind of man will become "an ocean / Of clear emotion," and in the "crystal palaces" of "Thought's crowned powers" the power and harmony of love will create the earthly paradise. The enlightened and emancipated man is now a reflective and illuminating center, both the undistorted mirror of the forms and the lamp ignited by knowledge which beams through the mists of ignorance, hate, and fear to renew and strengthen the faltering hopes of mankind. Such heroes when united can reform the world. They know and attain Utopia now, if only in those transient moments, when wrought into one identity and one will by love and the shared hopes, they see and feel their destiny.

X

The Revolt of Islam

In Shelley's second revolutionary epic, *The Revolt of Islam,* he adopts a more positive and poetic course than in *Queen Mab.* He looks more closely into the makeup of the revolutionary heroes and heroines who are to create the Heaven on Earth, and he tells a coherent story about an attempt to organize and run a real revolution very much like the French Revolution. Shelley's problem for the poem was defined by his study of the course of the French Revolution: How were liberals during the reaction against the Revolution to restore the former enthusiasm for the great abstractions of human progress? After the tempest how much desire to work for a better world remains? The older expectations had been pitched too high. Clearly the masses could not at once become enlightened, humane, and philosophical. But need the ideals be sacrificed because men had been unable to live up to them?

The audience for this experiment on the public temper is the "enlightened and refined" of the intellectual aristocracy, those who are most truly sensitive to possible change for the better, who, like the poet, have become aware of "a slow, gradual silent change" (preface). Assuming the presence of such an audience, Shelley offers them a projection of the noblest forms of ideal human passion and intellect. He pictures men and women whose quality, whose struggle, and whose defeat may arouse or renew a sense of the beauty in true virtue and enlightened politics. If such an audience can respond to his narrative, they may be incited to search for a nobler and more active moral and political creed. Shelley in *The Revolt of Islam* anticipates what men might be by presenting images of philanthropists aspiring to the highest human excellence. Perhaps a more generous enthusiasm for liberty and justice may be created and faith and hope in man's better nature be rekindled.

Unlike the didactic *Queen Mab, The Revolt of Islam* is organized as a narrative. It is a love story, both passionate and political, which ends both happily and unhappily, that is, with the lovers as united and in some sense immortal martyrs but also dead and politically defeated. Their defeat inspires feelings that better things are to come. The poem is also a history of a revolution. Probably the love story was inspired by the turmoil of the early years of Shelley's own relationship with Mary, but it seems also to have been influenced in detail and atmosphere by the romantic story of Louvet and his Lodoiska which the poet had read in Louvet's *Memoirs*, a source book for the personal drama and suspense of the Revolution during the Terror. There a revolution and the pangs of separated lovers were brought together.

The focus in Shelley's sketch of the course of an ideal revolution is on the work of "individual genius" (to a publisher, October 13, 1817, *Letters*, I, 564). He has a hero and a heroine whose ardors, successes, and failures he presents, but he also describes a "beau ideal" of a revolution which his lovers create through their own union, a "type of peace" (IX, 30). Every stage of the revolution is pictured: inception, planning, and organizing; early steps and procedures; capitalizing on opportunities for arousing and arming popular enthusiasm; stabilizing after initial gains; struggling against the bloody and reactionary tactics of priests and despots; and finally learning to face the violent obliteration of the newborn cause in a world of plagues, executions, and shocking inhumanities. The plot echoes many of the events of the French Revolution, and the terms in which Shelley outlined his poem were clearly suggested by the history of the French Revolution: "the faithlessness of tyrants" refers to the duplicity of Louis XVI; "the confederacy of the Rulers of the World" recalls the backing of the Brunswick Manifesto by European armies; the theme of the restoration of an expelled dynasty by foreign arms resembles the return of the Bourbons; and the reference to the judicial murder of the true patriots and advocates of liberty indicates Shelley's sympathy for the proscribed Girondists who died on the guillotine.

The vision of the nineteenth century which the poem records was granted to the speaker of the poem at a time after "the last hope of trampled France had failed" (I, 1). The poet's "visions of despair" over this failure were mitigated by the story narrated by Laon and Cythna, immortals who reside in a hall of spirits. These two spirits describe a Wordsworthian childhood in Greece during the sway of the Turk. Here the theme of *Hellas* and the later connection between Hellenism and Shelley's revolutionary idealism are anticipated. United by their nurturing close to the natural beauties of the mountain and the sea, the two also shared revolutionary sympathies which they learned through reading and observation of the effects of tyranny.

The idyll was ended when Cythna was carried off by hireling slaves provisioning the tyrant's seraglio. Urging his friends to fight for death or liberty in the struggle to save her, Laon practiced a rebellious violence which he learned to preach against. He was bound like Prometheus to a rock overlooking the town for having slain three soldiers. Perhaps his punishment, like that of Prometheus, was the symbolic result of violence in a world whose ills can only be cured by love and peaceful change. After a period of suffering he was released by an old man, inspired by Laon's published doctrines. His strength and his sense of mission were restored by a long stay in an old tower.

Laon returned to the fray when he heard reports of insurgent activity in the Golden City, which had apparently been inspired by his own early hymns to hope and freedom. He arrived at the scene of action in time to give a lesson of love and forbearance by taking a thrust from a spear which one of his associates had intended for a minion of tyranny, proclaiming as he did so that only ill can come from ill. This act of love seemed to do the job, for soldiers and citizens were joyously united, as in France, and universal peace and harmony briefly reigned though tyrants and reactionaries were fulminating in the background. Had not soldiers turned into citizens during the French Revolution when asked to fire on the people? According to Mackintosh, when the soldiers realized that they were citizens, despotism in France fell. Their "sympathy with the national spirit" produced "noble disobedience."[1] Mary Wollstonecraft too had described in her history the several such periods of contagious enthusiasm when the citizens and the "myrmidons of tyranny" embraced one another and produced the great ardors of the moment which accomplish more "than all the engines and batteries in the world" (*View of F. R.*, pp. 58, 193).

There followed a fete celebrating the triumph. Laon was hailed as a deliverer. The former tyrant was brought out, not to be guillotined, but to be pitied and even permitted a little harmless pomp, something of a mistake, one might think, in the light of what followed. Violence and revenge had been outlawed. Yet, after an unquiet night, like those following the fall of the Bastille in France, when the tyrants congregated in defense of their brother and the bloodshed began, Laon himself led the lovers of liberty to fight for their cause with such rude weapons, pikes mainly, as were available. These dedicated diehards united by "desperation's hope" battled for "native rights" (VI, 8, 13). As their cause was strong their might was great, even though they were finally overpowered by the weight of numbers. The slaughter was described by the poet with all possible emphasis on the ugliness of hatred displayed in the lurid carnage. Since the vividness and intensity of the struggle and the horrors of violent death so dominated Shelley's imagination in his account, it becomes difficult to comprehend what Shelley meant by referring to his revolution as a "beau ideal." We shall consider this question more fully below.

As the strife neared its fated end, Laon and Cythna were reunited melodramatically, and they retreated from the cause of helpless and hopeless humanity to a lovely isolated ruin where their passionate and ideal love was consummated. Shelley's account may well have borrowed something from the descriptions in Louvet's *Memoirs* of his occasional retreats from fear and despair to the arms of his Lodoiska, where he knew a peace, beauty, and security unattainable in a world where larger public hopes had dwindled.

The tyrant, having defeated the short-lived revolution, summoned a league of evil despots and priests. Plague was striking down those spared during the fighting. The oppressors decided that human sacrifice would be necessary to propitiate their god and to prevent their own corpses from being added to the maggoty heaps littering "the death-polluted land" (X, 13). As the counterrevolutionaries meditated upon their policies, Laon entered, his face masked, and addressed the parliament of priests and warriors with a stirring appeal to revolutionary ideals. The ardent young few who responded were quickly slain by the "men of faith and law" (XI, 19). Likely Shelley was influenced in his account of Laon's heroic stoicism and dedication to liberty by the descriptions he had read in his sources of the brave defiance of the great Girondists. Some witnesses, Riouffe noted, were convinced of the truth of the Girondist cause by their remarkable, martyrlike deaths. Husbands and wives, like Laon and Cythna, died together because they refused to survive their mates. Mme. Roland's husband killed himself when he heard of his wife's death by the guillotine.[2] In Shelley's poem, comparably, Laon offered himself for sacrifice if Cythna might be released to go to America, the land of hope. Laone or Cythna, however, felt, like Louvet's Lodoiska, that even if she and Laon were not allowed by a hostile world to live together, that they could die together. Louvet himself, like Laon, fearing that his absent Lodoiska may have been captured and doomed to the guillotine, thought of forcing his way into Robespierre's chambers and bartering his own life for Lodoiska's.[3]

Laon and Cythna were burned at the stake, but their death is described as a release into harmony. They drifted into a brighter world, their united souls steeped passively in scenery akin to that of *Alastor* and *Kubla Khan* where rich opposites are reconciled. On a charmed boat propelled by music and poetry and guided by a winged child claiming descent from them and the tyrant, they finally reached their shining destiny outside of the world of life and time. There they joined a noble senate of the heroes of the human mind to reside forever in a spiritual pantheon.

This sketch of Shelley's narrative may reveal some of the more obvious ingredients of his ideal revolutionary pattern: (1) the emphasis on environment, early study, and decision; (2) the need for sympathetic communion like that of lovers to forge the symbol of the ideal revolution; (3) the insistence on the ultimate supremacy of love over hate; (4) the difficulty of maintaining the new world against the deeply entrenched forces of anarchy and ruin; (5) the final turn to extramental and extrahuman consolations and sources of strength.

All of Shelley's characteristic images appear in *The Revolt of Islam*. At the very beginning the history of mankind is allegorized as a struggle between an eagle and a serpent. The serpent, emblem of eternity, sheds its skin annually and thus became for revolutionaries, Shelley would have learned in Barruel, an emblem of revolution (IV, 349–350). Spring and renewal symbolism is concentrated in the episode where Laon senses renewed power and hope as he anticipates his reunion with Cythna. It is a pattern to be developed more richly later in the description of Prometheus and Asia. The revolution seems to have faltered, but when the lovers retreat to the home of autumn's dead leaves, some notion of the ritual spell of hope and renewal which lovers may invoke is suggested. Power, beauty, and knowledge were kindled by their relationship. Though the "fearful overthrow / Of public hope" was snapped from their being by "wildering passion," the imagery of meteors and maenads and green domes which supports this intensity indicates that the blending of their "two restless frames" adumbrates ritually a glorious future for humanity (VI, 30–36).

The whole West-Wind complex of imagery is explored in *The Revolt of Islam*. In fact, the great ode might be described as an abstraction of the long poem, just as *Prometheus Unbound* is its symbolic and mythological counterpart. "Ode to the West Wind" dramatizes the elemental powers behind myth in a ritual invocation which omits the specific human clothing of story or event. The Laon of the spiritual senate is one whose brow shadows his eyes

like the morning sky
The cloudless Heaven of Spring, when in their flow

Through the bright air, the soft winds as they blow
Wake the green world . . .   (I, 59)

Cythna's hopes in her exotic prison were like the "prophetic dreams" of odorous violets. "The buds foreknow their life — this hope must ever rise" (VII, 37). When the unruly ocean and the quaking earth released her from her "crystal cave," she shared the elemental freedom of the wind which has power to unbind the tempest. Her voice, as she addressed the assembly at the fete of freedom and equality, was like a stream which sweeps autumn's dead leaves to a deep lake where they are transformed into the living and beautiful flowers of the blue spring (V, 53). So with the multitude of her auditors. Laon's poems were as winds which sustained Cythna's flights of fancy. The citizens congregating in the Golden City, drawn by Laon's wild songs floating on the winds, were like clouds gathered by distant gusts (IX, 12). At another stage they were compared to the multitude of waves in a tempestuous sea, weeping sympathetically over the plight of Laon and Cythna, their tears "like soft dews / Which feed Spring's earliest buds" (XII, 14). The plague struck the country in autumn after the failure of the uprising and poisoned all life. Frost stripped the trees of leaves. The ravaged citizenry are themselves described as dead leaves filling the "cold and sullen brooks" (X, 44).

These images were collected and concentrated in the scene of the lovers' retreat from this sick world. Their love prophetically clothed an otherwise wintry future with bright shapes. Now they know the blasts of autumn driving the "winged seeds" to the "frost of death" where they wait during the "flood of tyranny" and the stagnation of faith. In "the winter of the world" heroes perish at the guillotine and philosophers keep silence, but the spring returns which they "who made / The promise of its birth" shall not see, though within their hearts reigns a paradise "which everlasting Spring has made its own" (IX, 20–27). Thus they know satisfaction even in the defeat of their public hopes from the knowledge that they have scattered the seeds of hope for the eternal spring to come which begins to reign now in the hearts of the good and mighty. Laon and Cythna forget all about the revolution for two days or so. Thoughts of duty and public hope return, but now their love has redeemed and reinforced their hopes and given them a large calm immunity to the unrest and mutability of the times (IX, 19), without in the least diminishing their dedication to the great truths they have actively served.

The Cythna whose purity and beauty as a child kindled intenser zeal in Laon and converted his knowledge into wisdom by the power of ideal love became his partner and the central agent for the communication of Laon's revolutionary ideas. Shelley, the admiring reader of Mary Wollstonecraft's works on the revolution and the role of woman, demonstrates her influence strongly in *The Revolt of Islam*. He also reflects what he had read about Charlotte Corday and Mme. Roland. In the vision of the first canto a lovely woman soothes the injured serpent. At the great Hall of Genius, the woman and the serpent commingle in their new identity as the twin forms of Hope and Spring-born Radiance, the immortal powers known on earth as Laon and Cythna, or Laon and Laone. Later, when the rebellion inspired by Laon's writings broke out during his absence, it was Cythna, a more efficient Mme. Roland, who organized her "happy female train" to realize his prophecies (II, 38). By some, Cythna or Laone was regarded as a female messiah sent down by God to save the women.

When Cythna sang Laon's songs of hope and change he found his own sense of purpose strengthened. She felt fully the power of his conceptions and returned to him a richer sense of the meaning in his own liberating ideas. As an implied doctrine, the conclusions seem to be that human growth is not the product of isolated selfish concentration on the worship of intellectual beauty. The power for genuine development comes from the reflection of one's thoughts in other minds, for the meaning or energy of ideas is enlarged and extended through this process of sympathy. Love, knowledge, and progress are closely linked. As the poet testified in the dedication to *The Revolt*, though power and political hope were strengthened in him by study, he needed love to complete him for his work. Solitary gazing upon the beauty and mystery of the universe must yield to the deeper communication with the personal and ideal intermediary to the divine represented by female beauty and grace.

In terms of political doctrine, Shelley insisted, like Mrs. Wollstonecraft, that there cannot be lasting liberty and progress without equality of the sexes. Free children can only be reared by free women. Domestic tyranny is incompatible with social liberty. Men cannot be free if women are slaves. "Never will peace and human nature meet / Till free and equal man and woman greet / Domestic peace" (II, 43, 47). Moreover, on an ideally spiritual or metaphysical level, the supporting and enriching insights of two lovers make up a new creative synthesis in perception. The theme is launched in Shelley's dedication with his tribute to Mary for liberating him from despair and solitude. "Thou Friend, whose presence on my wintry heart / Fell, like bright Spring upon some herbless plain" (ll. 55–56). Love and wisdom become the keys to the future, for from the union of equal lovers comes the new heaven on earth. Lovers possess in and through their unity the key to eternity. Laon, contemplating his withered features after the years of madness, saw there the likeness of Cythna's face, which once had been the "mirror of her thoughts" (IV, 30). In the exalted bliss of love such as theirs, all faculties and feelings are confounded into one power which collapses time and blends "two restless frames in one reposing soul" (VI, 34–36). Evil is conquered by the "uniting minds" (II, 46) of the two lovers, for they live in a world outside change and death and political chance.

One must live "as if to love and live were one" (VIII, 12). In his poem, as Shelley says in the preface, "Love is celebrated everywhere as the sole law which should govern the moral world." The gradual extension of sympathy necessary to realizing true social goals depends on the general love of humanity. These social sympathies, one variety or level of love, are the object of the poet who tries to find the words and music "To weave a bondage of such sympathy, / As might create some response to the thought / Which ruled me now" (II, 16). His sympathies are given further strength and wider purpose by his more human and intimate relationships. Without them, he might become another abstract revolutionary monster like Robespierre. Here the French Revolution fell short.

When the larger social goals falter, true lovers can retreat to ideal paradises of their own and defeat those evils which are resistless to the oneness of love. Shelley would have known this theme of a retreat to the bower of bliss amidst the terror and cruelty of violent revolution from Louvet's *Memoirs*. Louvet and Lodoiska seized their moments of love in a hostile world. Thus they remained free in the midst of slaves: "nous avons dans l'asile secret, dans le profond mystère où les oppresseurs nous tenoient ensevelis, nous avons trouvé le moyens de rester libres" (we found a way to remain free in the secret retreat, in the mysterious depths where our oppressors had kept us buried).[4] As Cythna to Laon, Lodoiska remained for Louvet his divine inspiration in a sea of dangers. She kept him alive. For him "l'amour et l'espérance" were inseparable companions. Their retreats Louvet described in the luxuriant imagery of a romancer, and he may have influenced Shelley's similar descriptions in both *Alastor* and *The Revolt of Islam*.

Love operates within our perceptions to contract the world to a clear image of beauty: "from its beams deep love my spirit drank, / And to my brain the boundless world now shrank / Into one thought—one image" (I, 41). Love fills the world with its dazzling light. Love has the enduring, real, and positive power of so transfiguring the world about us that we do indeed see it in the radiance of eternity, wedded as we are both to our beloved and to nature our common mother. The beauty of a beloved person enchants faith and lends power to hope so that the union of lovers becomes at once a fulfillment and a prophecy in which other men may read their glorious destiny.

The power of love taught Laon the necessity of avoiding revolutionary violence. The hero must realize in miniature what society may not know and practice for generations. Unless liberals "cast the vote of love in hope's abandoned urn," the cause they advocate can claim no real moral superiority. By arming themselves and fiercely resisting the tyrant's guards, the partisans of liberty perpetuated the will of hate. "If blood be shed, 'tis but a change and choice / Of bonds" (IV, 22, 28). Confusion and despair did not weaken the ardor of the patriots until "revenge and fear" entered their hearts, and it took Laon's example of love and forbearance, taking in his own arm a spear thrust meant for a soldier, to rally his supporters and overpower the enemy, not by force, but by the power in the "truth of love's benignant laws." Thus was a nation "Made free by love" (V, 7–14). Laon fought, however, and shed blood when the enemy returned. Apparently Shelley did not think it inconsistent to distinguish between the way men may achieve the true society and what they must do when fighting for their lives, or perhaps fighting for their principles, since their lives were already given up, "As myriads flocked in love and brotherhood to die" (VI, 10). The time comes when passive resistance must end, and the law of necessity that ill will flow from ill loses its force of application.

In *The Revolt of Islam* Shelley wrote the epic of a hero as poet. He focused on the revolutionary leader rather than the revolutionized society. Laon's personal rebellion and his noble eloquence arouse the sleeping multitude. The ideas which govern him, "invested with the light / Of language" (II, 16), create a response wherever they break through the darkness of "tranced spirits." His weapons are words, and he springs forth on fancy's wings to rally secret hopes in his name. There are men who possess a "secret strength" which penetrates to the roots of unborn hopes: "young Laon's name / Rallied their secret hopes" (IV, 10). Such men are not, however, to be imitated passively. Laon's presence and his doctrines work inside human hearts and arouse activity. The thoughts aroused by the aspiring hopes of the poet-hero are doctrines of human power which nourish aspirations and bring the human faculties into living and unique relation.

The hero and those he inspires are fed by a vision of fulfilled hopes within the reach of humanity, the new order of justice, joy, love, equality, and peace which is to succeed the world of fear, faith, and slavery. Man has a continuing belief in some abiding good beyond the particular, the present, and the passing, Shelley suggested in his preface. Love and joy at least seem immortal (XI, 17), whereas there is a dreamlike unreality to "violence and wrong" (IX, 20). The old forms which have defrauded humanity for so long perhaps merely conceal the eternally available ideal forms which sanction the progressively penetrating work of science and the imagination.

There is considerable description of ritual and revolutionary pageantry in *The Revolt of Islam*. One is reminded of the fetes celebrated during the French Revolution. Discussions of ritual and poetry are prominent in the poem. The hero is a poet who brings about an ideal revolution, begun by men and women inspired by his poetry and given strength at the crisis by his example. Within the poem, the considerable pageantry and ritual help bolster, express, and empower the revolutionary spirit.

In the preface to his poem, Shelley outlined the revolutionary poetics. Like other men poets have active and passive faculties. Poets are partly shaped by their experience and environment, all of a particular age being subject to a "combination of circumstances" peculiar to their time, "though each is in a degree the author of the very influence by which his being is thus pervaded." Such passiveness, poets, allowing for their more highly developed sensitivity, have in common with all men. The true poet, however, having "a mind that has been nourished upon musical thoughts," can convert or transform his experience into images and harmonies capable of awakening in others sensations and ideas like his own. It was thus that Laon's poetry acted on Cythna's deep, aspiring, and sympathetic nature. The experiences and feelings recorded in his poetry came from a closeness to elemental nature, deep reading in rich mines of revolutionary lore, and his own shared love with Cythna. Laon's was the active, creative power. She was the profoundly receptive auditor able to sing and live those harmonies. In her they found the form and the contagious power for igniting the revolution. As Cythna sang she gave order and meaning to her world, creating a whole new poetry of occult images as her flights were sustained by Laon's hymns to freedom. She enriched the world with new thoughts and hence new perceptions, images and ideas with specific regenerative power which were capable of arousing power and hope. Thus can art and poetry rejuvenate a world of freedom, equality, and love.

Socially the forms of Utopia may be made real by rituals which give revolutionary abstractions a dramatic life and concrete form. When Laon's revolution achieved its first marked success, the moment and the associated feelings were memorialized through a great fete to the goddess of Equality and her attendant deities. Like the fetes of the French Revolution, Shelley's ritual Mass in canto V celebrating the descent of Equality invokes multitudes of worshipers; models its procedures on older techniques using altars, hymns, impressive statues, and veiled images; and has a presiding priestess, Laone, who, like the actress representing Liberty at the Feast of Reason, chants a hymn to Equality. Apparently women often performed the ritual offices at the revolutionary fetes and received the homage of the people in the name of the abstractions they personified.[5]

In the ritual at the "Altar of the Federation" Laone invoked Equality as a supreme principle or ultimate form which ministers to man through her "Angels" of wisdom and love. As a divine principle or a Grace, Equality was summoned by the priestess to descend to encourage her worshipers at the throne and altar of the human heart. Before and after the specific rituals there was general spontaneous gaiety, happy banqueting on fruits and vegetables beneath liberty trees, waving of bright pennants, singing and dancing. Like the fetes and pageants of the French Revolution, the rituals which Shelley describes were designed to consolidate and inspire the liberated masses, make them live the revolution ideally and emotionally so as to become one with the divine general will and escape the pull of ages of reaction, corruption, and indolence. Shelley's account emphasized the spontaneity of the occasion. His altar and the shapes it protected were erected overnight by the enthusiastic devotion of millions, just as at the first great French fete on Champ Mars celebrating the anniversary of the fall of the Bastille. Shelley's "sacred Festival, / A rite to attest the equality of all / Who live" (V, 37) was not the sort of thing to please Godwin, the apostle of reason and slow individual enlightenment. Shelley described not philosophers but vast enthusiastic masses.

> Now first from human power the reverend veil
> Was torn, to see Earth from her general womb
> Pour forth her swarming sons to a fraternal doom.
>
> (V, 38)

The spontaneous fete which grew out of the gladness and reborn hopes of the liberated people was quickly followed by the horror and desolation of an exceedingly rapid overturning by the leagued forces of faith and tyranny. Shelley omitted none of the stages of revolution. It began in radical doctrine and song, became active under inspired leadership, achieved its few moments of enthusiastic unity and happiness, and then declined rapidly to the accompaniment of mass carnage and bloody executions — the whole process rather closely resembling the course of the real revolution whose defects the poet hoped to indicate. He described his revolution as a "beau ideal," but not obviously because of any lasting practical success. It was, however, based on the right sources and emphasized the right models. Laon and Cythna personally enacted an ideal revolution of their own to which they remained faithful even in death. The true revolution is conducted by such people. Had there been more of them in France, the world's hopes had not now been desolated. Nor were a solitary Laon and a solitary Cythna enough to offset the recurring grip of fear and fraud over their followers. Their success was very brief as far as a truly revolutionized society was concerned, though they had made it real in their lives by their faithful service to its forms and it would remain real and alive in the minds of men thereafter, waiting for its final fulfillment in this world on the wider meeting of knowledge, love, and power when the great general will should at last act.

As in *Queen Mab*, the obstacles to ideal change are not lightly taken, but fully and quite specifically and dramatically considered. Shelley's revolution does as a practical movement fail, and the realization of human hopes is placed very nearly outside of space and time. The past has been dominated by evil, and man's victories have been tentative, incomplete, and somewhat illusory. The struggle between eagle and serpent may be conceived as a projection of the hostile but familial alliance of good and evil in man's "searchless heart." The primeval Cain who witnessed the tempestuous jarring of a blood-red comet and a morning star over the abyss felt a sympathetic strife within his own mind. When the star fell, he slew his brother. Also, when Laon's multitudinous rebels rested from their apparently successful efforts, the inner conflict continued.

> What secret fight
> Evil and good, in woven passions mailed,
> Waged through that silent throng; a war that never failed!
>
> (V, 2)

What Shelley made abundantly clear in *The Revolt of Islam*, markedly in the preface and quite strongly in the poem itself, was his awareness of the present strength of evil. He writes of a tainted age, whose prevailing gloom, misanthropy, and sense of moral ruin have made men feel hopelessly bound by circumstance. He writes of himself as of a person dimly conscious of a hope now gradually re-emerging, "which time nor chance / Nor change may not extinguish" (IV, 16), and the story he has to tell is not one of easy triumph but of heroism and unselfishness beaten down once more by despotism and religious depravity though attaining high moral and metaphysical status. He writes as one experimenting with the public temper, believing himself that the panic caused by the

Terror is "gradually giving place to sanity" and desiring to point out the workings of certain fundamental laws of human behavior which, when known, yield some nutriment for hope. It is true, Shelley noted in the preface, that there are "violent and malignant passions" in human nature always ready "to alloy the most beneficial innovations." The situation is not immedicable, however. Too much had been expected of men deformed by ages of despotism. Evil gives rise to evil. That is law.

> Necessity, whose sightless strength for ever
> Evil with evil, good with good must wind
> In bands of union, which no power may sever:
> They must bring forth their kind, and be divided never!
>
> (IX, 27)

The "ferocity and thoughtlessness" which the French showed revealed nothing more strongly than the necessity of the Revolution. By expecting too much of yesterday's trampled slaves, the early enthusiasts for the cause were hurled too readily into the other extreme of "melancholy desolation." Thus, a love too sanguine and too blind is ever followed by a desolation, as Shelley came to express it in a central doctrine of *Prometheus Unbound*.

When the tyrant in *The Revolt of Islam* summoned a league of vicious reactionaries to prop up his tottering throne, the fearful laws of burgeoning evil were revealed. "Strange natures made a brotherhood of ill" (X, 6). Slaves and savages also have creative passions capable of uniting them in sympathetic bonds with their kind, and in a world scourged by the habits of the past, such savage sympathies are easily forged. The reaction quickly desolated nature and humanity with plague and ruin. The world was sick. It has been pointed out that Shelley charges his monarch with responsibility for the subverting of the revolution, just as the extreme republicans in France had charged Louis XVI. The tyrant of Shelley's poem, like Louis XVI, is a weak and vacillating man who alternately cowers and threatens. Moreover, Shelley simply omits the Napoleonic regime and has the Bourbon regime restored. In Argolis, unlike France, there was no "sorry spectacle of tyranny broad-based on popular support." [6]

Shelley does accept the doctrine of mass conversion, that is, of immediate revolution, for his poem. However, when the "glorious madness" of a successful revolution has drowned "dark Custom's brood" of fears and cares (IX, 4), a second and ultimately greater problem faces the new leaders. How are they to maintain the effective enthusiasm generated by the atmosphere of change and reform and stave off the apparently inevitable reaction and corruption which return as the ardor of lesser men dwindles? Old, dark creeds and traditions breed a cultural apathy which is the particular enemy of ideal revolutions. Men falter and lose the assurance kindled by momentary success when the supreme tests come. Laon's followers, for example, were swept by panic at the first arrival of the tyrant's reinforcements.

Men prostrate themselves before the Anarch Custom. Quickly they lose their momentary glimpse of a freely and richly developing self. The benumbing cramp of custom, the absurdities of daily problems and arrangements, and various "low-thoughted cares" consume their hopes and lives. Habit or custom is before long converted into traditions; traditions breed fixed and distorting creeds; the result is that men's lives are poisoned at the source. Nature's divine laws cannot prompt such stifled beings to submit to her harmonies (VI, 40). Hence it is that even men tasting freedom for the first time defend their rights by slaughtering their foes in the field. Such carnage is all that the past has taught them. Even the noblest men have been subdued and bound by custom. Like Laon's aged disciple, custom has rendered their lofty hearts "blind and obdurate" (IV, 9). What has been they feel must always be, and it often takes, as it did for Laon's friend, the spectacle of a heroic believer's suffering and sacrifice to convince them that the truth is strong and might prevail.

It is true that corruption and slavery are not readily overcome — "evil casts a shade, / Which cannot pass so soon" (XI, 15). Men such as Laon, however, will also continue to rise and attempt to liberate a world now suspended in the trance of dogma by presenting a living truth which grows, changes, and discards outmoded ways and thoughts. One day perhaps the inert symbols men inherit from the past will lose their unreal power, and with them will go the dark passions which kept them powerful. Thus, Laon, when the people cried for revenge against their fallen monarch, turned their wrath. He told them that the King, a natural product of their evil passions, would merely become their scapegoat if they slaughtered him (V, 33–34).

The fear which ignorance gives rise to and which in turn helps create the other destructive passions or emotions was instrumental to the fall of Laon's revolution. "Then, none knew whence or why, / Disquiet on the multitudes did fall" (VI, 2). Laon rallied his followers, but the universal panic could not be quelled. The tyrant himself later testified to the strength of unknown fears in abetting his cause. The failure of the revolution had been mental and emotional before it was actual. The panic-stricken populace still possessed the latent power to triumph over hired assassins.

> Millions yet live,
> Of whom the weakest with one word might turn
> The scales of victory yet.   (X, 9)

When patriots and rebels rise to liberate humanity, they are met by "shafts of falsehood" and "cold sneers of calumny" which urge the dangers of freedom and democracy. It is said that tampering with the wise institutions created by tradition and prescription will remove the props essential to protect men from their own weakness, viciousness, and anarchy. Men like Burke and Malthus, teachers "who necessity / Had armed with strength and wrong against mankind," warn the fearful people of the confusion and corruption to come when society's safeguards are released.

> They said, that age was truth, and that the young
> Marred with wild hopes the peace of slavery,
> With which old times and men had quelled the vain and free.
>
> (IX, 14–15)

Even the hero, like Laon himself, may be tempted by evil thoughts. Hate wells up too readily in the best of men. Laon, preacher of liberty through love, slew three of Cythna's abductors (III, 10), an act of violence which his foul dreams of monstrous and ghastly shapes the night before probably anticipated. Such horrors are brewed in the mind of man before their expression in actions. When the champion of faith in liberty (III, 19) was chained to the rocks, he was visited by terrifying but formless visions, like the prospects the Furies unveiled to Prometheus in his agony.

Self-contempt in particular propagates these monsters of desolation, hatred, and despair within the human mind. Like the tyrant lusting for Cythna in his seraglio, men convert all best things to worst uses. They destroy beautiful things because they both dote on and despise the image of a clouded and polluted self with which an evil time and habits of fear and vice have replaced man's true form. This serpent self-contempt stings inwardly and strengthens with its venom the formless hate obscuring vision (VIII, 21).

Self-knowledge and adequate self-esteem promote true growth and help dissipate the reigning deities of hate and fear, shades, names, and abstract symbols temporarily governing our wayward wills. The "dark idolatry of self" (VIII, 22) may yet be relinquished and the weight of error and the duty of "vacant expiation" be forgotten, for the shadows on life — gold, thrones, faith — are, like all things, subject to human will.

> All shall relent
> Who hear me — tears, as mine have flowed, shall flow,
> Hearts beat as mine now beats, with such intent
> As renovates the world; a will omnipotent!   (II, 41)

In *The Revolt of Islam* Shelley measured with some care the real weight of the evils created by the weaknesses and mistakes of the past. He found matter for encouragement, even though his message of hope is placed in the discouraging context of a defeated revolution. The hopes of man have been desolated, he acknowledges, by the French Revolution. Enthusiasm dwindles before the fact of failure. But man's "faith and hope in something good" does not die even in the midst of the real horrors of the ill-fated insurrection which the poet chose to confront and describe. The "temporary triumph of oppression" is the "secure earnest of its final and inevitable fall." The present deformity of some men becomes the best argument for reform. Shelley pictured a completely successful revolution only in the abstract and ideal terms of *Prometheus Unbound*.

Shelley did not share Godwin's distrust of revolution. Strife and disquietude promote the circulation of fresh ideas. The triumph of the fiend may be "dearly won," may help bring about his end because men even in suffering and defeat learn nobler aspirations and discover their real strength. On the other hand, an observer of the visible results of Laon's revolution might well yearn for the peace of reaction. There is more optimism in the preface and the commentary within the poem than the mixture of plague, murder, drought, and rapine offered in the poem itself may seem to support. How the presentation of such scenes was to kindle generous enthusiasm for liberty and justice and develop the faith and hope in our better natures which the poet desired might not be so clear or sure as the confident outline in the preface suggests.

Shelley does describe unsparingly a fairly convincing revolution. How, therefore, was his poem to assist in the change to a better outlook which he thought was reviving? There was not so much wrong with the way Laon's revolution was conducted, but the results seemed to support the lesson given by the French Revolution that men as a mass were not ready for ideal changes. Where did the trouble begin in this poetic revolution? Was it inevitable because slaves cannot become free men overnight? Were the patriots foolish or mistaken in their leadership? Might it not have been good policy to execute the tyrant, for alive he became a rallying point for the league of foreign reactionaries? Perhaps Shelley agreed with those observers who felt that the guillotining of Louis XVI had unleashed the worst elements revealed in the Terror.

Revenge was dismissed. Therefore, Shelley's revolution failed politically but succeeded morally as an example or model. As one critic has pointed out, Shelley's people were not aggressive like the Parisian mobs. There were no outbursts of revolutionary fury. The aristocrats attacked first, and the people merely defended themselves.[7] The revolution failed, not because of defect in the principles, but because of the continuing grip of habits of despair, doubt, and fear. Love is enough, but there is not enough love as yet to insure the continuing dominion of the goddess Equality. For that matter, the revolution did not really fail. It has been achieved in the minds of men. Some few will continue to express in the life of time the forms of the ideal society, and this development may forge in the brighter future "a mighty brotherhood / Linked by a jealous interchange of good" (V, 14).

Part of Shelley's purpose was to show how much, in fact, the French Revolution had accomplished. What he read of the conditions of France before and after the Revolution clearly informed him of the tremendous acceleration in progress made by the breach with the past, after one discounted the desolations of the Terror and Napoleonic rule. A "wide enthusiasm" can "cleanse the fevered world." The avalanche of revolutionary passions begun and led by the ideal of liberty opens a "path through human hearts" which dark Custom had long subdued to the oppressor's rule. The contagion may be stopped, but a greater and brighter day has been anticipated. By their "steadfast will," the heroes of the revolution have bought a "calm inheritance, a glorious doom" for men who follow (IX, 3–5, 28–29). The survivors of liberty's martyrs acquire "the wisdom of a high despair," for the memory of such accomplishments, though followed by desolation, foretells "an eternal morning" (XII, 28–29).

The Revolt of Islam is a poem of special importance to this study, for it brings together Shelley's notions of revolutionary practices and his ideas of true revolutionary principles. It is a marriage of form and matter like the Revolution itself. It affords a positive view of the achievements of a real revolution which, however bloody and disastrous it seemed on the surface, did, like its historical prototype, stir up mental currents and create a sense of possibilities and hopes never again to be dismissed. It is closer in time to *Prometheus Unbound* than to *Queen Mab*, but it has interesting similarities to and differences from both poems. Unlike *Queen Mab* it has a story to tell. It attempts the project, presumably in Shelley's mind from the time of *Hubert Cauvin*, of presenting the story of men conducting a real revolution. *The Revolt* actually does describe the whole cyclic form of a revolution, as we have noted, though it emphasizes the role of the individual. Laon is a model poet-hero who does the right things mainly, unlike the leaders of the French Revolution. His failures are due to the same inertia of the human spirit causing the failure of the French Revolution. The poem accepts as its problem the ways of extracting hope and encouragement from failure.

The targets and the supporting doctrines are approximately the same as in *Queen Mab*, but in *The Revolt* there is more taking stock in progressively more subtle and concrete ways of the reality of evils both inner and outer. There remains some of the abstract rhetoric of denunciation and hope of the early poem, but mainly the poet uses symbol and narrative to convey his purposes. The numerous parallels to the events and personalities of the French Revolution give some sense of anchoring in fact and observation to the poem, though the facts are invested with an aura of symbolic value. *The Revolt* is no doubt a less fresh and appealing poem than *Queen Mab*. *Queen Mab* is entertaining because of the vigor of its youthful broadsides at every established thing. It expresses the spirit of complete revolt against every form and institution that has ever fettered the energy and enthusiasm of the young. It pounds away at the enemy with an assurance that the later symbolic poetry can't attain. It finds incredible the fact that such abuses can exist when their villainy is so obvious to the clear-sighted.

The merits of *The Revolt of Islam* are difficult to judge. It may not seem a very successful work, perhaps because it is tremendously ambitious. It has, as Byron said, "much poetry."[8] Like *The Faerie Queene* it is didactic, symbolical, historical, and heroic narrative in varying proportions. It contains striking, sometimes shocking imagery. It delineates characters, though perhaps for many readers they are not real or complex enough to be especially interesting. Laon and Cythna are mainly theoretic enthusiasms. The villains — priests, soldiers, tyrants — are too abstract and impermeable to be very convincing.

Perhaps it was impossible to succeed in what Shelley tried to do, except in the ways taken up in *Queen Mab* and *Prometheus*, that is, abstract and impassioned rhetoric or obscurely allusive, dimly great, and generalized symbolical action. In *Prometheus Unbound* Shelley will fuse symbol and narrative rather than separate them somewhat feebly. In *Prometheus* he was perhaps able to employ his characteristic strengths as poet without losing effect because of weaknesses in narrative construction and lack of insight into concrete psychology. *Prometheus Unbound* restores the cosmic sweep of *Queen Mab*, bears a similar freight of revolutionary doctrine, and brings together the elements scattered in *The Revolt of Islam*.

The Revolt is closer to the period than the other poems, and is in a sense the primary source for this study. It is more ritual and incantatory than *Queen Mab* and more of an anticipation of what it hopes for and a symbolic realization of what it practically preaches. It is less remote than *Prometheus Unbound*. If there is value in attaining such ends as it proposes, that is, to sketch the outlines of an ideal revolution and to suggest that there are genuine grounds for hope of human betterment, then Shelley's poem achieves a measure of success because it does seem to convey such experiences. The problem has been raised in this study as to what sense Shelley's revolution can be termed ideal, in view of the prevailing slaughter, the execution of his hero and heroine, and the general blighting of men and nature described. In short, how well did Shelley succeed in realizing one of his primary purposes? In the first instance he presents ideal leaders given energy by human love, unlike the inhumanity of such revolutionary leaders as Robespierre and St. Just. The means employed in the development of their revolution are ideal. Shelley stressed growth and reform through imitation of ideal human characters rather than constitutional maneuvering. The revolution is ideal in the Platonic sense as a reflection of the true forms. The failure is the failure of all achievements in the world of sense. Plato assumed that his own ideal state, if ever attained, could not survive in this world of flux and change. Shelley's revolution is ideal as something really achieved and permanent in the minds of men, which remains alive as an ideal and continues to attract the roving imagination because men have demonstrated what human powers can accomplish. Finally it is an ideal revolution Shelley sketches because after fully and clearly measuring the obstacles to progress, the poet succeeds in giving a sense that the lofty human hopes and the ideas they serve have been confirmed.

There are numerous symbolic and thematic similarities between *The Revolt of Islam* and *Prometheus Unbound*. Images, situations, events, and characters common to both poems appear in a context close to experience in *The Revolt*. *Prometheus Unbound* re-enacts the events of *The Revolt of Islam*. The basic plot is the same. Separated powers in human nature are reunited, and from their union arises the sense of a new and enriched and beautiful world which acts on human hopes as a guiding beacon. There also are numerous specific points of resemblance. Laon, like Prometheus, is chained to a rock and is seen as a Christlike, abused redeemer. In captivity he is tempted by evil thoughts, but comes to understand that love and pity are the means to the true revolution. Both Laon and

Cythna are visited by nightmare agonies of ugliness and doubt like the visions the Furies use to torment Prometheus. Vicious hireling soldiers who rend like Furies the liberated rebels seem to express the sum of human evil and despair. The soldiers, like the Furies, take their coloring from the element in which they have lived their lives. Laon's powers and hopes revive at the prospect of his spring reunion with Cythna. Laon and Cythna are complementary forces like Prometheus and Asia, whose reunion creates the brighter universe of act IV of *Prometheus Unbound*. Cythna in her oceanic prison dreams like Asia of being united with Laon, and her sense of their approaching unity is reinforced by her dream of a child. This child motif is fully developed in *Prometheus*, but the events and associated symbols are adumbrated in *The Revolt of Islam*. Cythna is in some relation to both the tyrant and Laon, and there is ambiguity in the child's parentage, the whole complex suggesting the rather kaleidoscopic identity of Prometheus and Jupiter and the notion of the blending and separating of masks and reality. Like Prometheus for Jupiter, Laon shows pity for the fallen tyrant. He thereby reveals the true means to the ideal revolution.

Generally, the underlying doctrines of the two poems are closely similar. The later poem continues the process of substituting suggestive symbolic identities for abstractions, though Love is in *Prometheus Unbound* also followed by Desolation. *The Revolt*'s analysis of the workings of Fear is replaced, for example, by the dominating figure of Jupiter. Ultimately the boat-dream-poetry symbolism of the conclusion to *The Revolt* leads directly into the world of *Prometheus Unbound*, where we find imagery of reflection, ideas of harmony, suggestions of the nature of true mental progress and the powers and sources which kindle and nourish it—all of which appear though less richly developed in *The Revolt of Islam*.

XI

Prometheus Unbound

In *Prometheus Unbound* the elements of a successful revolution are presented in an abstract and ritualized action. The poem enacts ideally the revolutionary victory it celebrates and would inspire. It unites the cosmic explorations of *Queen Mab* and parts of *The Revolt of Islam* with the basic heroic and humanistic messages of both poems. Shelley attempts to create by song "In the void's loose field / A world for the Spirit of Wisdom to wield" (IV, 154–155). His vision "can still trouble the imagination and raise hope" because, like other effective dreams, it seems true of a potential future implicit in human nature.[1]

Shelley no longer wrote in England and was no longer under the immediate impress of reform developments and pressures, though his interests remained strong and practical. He still proclaimed his "passion for reforming the world," but as a poet he conceived his purpose to be to present "beautiful idealisms of moral excellence" before the moral imagination of readers who might thus be prepared to lead the battle against the "advocates of injustice and superstition." He selected a story which had never, he said in the "Vindication of Natural Diet," been satisfactorily explained though "universally admitted to be allegorical." Prometheus is the representative hero of humanity (Clark ed., p. 82). He is, Northrop Frye has commented, a favorite mythic hero for poets of the industrial age, for it was he who stole the fire from Mount Olympus for man.[2] Shelley decided on a hero who would image the form of ideal human excellence, who would reconcile Christ and Satan, the redeemer and the rebel. Prometheus would be free of the taints of character which "interfere with the interest" we have, Shelley said, for Milton's Satan.

The narrative in Shelley's treatment of the myth is essentially simple and clear. The symbolism is complex. The opening scene finds Prometheus bound to an icy ravine in the Caucasus, a "Mont Blanc" world of barren and fearful images, perhaps the world not yet redeemed by the value-endowing visions of poets and prophets. In reviewing his sufferings, Prometheus regrets his curse on Jupiter. This expression of pity and remorse may be regarded as the first movement of the regenerated will. The mythic machinery then creaks through a series of trials, probings, and temptations in the process of giving power and substance to the reformed will. The Prometheus who defied omnipotence like Milton's Satan appears in a vision of a phantasm of Jupiter who resembles Prometheus as he pronounced the curse. The words of the curse retain their power to reveal and anticipate mysteriously even though Prometheus now regrets his violent passion. Apparently the curse has already performed its task in the economy of history. Earth ironically regards Prometheus' remorse as an admission of weakness and defeat, nor does he himself understand its significance.

Mercury appears to urge upon Prometheus the conservative doctrine of acceptance and resignation to the inevitable evils which visit men as part of the nature of things. Mercury is a pleasant and regretful gentleman, remorseful but helpless before his own weakness and lack of principle. Behind him, however, come the Furies. Prometheus' ancient curse has continued to fret Jupiter. The Furies, creations of miscreating Jove and reflections of Prometheus' own agony, give the champion of humanity a vigorous sense of his own weakness and increase his despair by showing him the fate of heroes and heroic ideals on a corrupted planet. Yet he survives these torturing visions somehow. Comforting spirits partly restore him. They foretell a glorious future wrought by charity, self-sacrifice, and poetic vision within man's complex of love and desolation. At the end of act I, however, Prometheus ironically shows little aware-ness of how much has in fact been accomplished by his re-nunciation of spite.

The initial results become obvious in act II. Here Shelley describes "the workings beneath the surface of history of those forces which are gathering up, as a result of the movements engendered by the American and French revolutions, for the overthrow of the aristocratic state and the establishment of a new order."[3] Prometheus does not appear in the act, but the effects of his inward regeneration are expressed in the sense of hopes reborn which dominates the spring and renewal world of Asia. Panthea conveys two dreams to Asia that she has ab-sorbed from Prometheus' dominating imagination. They sum-mon Asia to fulfill her role in effecting Prometheus' release by the revolution of love. A voice below waits on her requests. The depths are approached through enchanted scenery as Asia and Panthea are drawn by spirit song beyond the veil of phe-nomena to Demogorgon's throne. After a somewhat puzzling interview, Asia or Love is released by song and poetry to trans-figure the world.

At the beginning of act III Jupiter from his throne proclaims that he has wrecked finally the hopes of men. His newly be-gotten son will join with him to complete the suppression of humanity. Ironic parallels to the Christian story are obvious. There is effective dramatic irony in the presentation, for quickly Demogorgon appears in the name of Eternity to wrest Jupiter, the latest child of time, from his throne. There is a brief struggle as the two sink, like a vulture and a snake, into a "shoreless sea." The strife dimmed the sun and illumined heaven with "sanguine light." In short, there was violence.

The first proclamation of the liberated world was delivered from the shores of Plato's Atlantis by Ocean. Apollo hailed the rise of the young spirit of Hope that sits in the morning star, and various testimonies were offered on the change occurring in and on earth after Prometheus had been released by the strength of Hercules. Before a redeemed world can be beheld by the reflective imagination, there must, it seems, be an active revolutionary phase. Prometheus and Asia retire to a cave where apparently they are to think and feel the new universe progressively into being. In act IV the cosmic excitement of the liberated macrocosm thus renewed from within is expressed in joyous pageantry, reminiscent perhaps of both revolutionary fetes and Spenser's processional imagery. At the end of the poem Demogorgon arises to dash a little cold water on the universal enthusiasm by reminding all creation of the possibility of another failure and indicating the specific spells which brought about this successful revolution and may be useful in subsequent revolutions.

Shelley defined the idea of revolution in *Prometheus Unbound*. It must occur within the mind of man, perhaps within the mind of every man before the true change can be expressed in nature and society. The avalanche of the ideal revolution ultimately occurs in society after an accumulation of insight "in heaven-defying minds / As thought by thought is piled." Once the great truth has acquired sufficient force and momentum, the nations are freed from the bondage of ignorance and superstition (II, iii, 36–42). The movement is from the darkness and despair of revolutionary failure to visions of hope which create their objects out of the impulses and suggestions brought into being by such apparent failure.

The action of *Prometheus Unbound* is less involved with this world than is *The Revolt of Islam*, but the indictment of the enemy is broadly similar. The scene of Prometheus' torture reveals the barren and indifferent natural order in which men live when they lack the power of vision or imagination. It is a world of blood and desolation, "slavery and command," which has been laid waste by the "dark yet mighty faith" served by kings and priests (III, iv, 173–175). The Furies, creatures of hatred, despair, and self-contempt, mount to their work of torturing Prometheus from battlefields, famine-wasted cities, and reactionary conclaves such as those Shelley described more minutely in *The Revolt*. The great cities of the industrial revolution vomit smoke into the bright air. The lives of the inhabitants are blighted by the dirty machines they serve, and their plight is made even worse by the defeat of ideals, like those of Christ and the initiators of the French Revolution, which were to liberate them from their sullen slavery. Thus are men in this world ever consumed by glorious hopes, loves, and desires that seem to generate their opposites of despair, hate, self-loathing, and satiety. To Jupiter, the soul of man seems "Aspiring, unrepressed, yet soon to fall" (III, i, 17).

The French Revolution, man's noblest hope and promise, had resulted in the confusion of all best things to ill. The ideals of truth, liberty, and love were proclaimed, and then confusion and anarchy fell from heaven to create opportunities for new tyrants (I, 648–655). The social and political movement of France is the backdrop for the simple action of *Prometheus Unbound*, which on a grander and remoter scale than *The Revolt of Islam* stages another ideal revolution but in a world where reactionaries and doubters cannot interfere, the mind of the regenerated man. It was apt that Shelley should find in his sources the comparison of Napoleon to both Jupiter and Prometheus, for man in history had been both. The comparison of Napoleon with Prometheus was familiar to Shelley from Byron's "Ode to Napoleon," and Lady Morgan likely reinforced the comparison by her criticism of the English mistreatment of the Emperor, "chained to a solitary and inaccessible rock, with no object on which to fix his attention, but the sky, to whose inclemency he is exposed."[4] Napoleon himself is said to have worked on his lonely Atlantic rock to create a legend of himself as the "new Prometheus" who sought to be the savior of the Revolution and lead the way for all nations to peace and world government. Lady Morgan also mentioned having seen a chariot representing Napoleon as a "Jupiter Tonans."[5] In *Prometheus Unbound*, Hercules and Prometheus, strength and humanity, are united. Shelley's Prometheus becomes a Napoleon with mind and humanity and poetry to direct his all-powerful will, just as he had once been a Jupiter, a creature of ignorance, hate, and fear like his creation. Here in part lies the explanation of the ambiguities of identity between Prometheus and Jupiter in the early scenes of the drama as Prometheus recalls his curse. Historically Prometheus has played all these roles — benefactor as well as betrayer of man. He has been both Christ and Judas, but in the action of *Prometheus Unbound* he finally becomes king over himself and quells the "torturing and conflicting throngs within" (I, 493).

In *Prometheus Unbound* Shelley's views of evil have further deepened and added subtlety, again without essentially changing. How now does he describe the obstacles to human fulfillment? Clearly the old iniquitous institutions are still iniquitous, but the focus of criticism is, even more than in *The Revolt of Islam*, on the passions and errors in man which create them. Much confusion and misunderstanding has resulted from Mary Shelley's prefatory note. She said that Shelley viewed evil as accidental rather than inherent, something which might be expelled by the will. "Shelley believed that mankind had only to will that there should be no evil, and there would be none." The "only" suggests a more casual view of the problem than the poem warrants, especially in view of its emphasis on the subtle process of regeneration within the mind. Mrs. Shelley's statement is true of the poet's position in the most general possible sense. Shelley does profess to believe that man may accomplish the goals he can contemplate. Inner vision and outer fact may be made to correspond, but not without protracted agonies of struggle and near-defeat which the poet now largely describes in terms of a conflict within the mind of man with destructive passions.

Shelley's view of the sources of evil as darkly entangled in individual and racial development is delineated in Asia's historical sketch. She seeks through dialectic with Demogorgon the answer to the problem. Asia asks Demogorgon, not to explain the natural evils of death, physical afflictions, earthquakes, and the like, but to identify the cause of psychological or man-created aberrations — "terror, madness, crime, remorse" and yet worse —

> Abandoned hope, and love that turns to hate;
> And self-contempt.   (II, iv, 19–25)

Why are creative and useful passions so readily converted into their opposites? The answer is, "He reigns." These evils are created in a world of masters and slaves where men blindly and fearfully subject themselves to and worship creeds, abstractions, anthropomorphisms which limit the will and restrict the searching genii of science and poetry. These evils are the work of Jupiter, but Jupiter is man's corrupt mask and self-imposed oppressor. Why such things should be is perhaps not a question that can be answered abstractly. To see how it came about is to review with Asia the history of progress and civilization.

Asia's mythopoeic outline moves from the Saturnian Golden Age of thoughtless joy and innocence to the period of Prometheus' early benefaction. Prometheus endowed Jupiter, a higher being than Saturn, with a nobler wisdom; but wisdom during Jupiter's permitted reign mainly gave men an awareness of their suffering in a world of death, disease, and strife. Such was the state of savagery unredeemed by loftier feelings and creature comforts. Then Prometheus brought further gifts to men for reducing the privations and terrors of existence. Hope shielded them from the fear of death. Love softened their hearts. Science began to discover the powers of industrial development in fire and metals. But Prometheus' greatest gift was language; for thought was created and man learned to take the measure of his universe and to harmonize his insights in "all-prophetic song" and the arts and sciences. Commerce flourished, and ultimately lovely cities grew which contained and nourished man's noblest arts, helped, as Mary Wollstonecraft said of European cities, to "light up the sparks of reason, and to extend the principles of truth" (*View of F. R.*, pp. 493–494). Prometheus' work therefore was, as Mrs. Shelley noted, to lead mankind "beyond the state wherein they are sinless through ignorance, to that in which they are virtuous through wisdom."

In a sense, however, Prometheus' benefactions worked to fill in Jupiter's hand, for, as the Furies tell the Titan, the clear knowledge he awakened in man kindled yet more powerful thirsts and ardors and aspirations which, with their opposites, but consume his being (I, 542–545) the more and bring a despair in which he subjects himself the more deeply to the death-life peace of Jupiter. In our corrupted world desolation follows closely behind hope and love. Thus was Prometheus punished by Jupiter. History remains the answer; history, the product of man's erring but progressively more profound attempts at self-knowledge and command of nature, punishes man for his insights and inventions by tainting his noblest hopes with despair, by corrupting and converting his highest knowledge to the work of destruction and oppression. Man accumulates a large class of self-created evils. Why this fatal imbalance? Why must love be followed by desolation, creation by destruction, self-knowledge by self-contempt? There is no answer in terms of either doctrine or experience — "the deep truth is imageless." We must accept what we can see, and what we see is a "revolving world" in which all things but "eternal Love" are subject to "Fate, Time, Occasion, Chance, and Change" (II, iv, 118–120). But even there it seems is our saving grace and the foundation for ever-recurring hopes. The way of love in illuminating a bright paradise for the mind of man kindles fresh assurance in the midst of doubt and despair that Jupiter may be finally and completely "dragged captive" and in that day

> Love, from its awful throne of patient power
> In the wise heart, from the last giddy hour
>   Of dread endurance, from the slippery, steep,
> And narrow verge of crag-like agony, springs
> And folds over the world its healing wings.
>
> (IV, 557–561)

Failures reveal strength, and perhaps even desolation, ruin, and destruction thus become mediators to the rule of love when Prometheus and Asia build the "bright pavilion" of reunited humanity over the "waste world" (II, i, 125–126).

All the static and dogmatic forms of worship, all that customarily passes for theology or ultimate and absolute truths of divinity must be eliminated. Jupiter is the one name for the older names and forms of worship.* Jupiter is created by human ignorance, and his rule is sustained by man's fearful defiance, self-contemptuous hatred, and despair. He gains strength even from the resentment against his oppressor which Prometheus felt at the beginning of the drama. That is a passion which merely continues the domination of man by progressive generations of tyrants as the change of oppressions in the French Revolution demonstrated. Man has a penchant for subjecting himself to the sense of his weakness and settling for the security and rigidity of final images. These are his true crimes. Thus is Jupiter an anthropomorphic creation continued in power by man's corrupted will.

Although his argument draws from the great stock of philosophic commonplaces developed in the thought of the Stoics, Epicureans, Christian humanists, and eighteenth-century rationalists, the ideas are freshly handled in Shelley's myth and some of their strength renewed. The real power, however, of Shelley's presentation comes from his emphasis on the element of terror and hopelessness which such black passions inspire in their victims. His most memorable passages stress the reality and immediacy of psychological evils and their intimate alliance with the good. Evil has its own sources of strength and growth. It can transform good into its own nature, as Prometheus was enslaved to Jupiter, his tyrant double created by the fear and hate in his own mind. Prometheus was nailed to his mountain as long as he, "eyeless in hate," contemptuously defied his foe (I, 9–11). He had to learn, like Laon, to see

---

* "Jupiter has to go because he is a characterization, and a particularly vicious and poisoning characterization, of that which can in no way be characterized"; I. A. Richards, "The Mystical Element in Shelley's Poetry," *Aryan Path*, XXX (June 1959), 252. Cameron says that in the political allegory Jupiter represents specifically "the tyranny of the Holy Alliance" whose downfall Shelley was anticipating; "Political Symbolism," p. 748.

the tyrant himself as a creation of human weakness, deserving pity rather than scorn for his false eminence.

The reflex action of vicious prejudices and passions was emphasized by Godwin as a liability of movements like the French Revolution. Periods of such civil anarchy do generate a sense of independence and individuality. They loosen faith and prejudice, but they do "not instantly convert ordinary men into philosophers." In fact, some prejudices, converted into Furies, become instruments of vengeance against freshly sown hopes (*Political Justice*, III, 205). Similarly, in Shelley's doctrine of negative perception the Furies are endowed with the gorgonlike power of transforming their beholder into what he contemplates by "loathsome sympathy." * Thus, Prometheus after repenting of his curse becomes for a time passively subject to the images imposed on him by an evil world and a corrupted will, like the leaders in the early years of the French Revolution. He suffers from self-contempt, the powerful inward antagonist of hope and progress.

Men do become what they contemplate, as the environmentalist strain in both Platonic educational theory and eighteenth-century empiricism assured Shelley, but that they may in time throw off the weight of the past is the lesson of Prometheus or progressive humanity. Men are now prey to the inward destructive work of the Furies, evil principles who delight in their own corruption, and, like Count Cenci, feed and grow on it. The Furies exult in the perception of their own evil. They or their subjects progressively take on the form, odor, and color of the poison they are and know.

---

* The more violent and fanatical women of the French Revolution were often called Furies (Lacretelle, III, 274). Of the enraged masses who butchered the Swiss guards, Dr. Moore said, "such furies do not deserve the name of citizens" (I, 60). The author of *The Female Revolutionary Plutarch* had a chapter entitled "Furies of the Guillotine." It described the activities of an organization so named by Robespierre.

The beauty of delight makes lovers glad,
Gazing on one another: so are we.
As from the rose which the pale priestess kneels
To gather for her festal crown of flowers
The aëreal crimson falls, flushing her cheek,
So from our victim's destined agony
The shade which is our form invests us round,
Else we are shapeless as our mother Night.

(I, 465–472)

Evil, like physical agony, can be viciously linked to every thought and feeling. It astonishes Prometheus as it wells up within to drench his aspirations in its poison, the "foul desire" in his "astonished heart" (I, 489). Perhaps man need only to will that there shall be no evil, but slaves do not become freemen overnight, and the description of the work of the Furies in *Prometheus Unbound* suggests that Shelley grasped fully the strength and savagery and lasting power of evil passions and views. There is in man "an unwilling dross that resists imaginative redemption." [6]

Prometheus kindled in man a consuming thirst for knowledge which outstripped man's ability to use his knowledge humanely. The result was the darkness of industrialism blackening the air with smoke while men bewailed the ascendancy of their newly created monster-tyrants. Thus, philanthropists and martyrs, rather than improving and redeeming man, "heap / Thousand-fold torment on themselves and him" (I, 505–506). Witnessing such torments persuades even enlightened and sensitive men that reform is dangerous and impossible. They become subject to their own worst fears and see latent and ineradicable evils deep-dyeing their own souls.

Yet the man-created ills of the world summed up in the name of Jupiter must fall before the progressively enlightened will of men. Jupiter must give way to Demogorgon, the son who is greater than his father. Jupiter made a serious mistake about the identity of his "fatal child." He thought he had bred anarchy, the "child and chastiser of misrule," continuing and confirming the unending cycle of despotism-anarchy-despotism; but Demogorgon proclaims himself a child of Jupiter in a different sense. Despotism breeds the conditions that overthrow it. This, as Professor Cameron develops the point, is what Prometheus foreknew: "despotism sows the seeds of its own decay and will inevitably, in spite of all its efforts to survive, be banished from the earth."[7] In Shelley's view, the tyrant, a creature of solitude and self-contempt, is destroyed when recognized as a corrupt mask. Love and Necessity then unite to forge the true and enduring revolution. Demogorgon, that greater son, incarnates eternity in the world of time and liberates man from the bondage of worship because he is the idea of order, not a personal deity. Doomsday for Jupiter can, of course, be now in the mind of the truly enlightened hero of humanity, whose realization of error and needless subjection may well come suddenly though long prepared for. The knowledge that the son will be greater than the father sustains our hopes. That is Prometheus' secret and the content of the idea of progress.

In Shelley's version of the Prometheus myth, reality or Demogorgon is a voice which waits below and beyond "the veil and the bar / Of things which seem and are" (II, iii, 59–60) to answer the right questions when men are prepared to put them, that is, when they have developed the power and wisdom needed to know the true forms and to act on such knowledge. Thus, Asia comes to the Cave of Demogorgon, bearing in her mind an image of an arisen Prometheus, and to her in this retreat beneath the spinning busy orb and beyond all worlds known to the senses are awarded a destiny, a meaning, and a knowledge which swiftly create their objects. The shadowy figure of Demogorgon recalls the *Queen Mab* doctrine of Necessity, but invests it with more mystery and creative force.* On his throne at the still point in a world of process, Demogorgon awaits the arrival of those who contemplate and question, and to those questioners who unite love, humanity, and knowledge, he discovers and releases a destiny which must be known in the mind before it can be fulfilled in nature.

According to Professor Baker, Demogorgon's "mighty law" asserts that the forces of moral good can be activated only through a regeneration in the mind of man.[8] He represents the sum of laws and forces which make revolution inevitable, though both thought and love, both intellectual and moral enlightenment, must be united, as Prometheus and Asia are united, before the revolution can be successful. According to Wilson, who provides an excellent study of these relationships, Demogorgon's law makes a French Revolution inevitable, but the presence of Asia averts a Terror and a Napoleon and a Restoration by creating the Promethean revolution.[9] Cameron comments similarly: "Demogorgon can overthrow the old order without the aid of Asia, but he cannot build a new one unless she assists him."[10]

When man is liberated from his self-imposed tyrants, his mind can conjure new worlds of beauty and truth. The crystal

---

* G. M. Matthews sees in Demogorgon an emblem of a volcanic force which violently erupts to overthrow Jupiter. Demogorgon, he says, is an image of that "irrepressible collective energy" which Shelley in his preface said was rising all over the world to end tyranny; "A Volcano's Voice in Shelley," *ELH*, XXIV (September 1957), 222. Certainly the image of a volcano was popular, quite inevitably so one would think, during the French Revolution. Lacretelle described Condorcet as "un volcan couvert de neige" (II, 29). When Burke charged that the French Revolution left a great void in Europe, Mirabeau is quoted as having replied, "Ce vide est un volcan" (V, li).

palaces and "skiey towers" of mind will be "an ocean / Of clear emotion" (IV, 96–97). Energies will be marshaled which, when their "congregated might" is unleashed, will restore strength to "unawakened earth." Then the work of creating a golden world surpassing the order of necessity may begin, the lead being taken by the poets who create from the shapes haunting "thought's wildernesses"

> Forms more real than living man,
> Nurslings of immortality!   (I, 748–749)

Such forms are known and connected in the mind of Prometheus, the hero as ideal revolutionary poet and liberator. He is described in the preface as "the type of the highest perfection of moral and intellectual nature, impelled by the purest and the truest motives to the best and noblest ends." For a few lines at the beginning of the poem Prometheus expresses some ordinary human impulses, and in his bout with the Furies he develops or reveals awareness of the evils preying on his representative mind; but for the most part Shelley's hero acts as a radiant projection of the ideas, hopes, and joys nourished within the mind of man. Mrs. Shelley described Prometheus as Shelley's latest hero-warrior against the Evil Principle, who, though scorned and oppressed by the conservatives who accept evil as man's necessary portion, ultimately triumphs through hope and fortitude over the destructive passions which abort man's visions. She saw him as a more idealized Laon, and indeed he is in that line. Like Shelley himself in Italy, Prometheus is at some distance from the strife of reform, challenge, and revolution in which he had once participated as a Laon leading his patriots.

When Prometheus, the benefactor of mankind, is liberated by Hercules or regenerated by the denial of revenge, Asia's

spirit is released to illumine the world as of old. Prometheus
and Asia reunited turn outward the radiance of their love and
beauty. With this world seen anew by the light of Asia, the
rekindled "Lamp of Earth," hate and fear and pain — creatures
of man's once distorting perceptions — are banished. Asia, like
Cythna, represents the element lacking in the French Revolution, the energy and beauty of love which would have prevented the excesses of fanatical rationalism.

"Most vain," Prometheus says, is "all hope but love" (I, 808).
Love, like other passions, is, as Keats said, "essentially creative."
The energy released by the love of Prometheus and Asia transfigured the universe, and the world was seen anew by the
light which Asia, Lamp of the Earth, shed, "clothing with
golden clouds / The desert of our life" (II, i, 11–12). Reunited
in the Cave of Mind, Prometheus and Asia (man and nature,
humanity and love, and perhaps even man and woman) will
be a still point of contemplation in the world of Change.

> we will sit and talk of time and change,
> As the world ebbs and flows, ourselves unchanged.
> What can hide man from mutability? (III, iii, 23–25)

The true progress starts with the reformed will of man,
reformed because it no longer follows a corrupted intellect.
Guilt and pain existed because man's will "made or suffered
them" (III, iv, 198). Men may alter their views and govern
themselves by self-created values. Prometheus' will had once
negatively withstood Jupiter, and this defiance was necessary
to limit the further extension of the tyrant's reign, just as the
violence of revolution is better than external submissiveness to
injustice and anarchy. But Jove could not be overcome until
Prometheus' inward regeneration through suffering, endurance, and forgiveness had banished the shadows of hate, fear,

and despair and had added the power of Asia or love to thought. There is a law of necessity involved in the dialectic of moral improvement or genuine progress which makes each revolution produce more lastingly beneficial results than the previous one. The greater the challenge of evil, the greater the despair and the hope. The greater the play of intellect and imagination called forth to defeat the demon, the greater the subsequent growth and attainment. This is the irony of history or of Shelleyan theodicy which neither Jupiter in his hour of triumph nor Prometheus in his despair quite grasp.

Now the matured Prometheus, who has learned through suffering, directs with Asia the positive and reformed will of humanity as it begins to acquire power and substance and penetration in colonizing the "hoar deep" (IV, 143). The power of sympathetic participation in the life about us is extended as the mind acts upon all thoughts "so as to color them with its own light." A new language "marks the before unapprehended relations of things" or unveils the "permanent analogy of things by images which participate in the life of truth." Such is the program for the Promethean world foreseen by the "unacknowledged legislators" whose pure laws will govern the burgeoning universe to come. "For he not only beholds intensely the present as it is, and discovers those laws according to which present things ought to be ordered, but he beholds the future in the present, and his thoughts are the germs of the flower and the fruit of latest time" ("A Defence of Poetry," Clark ed., p. 279).

Imagery of cave, stream, and bright pavilions — all emblematic of the nature and activity of mind — is frequent and rich in *Prometheus Unbound*. Shelley uses stream imagery to suggest the unceasing flow of thought and its continuous interchange with its objects, an activity in which thoughts and their objects tend to merge or become consubstantial. The cave represents mind somewhat closed off from and creating its world of dim and elusive shapes independent of the changing life of nature, but this isolation may be broken into. Caves are also described, however, as prophetic (I, 252). Forces and possibilities are stored there — "Like a diamond, which shines / On the dark wealth of mines (II, iii, 85–86).

Echoes beckon Asia and Panthea to follow their voices through interwoven bowers and hollow caverns to a world of vision, dim possibility, fleeting and both scarcely and subtly realized insights. The "mighty darkness" of Demogorgon pervades with meaning the gloom of his cave in the deep centers of being. The movement of the perfected soul of Asia back through time into an elysium beyond time passes through "Age's icy caves" into a bright paradise of beautiful shapes. Prometheus described to Asia their own fountain-lit cave where the immortals will retire, like Lear and Cordelia, to "talk of time and change" (III, iii, 23). In this cave, mind in the embrace of beauty will remove the veils of error, guided by the spectacular but "doubtful light" yielded by a leaping fountain and gleaming emerald and diamond.

The most important imagery in *Prometheus Unbound* is drawn from music. Shelley translated one passage of the *Symposium* as follows: "Music is then the knowledge of that which relates to Love in harmony and rhythm." [11] The music imagery provides something of a key to the poem and helps explain the poet's emphasis on the primary role in reform and progress of a poet who is both "a hierophant of an unapprehended inspiration" and an "unacknowledged legislator."

Shelley wrote a lyric drama to convey his ideal revolution. The numerous songs in it bring the work close to the condition and effects of music, just as the impalpable imagery eludes the too-precise formulation which reduces poetry and religion to dogma. Shelley's imagery has often been criticized as thin, vague, and overly elusive. He may be defended in terms of his intentions. For a revolutionary poetry, images too precise and self-contained may lead to hardening of the concepts. In definite shape, the thoughts may lose some of their ethereal quality. Strenuously concrete imagery introduces the danger of dogma, the possibility of associating image and belief too strictly in the attitude of worship.[12] *Prometheus Unbound* makes much reference to a sense of an ineffable, complex, and subtle music or sound which rises from profound sources and approaches but does not quite achieve articulate meaning. To hear such music requires a sensitive passiveness, a capacity to steep one's being in delicate harmonies and their associated ideas without obtruding the rational and divisive intellect. The auditor of such music may express his sense of it, as in Shelley's poem, in semiritualized invocations of sources whose meanings only patience and time can develop.

Poetry which approaches the condition of music records an impression of a total, undivided, and rich meaning not analyzable or reducible even by the poets themselves when, released from their inspiration, they examine "the words which express what they understand not" ("A Defence of Poetry," Clark ed., p. 297). Understanding is a partial, calculating, abstracting activity. The imagination communicates with as little tempering and tampering as possible the forms it apprehends in all their contingent and necessary coloring and relatedness. Earth spoke to Prometheus through her "inorganic voice" in the form of dim shadows of awful thoughts, a mixture of sound and sense ultimately echoed in the Promethean music (I, 135, 146–147). These difficulties of communication are not, as some commentators have urged, clumsy plot devices for externalizing Prometheus' curse, but indications of the problem of the poet-seer, passive to his dimly felt inspiration, in communicating the experience. What Demogorgon imparted in his final injunction came as "a sense of words" or "an universal sound like words" (IV, 517–518). Earlier, after the departure of the comforting spirits of the human mind, Panthea said that the experience occupied the "labyrinthine souls," "like the omnipotence / Of music" (I, 801–804). She also spoke to Asia of the world waiting the descent of subtle harmonies heard when one is receptive. "Hearest thou not sounds i' the air which speak the love / Of all articulate beings?" (II, v, 34–36).

Such is the sense that men may have of the source of all energy and meaning, a sense that Shelley can convey only in imagery of a fundamental music or harmony. It is a music which a poet hears because he has been nursed on musical thoughts, and it comes as an incommunicable sense of being and meaning, misty and elusive, yet the apparent source of all that matters in this world. When Demogorgon rises at the end to pronounce a benediction, his voice penetrates to the depths of all things. "Thy voice to us is wind among still woods" (IV, 548). All creation receives this shaping order and force from the center of being, conveyed dramatically or mythically as a Demogorgon, rationally as necessity or the absolute, sensitively as a scarcely heard music which blends idea, image, and sound as it passes into the receptive imagination. Thus, the music which in this world even now may exempt man from mortal cares and render him receptive to the arts and the "all-prophetic song" of "the harmonious mind" (II, iv, 75–78) becomes the central emblem for the restoration to man of the power to hear and be attuned to the music of the spheres.

There is in man, however, also an active power which serves the cause of good, which from the richly passive participation of the sensitive agent in the deeper life of love and harmony abstracts the forms which must truly govern the ideal revolution. In Fogle's description, the poet makes an active and conscious arrangement and composition of his perceptions. His intellect labors to capture and compose elusive meanings, but his abstract statement of them is kept provisional and alert by being steeped in the experience of motion and speed. Shelley's truth is a "shifting, tantalizing, elusive" thing which cannot be quite clothed in words.[13] However, the more faithful the seer is to the unseen and unattainable in shaping and sensing its forms, the more successful will be the movements he anticipates and directs. Man is both like and unlike the Aeolian lyre. Like the lyre he is moved to melody by the reception of "a series of external and internal impressions," but unlike the lyre he makes internal adjustments to experience which give that experience its specific form or harmony. By his ability to subject himself to shaping impressions he may become receptive to richer, more comprehensive, more harmonious forms. What he communicates of this experience may be a feeble shadow of his original conception — "when composition begins, inspiration is already on the decline" — but that residue, distorted as it may be by the active, shaping mind is the Promethean source of the "light and fire" ("A Defence of Poetry," Clark ed., p. 294) of all knowledge, all beneficial social change and revolution.

The poet must be a shaper, and, at least in the form of an "unacknowledged legislator," a revolutionary who actively serves in society the cause of the ideas whose larger music and bearing in reality he has caught. Man is inspired when he forsakes revenge and fear and attunes his combined senses to the larger music which invades his passive spirit, but he also composes from his inspiration the thoughts which become "the germs of the flower and the fruit of latest time" ("A Defence of Poetry," Clark ed., p. 279). Thus, Prometheus and Asia are to create the music for the world to come as they search in their

cave for "hidden thoughts" and weave new and divine harmonies. It will be a world of "music soft, and mild, free, gentle
voices, / And sweetest music, such as spirits love." The Spirit
of the Hour loosens such a mighty but lulled music sleeping
in a "mystic shell" on the cities of man (III, iii, 34–39; ii, 33–
34; iii, 70–81).

> Soon as the sound had ceased whose thunder filled
> The abysses of the sky and the wide earth,
> There was a change. (III, iv, 98–100)

In act IV Shelley writes the rituals for the newly liberated
macrocosm. As a revolutionary, he rehearses the arguments of
Spenser's Mutability, but as a poet celebrating a new ideal
order he defines a kind of change which progressively reveals
an inner perfection and flexibly works toward the unimagined
radiance of beauties as yet unbeheld. In particular, the two
"visions of strange radiance" which float before Panthea and
Ione upon the new harmony of Promethean-Asian sound provide a mysterious and difficult culmination to the action and
imagery of his poem. Perhaps Yeats's description of both visions
as "a passage which reads like a half-understood vision"[14] comes
closer to the mark than the many laboriously specific interpretations available in Shelley scholarship. Here we shall consider
the passage as a poet's account of the reality which informs the
ideal revolution or perhaps better as an account of a poet's
perception of that large, unknowable epiphany of speed, light,
and music. Shelley blends earth and spirit, matter and mind,
in an obscure emblem of complex human consciousness.

The setting for the vision is described by Panthea. From two
openings in a dark forest two streams proceed, making a "path
of melody." The sense of a rich and complex intertwining of
sensations dominates. The two visions are said to float upon

the "Ocean-like" enchanted melody of "strong sound." Ione then describes the chariot of the moon, a description partly scientific, partly poetic, the whole a somewhat unrealizable blend of image and personification.

In the first vision the moon transforms objects perceived by its veiled light into "shapes in an enchanter's glass" (IV, 213). The wheels of this chariot of the imagination are clouds with an inner elemental life of their own. In the chariot sits a white-winged infant, a cloud-wrapped creature of wind and light, with eyes of "liquid darkness" pouring, as it seems, from the divinity within a tempering fire upon the atmosphere without. The infant guides its chariot over the clouds with a "quivering moonbeam." Sweet sounds, like "a singing rain of silver dew," are kindled by the movement of the moon. Such is the vision of the moon's chariot and its guiding power.

The second vision created by the enchantments of "strong sound" is of the dominant earth sphere, spinning rapidly "with loud and whirlwind harmony" within its atmosphere and through infinite space. A new abstract pattern for cosmical experience in the renewed Promethean scheme of things is suggested by Shelley's imagery of music and light, color and motion. The imagery may be thought to reflect and describe the united workings of nature and mind in the acts of imginative perception being conducted in the nearby cave of Prometheus. The sphere's activities are like those within the human mind; perhaps they are emblematic and descriptive of the operations of the imagination. The interinvolved spheres within the master sphere are a solid crystalline mass of lesser orbs, reflective of the music and light and color given off by each other.

Shelley describes an ultimate perception in which subject and object are nearly consubstantial. There is both order and richly involved complexity in these new forms, forms which agree with no static formulation but, like the activity of mind in the age of Prometheus and Demogorgon, are elusive, iridescent, and subtle. The spaces between the spheres are said to be "Peopled with unimaginable shapes," the material perhaps of those as yet unimagined arts which Prometheus had promised Asia would become further mediators between man and "that best worship love." By this solemn and sublime pageantry of "music and light" are kindled and kneaded from the matter of all refined and intensified sensations the "Intelligible words and music wild" of the new Promethean harmony. The process is summed up in an image of the activity of this visionary sphere reducing the brook over which it floats into something akin to its own ethereal substance.

> With mighty whirl the multitudinous orb
> Grinds the bright brook into an azure mist
> Of elemental subtlety.   (IV, 253–255)

Within the orbit lies the sleeping earth spirit, its lips moving in smiling speech. The child image may signify, as Knight suggests, the idea of a purified consciousness, a renewed sense of wonder,[15] as in Asia's earlier prelapsarian vision. From a star on its forehead shoot whirling beams "swifter than thought." This penetrating and whirling light is, like the wheels of Ezekiel's chariot, emblematic of the prophetic insight which unites heaven and earth. Imagination kindled by love has power in this revolution of the mind to penetrate the abysses of time and space with its "sun-like lightnings." The grimly warning relics of a dark and cruel past are uncovered, and the unimagined secrets of a reborn world are exposed to the forming light of science and poetry as the poet labors, in Hughes's phrase, "to bring to full reality as much as the mind of an already liberated mankind can conceive." [16] It is man, however, who is fully aware of all the suffering revealed in "the melancholy ruins / Of cancelled cycles." He knows that the "Sceptred curse" may return with its mean passions and shadowy death to muffle this bright universe with "black destruction" once more and reduce this world of love to one void and battered mass, but he has learned the spells capable of enfolding the world in the healing power of love.

The spirits of the human mind have built in the void by their singing the "new world of man" governed by "the Spirit of Wisdom" (IV, 153–158). Such is the true revolution which the imagination, beholding the beauty of such an order, creates out of itself. Shelley sings in his *Prometheus Unbound* of both the genuine achievements of the age of revolution in France and America and the continuing impulses to social and individual progress which poetry may serve and abet as the energy in true renovation. Demogorgon's proclamation of victory, warnings of danger, and enumeration of the spells for reassuming control of the serpent resemble in spirit and content Shelley's appraisal in "A Defence of Poetry" of the new and beautiful order emerging from the chaos of the past. "How the world, as from a resurrection, balancing itself on the golden wings of knowledge and of hope, has reassumed its yet unwearied flight in the heaven of time. Listen to the music, unheard by outward ears, which is as a ceaseless and invisible wind nourishing its everlasting course with strength and swiftness" (Clark ed., p. 288). The passage recapitulates the central theme and the imagery, especially the music imagery, of *Prometheus Unbound*.

Shelley had "a passion for reforming the world," but he saw the ideal revolution as a progressive attainment achieved by maintaining an equilibrium between institutions and opinions. Prometheus cursed Jupiter, but a conversion three thousand years later led him to renounce hatred and revenge.

> I hate no more
> As then ere misery made me wise.   (I, 57–58)

The reality which Prometheus' words adumbrated was wedded to experience only gradually. The process is gradual, though the actual sense of understanding and illumination may seem quite sudden in the hour when, as the Titan prophesies to Jupiter, "thou must appear to be / That which thou art internally" (I, 298–299). The "destined hour" arrives when Asia is prepared to behold what Shelley describes as "some unimagined change in our social condition or the opinions which cement it."

When it comes, the change does not seem especially dramatic. It is not a single event but the product of many events, many partial insights — "all / Were somewhat changed" when the ugly masks floated away. A closer examination revealed kingless thrones, sincere and liberated men, and women as "gentle radiant forms" freed from "custom's evil taint." "All things had put their evil nature off" (III, iv, 70–71, 98–156, 77). There were no more hypocrisy, no further extremes of self-love or self-contempt, no more blind faith. When the foul shapes and loathsome masks which have interposed between man and man and man and reality have fallen away, men and women self-governed by love, hope, and a freely ranging imagination are left. Like Godwin, Shelley saw sincerity as "the most powerful engine of human improvement." "In reality the chains fall off of themselves, when the magic of opinion is dissolved" (*Political Justice*, I, 99, 333, 335, 340).

In individuals change may well seem real, intense, and

frequent — however long it may be prepared for within. There is sudden illumination like the intoxication of revolutionary enthusiasm. Men do get reborn and rediscover their destinies. In Panthea's description of the Promethean epiphany beheld in her dream she spoke of the sudden falling away of the veil of corruption from his body

> and the azure night
> Grew radiant with the glory of that form
> Which lives unchanged within, and his voice fell
> Like music . . .   (II, i, 63–66)

The bloodless revolution at the end of act III is the equivalent in the social macrocosm of Prometheus' transformation. Once liberated from their bondage to guilt or pain, men and societies are seen by Shelley as able to confront with Lucretian imperturbability the clogs of "change, and death, and mutability" which restrain humanity from oversoaring

> The loftiest star of unascended heaven,
> Pinnacled dim in the intense inane.
>   (III, iv, 200–204)

The new man will be drawn into his own profound depths by the power of the liberated soul's harmonies, echoing or reflecting the imageless deep truths outside. His thought will be illuminated and his feeling refined. Through progressive meditation and the creation of new beauty, perception will be transformed as the enriched imagination partly projects, partly reflects its colors and its warmth upon what had once been the cold blank world of "Mont Blanc" or the icy ravine of the Caucasus.

Such are the general outlines of the new world of achieved

vision. The outward changes caused by the new unity of man with himself and with nature were neither dramatic nor radical. When men summoned by poetry and music put off their evil natures, the ugly masks simply faded. With the discarding of all the old and debasing forms for worshiping Jupiter, the tyrant of many names, man alone remained — free, equal, and good. Shelley, like Godwin, disagreed with Malthus' contention that the evils in human institutions are light and superficial in comparison with the deeper-seated evils involved in the natural situation of man on earth. The truly crippling evils are created by man's distorted thoughts and feelings and maintained in power by his infirm will. Like a Lucretian or a Stoic philosopher, the Promethean liberates himself from hate, fear, and the faith they create. He does not distress himself over chance, death, and mutability. Even these evils, once labeled natural, become less fearsome, scarcely to be considered in fact, when superstition's reign is ended. Life may be extended, as Bacon and Condorcet suggested, by progress in medicine, or, as Godwin believed, by greater control by thought over the matter of the body. Man is not, however, as in the ideal of Lucretius, the Stoics, and even of Godwin to be a passionless wise man who eliminates irrational fears by ignoring them. Shelley stressed, not contraction and avoidance, but aesthetic, emotional, and imaginative growth and receptiveness. The all-harmonizing imagination of the Promethean poet, inspired by the cosmic excitement of the ritual invoking a new world into being, banishes the shadows of time and imperfection.

XII

Hellas

Hellas is Shelley's last revolutionary drama. A real revolution, observed as it developed, figures in the poem, and, perhaps as a result, the revolutionary element and its associated faith and hope become shrunken, tentative, and subjective. The poem moves back and forth from scenes of ruin, hatred, and war to choric claims of the superior power of love and hope. As one writer has commented, "The eternal reality of Thought is asserted, but it is the rise and fall of generations which dominate the foreground."[1] As with *Prometheus Unbound* Shelley finds a model in Aeschylus, this time in *The Persians* for his "series of lyric pictures" and "figures of indistinct and visionary delineation" (Hutchinson ed., p. 446).

The Greek revolution against Turkish rule was the latest phase in the post-1820 rebellions in southern Europe which Shelley had been observing. *Hellas* reflects the ambiguities of his political and emotional experiences in his last years, his prolonged physical separation from active political movements and pamphleteering in England, and his greater devotion to Plato and poetry. It is a rather remote, shadowy, and on the whole unsatisfactory poem which lends some support to the belief that Shelley's poetic vein, at least as far as revolutionary sources are concerned, was approaching exhaustion. He could of course make fine poetry out of political and personal frustration. Peacock judged that had Shelley lived longer, he might have overcome the one real deficiency in his poetry, a "want of reality in the characters," but, on the other hand, "the more clear development of what men were would have lowered his estimate of what they might be, and dimmed his enthusiastic prospect of the future destiny of the world."[2]

Shelley predicted the final triumph of the cause and related this movement of liberty to the general progress of civilization. He looked, Mrs. Shelley says, on the struggles of the Spaniards, Italians, and Greeks "as decisive of the destinies of the world, probably for centuries to come." He had some notions, as always at such times, of personal action. Trelawny said that it was "the peace-loving Shelley" who suggested the Greek mission to Byron, and, according to Kennedy, Byron said that Shelley was to have accompanied him to Greece.[3]

Shelley's historical perspectives, however, seem to have shifted somewhat in *Hellas*; as a result his estimate of the importance of eighteenth-century political thought and the revolutions it created is changed. As he became more of a Hellenist, the French Revolution receded further into the status of a transient incident, illustrative and monitory to be sure, but important mostly for the positive passions it helped rekindle. A note in the preface on the present state of France commented that the country had at least attained a "partial exemption" from old abuses which the restored Bourbons labored fruitlessly to revive. Shelley read French papers in Italy and followed the fortunes of the country and the policies of Louis XVIII closely. He expressed pleasure at the news of an insurrection in Paris in 1820. In general during his last years Shelley showed marked antipathy for France for having once achieved so much and then returned to despotism and the church. Certainly he gave France, "that tame serpent, that poor shadow"

(l. 968), no great credit in *Hellas* for its contribution to the cause of freedom.

> France, with all her sanguine steams,
> Hid, but quenched it not.   (ll. 72–73)

Shelley declared in the preface that he had witnessed the spirit of revolution abroad once more in all nations. He saw a new race of Europeans emerging who love liberty and will or may accomplish the destiny which even tyrants can now foresee. From Europe the flower of Greek youth had brought back the good news of the attainable "social perfections" their ancestors had once known. Now the lamps of liberty are gleaming from Spain to Germany. There is a "general fever" (*Hellas*, l. 590). The tyrant-anarchs who have allied themselves to suppress the "many-headed Insurrection" are themselves disunited, no surprise to seers who know that "what was born in blood must die" (l. 811). These are the elements supporting hope, but an outline of the submerged events in Shelley's drama suggests that these hopes are filtered, in an obscure and shadowy fashion, through a deep awareness of necessary suffering and possible ruin.

Shelley's prologue opens upon an assembly in a heavenly pantheon of great men of thought and action of the past. Christ, Satan, and Mahomet debate before it as to the best conclusion of the present war. Then the drama begins with a scene of Greek captive women singing over sleeping Mahmud, the sultan from whose perspective as beleaguered tyrant most of the action is reviewed. The women sing of Shelley's favorite revolutionary and Platonic abstractions. Outside the seraglio the Janissaries are clamoring for their pay. To satisfy them Mahmud has to unlock a treasure hoard before they can be led "to the rivers of fresh death" (l. 258). Mahmud is in despair. Hassan attempts to hearten him by pointing out their superior strength, their troops gathered like lightning-laden clouds, their many triumphs, their European anarch allies. Mahmud, however, sees his empire fading, a lamp without oil, smitten by a star. The accounts suggest a dubious issue. We hear of a naval battle, described with a zest for concrete energy and action not much credited to Shelley, won by the followers of the cross. Ahasuerus or the Wandering Jew is brought in to add ambiguous testimony about thought, mutability, and history. Behind his cryptic pronouncements come further visions of horror and ruin in all times and places. The conjured phantom of Mahomet the Second comments like Volney on the ruins of empires. Then the curious mélange ends with the magnificent final chorus, a recapitulation of the ambiguities and obscurities of image and feeling.

It may be that *Hellas* can be regarded as a delayed expression of the damage done to Shelley's revolutionary ardor by subjective idealism and Godwinian gradualism. Woodman says of Shelley that "in his visionary works, his desire to reform the world is always crossed by a desire to transcend it." Woodman sees an irreconcilable conflict between the radical vision of the millennium and the Platonic vision of the apocalypse, one linear, Godwinian, and progressive, the other Greek and cyclic.[4] An examination of the theory of knowledge presented in the poem tends to confirm the impression that philosophy and experience were undercutting enthusiasm for causes. These views are stated most fully by Ahasuerus. Space, time, and change — all the cycles of "desolation and of loveliness" are unreal, visionary "motes of a sick eye, bubbles and dreams" created by thought in its "eternal flight" (ll. 746–747, 780–784). On the one hand, this philosophy makes revolution easy, and on the other, meaningless. Surely progress and revolution require that time and change be accepted as real if the struggles of rebels are to be more than idle shadows. A perspective which shows worlds constantly rolling from birth to death like sparkling and bursting bubbles on a river cannot command much confidence in the cause of reform. Nor will a revolution readily achieved within the mind inspire the unconvinced and adamant. Hopes should get realized merely by being expressed if nature is reduced to thought. If the world of experience is illusory in the light of the one, the eternal, the unconditioned central mind, which is both infinite and somewhat remote from the world of appearances, why should one attend to the meaningless turmoil and complications involved in trying to make this world better? Unless thoughts have objects other than themselves, there seems little foundation for believing that Islam or any other tyranny will fall to a "greener faith" (l. 871).

Contradictions implicit in revolutionary philosophy, unconvincingly reconciled in *Queen Mab* and *The Revolt of Islam,* are confronted with deeper awareness in *Hellas.* Faith in freedom continues to be asserted, but perhaps unconscious doubts and disillusion are reflected in the perspective and the imagery of the poem. "Nought is but that which feels itself to be" (l. 785), but it is with considerable effort that true feeling or being is associated with the ascendant spirit of freedom. Perhaps the skeptic and the subjective idealist have something in common. Both of them may quite logically elect to retreat from a world either hostile or unreal to create the island paradise. Shelley's thought does seem at times to be a puzzling mixture of skepticism and subjective idealism.

But Shelley also covertly suggests in *Hellas* some belief in Platonic or objective idealism. In Platonism the world of life, time, and change is only relatively unreal. Whatever in nature is intelligible, is so because of "the formal elements which are immanent in them." [5] Freedom, hope, truth, and love are such signs in Shelleyan Platonism, and their presence can still support some battered faith in the ideal revolution of the future. They can make "this obscure world splendid" (l. 980); the ideal city of Athens, rebuilt "above the idle foam of Time" (l. 1007), can yet kindle the imagination of those ardent poets and prophets who can overleap "the actual reign of evil which we endure and bewail" (Hutchinson ed., p. 479n). Certainly Platonic idealism and revolutionary hopes and ideals offer each other some support. One must believe that his ideas have some sort of ontological status to be much motivated by them. Shelley does insist in a note that the poet must contribute to the destruction of inadequate hypotheses about the nature of God, evil, and immortality without weakening the "inextinguishable thirst for immortality" which compels men to conjecture about futurity.

In general, in *Hellas* Shelley projects a larger cultural awareness than heretofore and offers rather less in specific revolutionary content. He uses words like "indistinct" and "obscure" to qualify his own sense of the objective. *Hellas*, is, however, a Greek poem. It is the great age of Greece which has been reborn. Shelley's intense sympathy for the "cause of civilisation and social improvement" (Preface to *Hellas*) is at least partly rekindled by the association of his old passion for revolution with his mature Hellenism. *The Revolt of Islam* had anticipated a rebellion of the Greeks against the Turks, and *Prometheus Unbound* had its kind of Greek setting. As Shelley said in his "Discourse on the Manners of the Ancients," the greatness of Greece was "a reality, not a promise," and it has since been the source of our notions of what we may "hope to be" (Clark ed., p. 219).

Abstractly Shelley's statement of the moral means to true revolution has shifted very little if any. Love and renunciation may overpower wrong and hatred which minds ridden by guilt and despair sustain as sources of continuing evil. The differences are mainly in treatment. The hero is still necessary. The Promethean principle, however, seems in this poem to be dissociated into the rebel and anarch figure of Satan, exulting in the prologue over the anticipated ruin and destruction, and into the Wandering Jew, symbol of a powerless redemption of understanding through suffering. The hero is a poet-prophet whose eyes pierce beyond time. He is remote from common humanity, or at least that is what Shelley's description of the Wandering Jew's isolated and inaccessible ocean retreat seems to suggest. The return to this spokesman is puzzling and interesting. He is a symbol of human suffering and persecution like Prometheus, but largely negative in his history and development. He is aged, has seen much, and learned a bitter wisdom about "strong and secret things" (l. 160). He is a scientist, philosopher, and observer of the cycles of historical change. He disclaims "all pretension, or even belief, in supernatural agency." Through his eyes one may learn to see the future in the past and present. Time is collapsed in his vision.

Another share of the heroic duty in the poem surprisingly is held by "the sublime human character" of Christ. Shelley gives qualified praise now even to popular Christian doctrines as at least relatively true and certainly superior "to the worship they superseded" (Hutchinson ed., p. 478n). In the prologue Christ is presented sympathetically as a man who suffered for such truths as Plato had foreseen. One chorus describes him as a Promethean power coming from "the unknown God" to tread in triumph his "thorns of death and shame" (ll. 211–216). His life gave the cross its powers of "killing Truth" (l. 234). Hassan reports a specific action to his master where the Greeks, though defeated, died professing constancy to their Christian God and the political hopes their faith in Him sustained. The cross may make an effective battle ensign to dry up "the strength in Moslem hearts" (l. 503), but the final chorus looks ahead to a reign of heroes "more bright and good" than Christ. Insofar as Christianity arms the Greek rebels with energy and hope in their fierce struggle with their Moslem tyrants, it is good. Like Byron, as reported by Count Gamba, Shelley saw this latest contest as between the principles of barbarism and civilization, Islam and Christianity.[6]

Shelley's views of the origin and nature of evil are not markedly altered. He can still speak of political evils as the products of inhibiting and distorting circumstances. Given their pernicious institutions, the modern Greeks could not be other than degraded by the "moral and political slavery" they have known (Hutchinson ed., p. 447). With the forms of ancient Athens to mold them, they might be as noble as the Greeks of that Golden Age. Nevertheless, it might well seem that Shelley by his admiration of the Greek Golden Age has become something of an "ancient." The fragments of their productions, he claims, "are the despair of modern art" (Preface to *Hellas*). Perhaps indeed, the more intense his Hellenism became, the less optimistic his evaluation of the chances for further progress beyond the mark set by the Greeks. However, his interest in modern science and his belief that circumstances create men seem to have prevented his acceptance of any thoroughgoing theory of historical decline.

Yet the large question remained: Why should such attainments as those of ancient Greece fail to endure? They do of course live on in the world of thought as monuments, but in this world of cankering time and space they fly before the night of sanguinary tyranny. Shelley had asked and answered the question many times and in many ways, and now in a note to *Hellas* he made one of his frankest and most realistic statements. He declared that the problem of the origin of evil is a Gordian knot man cannot yet solve. There must be "a true solution of the riddle," but at present one can perceive only that it is well to believe in perfectibility and the possibility of immortality (Hutchinson ed., p. 478). As a poet Shelley continued to conjecture through his rhythms and images about a future when the veil shall be removed. Our passion for immortality directs us toward optimistic answers. The universe is mysterious, and when our imagination penetrates deeply enough we seem to achieve acquaintance with an order of things in which our evil loses metaphysical substance. It would seem, however, that the revolutionary who doubts the ultimate reality of evil might suffer some proportional loss of faith in the reality of the good cause. Possibly Shelley was so affected to a degree. Revolutions are made in time by men convinced of their cause and sure of their enemy.

At best it does not seem that things work quite as they ought in the world of mutability. Though Nature is seen as an order of strength and freedom set against tyranny (ll. 441–442), this order neither prevails nor endures because of the faults in man's moral nature, his penchant for slavery, and his weakness of will. Very likely the historical expressions of the spirit of anarchy are not absolute and may be overcome, but the lag between vision and realization is terrifying. Heroes like Christ lead men to a sense of their power and destiny by accepting their "thorns of death and shame" in order to communicate with the "killing truth" beyond the veil, but dogma and desolation following hard behind create religions of "Hell, Sin, and Slavery" which bind men in their self-created prisons of hate, fear, and despair more tightly (ll. 211–234). Evil is as fruitful as good. "Revenge and wrong bring forth their kind." Satan figures as prominently as Christ in the prologue, makes his claim also to the "worlds of golden light," and invokes a destiny of anarchy and tyranny for Greece (ll. 120–150). The principle of ruin can still pit its strength on nearly equal terms with the principle of revolution. Tyranny recovers lost ground because the storm of faction weakens the "solid heart" of energetic and enterprising freedom-lovers, until "desolation flashes o'er a world destroyed" (l. 956). Then, to confound further the hopes that rebels have of embodying their visions in the world of space and time, the skeptical and solipsistic idealism of an Ahasuerus casts "on all things surest, brightest, best, / Doubt, insecurity, astonishment" (ll. 790–791).

It is said that the solution lies at hand. Poets and prophets have unrolled the scroll of the future. But the doing is difficult, that first real movement of the will to good. In the human soul rent by conflicting fears, passions, and hopes, knowledge is not enough. The burden of time and history and corrupting circumstance remains. Thus, the image Shelley suggests of himself in *Hellas* is of an optimist consumed by despair. As Mrs. Shelley said, "he resolved to believe that Greece would prove triumphant," but it was a resolution his reason couldn't support as "auguring ultimate good, yet grieving over the vicissitudes to be endured in the interval, he composed his drama" (Hutchinson ed., p. 481).

A special interest of *Hellas* is the attention devoted to the psychology of the tyrant. Mahmud becomes a real and convincing symbol of human incompleteness. He is fearful, doubtful, restless, and cruel, but he is also a fully self-aware tyrant who, in examining his plight, commands some sympathy for his unnatural isolation. Shelley chooses to make him his central character. The action is seen from his perspective, one reason, doubtless, for the focus on ruin. He is not self-deluded like Jupiter. His convulsed spirit envies the skills and insights of the adept Ahasuerus, but he recognizes his subjection to his destiny (ll. 750–752). His strong sense of history weakens his will to fight back. He speaks of himself as a hunted and shaken creature, tormented by gloomy visions of fierce ruin, wearied by the ceaseless strife about him but unable to find the repose he covets. He believes in his god and his prophets (ll. 261 ff.), and knows with regret the sanguinary turbulence that is and is to come; but he fears like others to reject the "Chalice of destruction" (l. 270). Mahmud is very much a determinist. Like other men, his hopes and his fears create their objects, but ultimately he says, we can suffer nothing "Which He inflicts not in whose hand we are" (l. 647). Now fearfully he beholds the coming of the "omnipotent hour" (l. 189) which will end his "gloomy crag of time" (l. 926). He has a strong sense of change. Men before him had looked to his hour as a glorious fulfillment of hopes, and he in turn is consigned to the dustbin of history (ll. 923–928). Knowing this much, he yet turns with dignity to his present duties. Defiant like Jupiter as he fell with Demogorgon, he will take as many of his conquerors into the abyss of ruin as he can.

It is, Shelley says in the preface, "the province of the poet to attach himself to those ideals which exalt and ennoble humanity," and it should probably be acknowledged that he works hard at the task in *Hellas*, however much energy the subsurface sources of doubt may have drained from his faith. Certainly *Hellas* does not seem useful for invoking the gods of revolution, encouraging aspirations, and generating activity. Its repeated scenes of ruin and hatred as cities, past, present, and future, topple into the abyss and "Bow their towered crests to mutability" (l. 846) create a perspective where the universe seems as a bubble or "a print of dew" (Prologue, l. 7). Thus, the poem reflects more clearly old inconsistencies and ambiguities in the revolutionary position which Shelley now recognizes and acknowledges. A larger measure of such awareness seems to have driven a wedge between his hopes and his observations. Doubt and despair increase about faith in this world as the poet labors to live more richly in a better world where "Paradise islands of glory gleam" (l. 1052). It is, Shelley asserts in a note, a hazardous exercise of the imagination "to anticipate however darkly a period of regeneration and happiness" (Hutchinson ed., p. 479). The poet, however, obliged himself still to retreat to his visions and create therein a world less vulnerable to the cycles of desolation and of loveliness in human history. Shelley's last poems impress one vividly with the sense of the triumph of ruin and desolation.

Like the *Triumph of Life*, Shelley's poem reflects his latest mood of doubt and indecision. While the later choruses tell us that freemen may possess a Paradise within and that tyranny is sterile and impermanent, the content of the ideals described implies a veiled and distant realization, in a visionary dream world. Thus, in *Hellas*, Shelley's "mere improvise," inconclusive doctrines and shaken hopes seem united with uncertain form. The ideal Greece thus remains below or beyond the passing show, waiting passively for the day of revelation. Men remain slaves here and now, whatever they might be ideally. Shelley's movement is from uncritical enthusiasm for revolutionary abstractions to subtler and more realistic appraisals of man's situation and possibilities. This shift of emphasis is sound enough doubtless, but hard on hope and the visionary gleam. For all his "intense sympathy" with the latest rebellion, his sense of the inert weight of tyranny and reaction has depressed Shelley's practical hopes and ambitions. The vision of an ideal Athens which the mind creates to combat time and change recurs, but the ruins of Greece may have to be reassembled in a remoter and diviner clime. If evil, like all objects and passions beneath the cope of heaven, is unreal in the light of the one, why should another Athens not arise, if only in the sustaining universal thought which weaves the world of mutability out of itself? More positively and classically, Shelley's later and conscious Hellenism, emphasizing the rich and complete civilization of great golden cities, separates itself from romantic and revolutionary radicalism.

The final chorus brings together the basic motifs, images, and emotions of the poem. The Golden Age revives. The earth renews itself "like a snake," a favorite image but cyclical. Old faiths and empires gleam and die in the smile of Heaven. It is a brighter, serener, fairer, sunnier scene than ever before. The whole burden of aspiration, adventure, and revelation occurs once more. Shall it indeed be brighter and fairer, however, the poet questions. Must freemen when they rise break their chains over the heads of their tyrants "with Laian rage"? Must the epic of liberty be reduced and despoiled by bloody purges renewing "Riddles of death Thebes never knew" (1. 1083)? Moods alternate. There is a rising and falling movement in the chorus as in the poem. The image of hope brightens once more with the vision of the newly arisen Athens bequeathing added splendors to the future if such visions can not endure in this world of mixed fortunes. Then once more the poet hails the more glorious advent of the new age of Saturn and Love, superior to all the luminous forms it succeeds because it is founded not on gold and blood but on the long schooled emotions of love, hope, and forbearance. But the poem in the final stanza returns to the sense of doubt, fear, and despair underlying the whole work — that with each revolution of Destiny's wheels may come back the hatred and death of every earlier one.

> The world is weary of the past,
> Oh, might it die or rest at last!

XIII

Conclusion

Shelley accepted the central political propositions of rationalist thought. He believed in the near omnipotence of truth when adequately communicated. He felt that man was perfectible. He believed that change must come gradually, since true progress moves by the conviction of individuals, that there should be many reforms rather than the anarchy of revolution. Man must be educated in the proper use of freedom. Revolutions, which excite turbulent passions, must be avoided as long as possible, so that the quiet work of intellectual conviction may proceed incessantly and surely toward the far goals of universal enlightenment and equality.

The poet shared the general British sense of the need to moderate between the extremes of revolutionary radicalism and conservative acceptance of process and evolution. Evolution might be a good word for his views of social and political progress, except for the implications in the term of conservative acceptance of obscure processes which men do ill to meddle with. Revolution means that men make changes guided by their insights, ideas, or sudden realizations of value. For Shelley, however, the idea of revolution is or at least comes to be tempered by consideration of the immediate and practical needs of existing societies and of the necessity to introduce reforms gradually as men are conditioned to profit from them. "I am one of those whom nothing will fully satisfy, but who am ready to be partially satisfied by all that is practicable" (to Leigh Hunt, November 14–18, 1819, *Letters*, II, 153). Ultimately he acquired sufficient historical sense to understand the true nature of progress as something more than a mechanical process to be set in motion when sufficient right-thinking liberals are congregated.

Shelley also, however, saw the need for a day of reckoning, the destruction that must come before creation. Perhaps reason can do the job gradually, but important changes are often the work of revolution. Tranquil reformers watch dispassionately while abuses accumulate which, in the heat of revolutionary ardor, when public spirit is aroused and irresistible, might be rooted out. Shelley had a good deal of that ardor, and it flamed up most intensely at those times when the chances of producing good were most promising. Perhaps he felt when most responsive to revolutionary hopes that the kind of advice that Godwin offered him in moderating his enthusiasm, "to put off self, and to contribute by a quiet but incessant activity,"[1] reflected too much conservative dislike of the shocks of change. Shelley is less cautious and fearful than Godwin, who traced the "dreadful convulsions" and "public calamities" that disfigured the Revolution to the premature abolition of injustices which had become incorporated with the basic principles of social existence (*Political Justice*, II, 448–449).

He stresses the need for moral preparation for change. Prometheus' conversion is gradual. When the will is not morally prepared, revolutions falter. The early Christian communities made this mistake. "The system of equality which they established necessarily fell to the ground, because it is a system that must result from rather than precede the moral improvement of human kind" ("Essay on Christianity," Clark ed., p. 212). The French people, like the early Christians, were far from being prepared for the state of equal law "which proceeds from consummated civilization" ("An Association of Philanthropists," Clark ed., p. 67). If institutions inhibit and restrain human and social development, they are evils; but they are useful and necessary when they help form the new shape of man, when they afford continuity with the past as a ground for the future.

Like most other disciples of the Enlightenment, Shelley often seemed to regard progress as something about to begin once men freed themselves from the worship of tradition and prescription. The past was a burden rather than a process of development from which something might be learned. Godwin and Condorcet erred less in this respect, and ultimately Shelley himself came to appreciate more the contributions of the ages. During his early period of "Écrasez l'infâme" he rather accepted Voltaire's view in *Essai sur les moeurs* of the history of great events as "a history of crimes." [2] He told his publisher Hookham in 1812 that he was about to begin the odious study of history, "that record of crimes and miseries" (December 17, 1812, *Letters*, I, 340). As late as the "Philosophical View of Reform" (ca. 1819), he described history as a record of man's mistakes and the suffering caused by them (Clark ed., p. 235). He was apt in his occasional brief incursions into the philosophy of history to leap from Athens to Lord Bacon, granting no more than an occasional fluttering of liberty's pulse to the ages between.

In Italy, however, Shelley's radical temper was eventually leavened somewhat by the historical sense. He appreciated the dangers and difficulties of revolution, without deserting the cause or leaving the hopes of man in the hands of blindly working necessity. He did come finally to understand the lessons in gradual progress taught him by Godwin in 1812, though he was never so ready as his mentor to wait upon events patiently nor did he share his opinion concerning the content of progress, which for Shelley was measured in poetic or imaginative terms.

Shelley blended the Godwinian equalitarian state with the Platonic ideal aristocracy by stressing the role of the poet-hero in bringing all men up to his eminence. Poets must kindle hopes by renewing the sense of human power and glory. Optimism is important, as Shelley stressed in many works. He believed, Mary Shelley noted, in man's capacity to attain "the highest grade of moral improvement" once the weight of custom and prejudice was thrown off (Hutchinson ed., p. 835), and he insisted on the danger of losing hope and the necessity of pressing on toward the best we can conceive. Moral perfection, the power to be governed continually by adequate motives, comes before the attainment of social and intellectual quality. We will steadily improve when we are no longer impressed by factitious distinctions. Mind may control matter in the "golden age" (to Elizabeth Hitchener, October 19, 1811, *Letters*, I, 152). None of these noble goals is to be accomplished truly in other than a gradual manner, for moral perfection is attained slowly through the conversion of the few liberally educated and reflecting individuals who may then in turn guide and instruct the people, partly through direct admonition, partly through example, and partly through the steady application of reformed institutions. Not to abolish institutions but to make them properly expressive of the best available insights was Shelley's ambition. Institutions which approach the ideal character of philosophic and philanthropic associations would be educative forces for the mass of the citizenry.

The minds of men are so warped by the dogmas and the restrictive institutions of the past that considerable time is needed for them to emerge, like Prometheus, from their slavery to ancient forms and the evil passions they foster.

Given the psychology of Locke with its renunciation of innate

ideas and emphasis on the passiveness of the mind in experience, progress in enlightenment would necessarily be defined
as gradual and individual. The mind grows impression by impression, and the process begins anew with each individual.
The idea of perfectibility seems dependent on these conclusions
about the nature of mind. There are some curious inconsistencies or contradictions, however. A sensationalist can scarcely
expect a healthy growth of right-minded citizens without a
favoring environment. Men are the passive results of particular
circumstances. French thinkers, consistent with their conclusions, stressed the role of good laws or benevolent despots in
shaping just communities. If environment and education are
the villains, then a rapid and thorough alteration ought to
produce practical progress and the ideal society without the
required generations of steady growth implied in views like
Godwin's.

Godwin and the French thinkers shared the belief in the
power of education to eliminate superstitions and wrong habit
patterns. They differed on the question of how much time
should be allowed for the changes, and the difference probably
reflected the contrast in their attitudes toward mind and experience. Godwin probably had Platonist leanings toward belief
in the attractive power of eternal and immutable ideas which
gradually draw our latencies on to realization. Shelley went
even further in this direction, and to a large extent rejected the
inadequate psychology and metaphysics of Godwin and the
French. Nevertheless, he somewhat inconsistently continued
to express a strong abstract faith in the power of social institution to put a period to human suffering and degradation, while
in practice stressing the primary importance of individual moral
culture. He accepted a reciprocal relation between the individual and society which was not really developed in Godwin's
ideal anarchism. Men do create society and build its institu-

tions in their own image, but conversely they are also the creations of these shaping forms.[3] The theory leaves room for practical reform interests, for visions of a Promethean age which will guide us in current change, and for acceptance of the necessity for gradual progress. Specific reforms or revolutions would occur when men become strongly aware of the gap between political knowledge and political practice. If men were mere products of circumstance, it would be folly to urge improvement and reform while denying freedom of action. They must be seen as fundamentally free and capable of freely creating visions of a Golden Age to which the imagination responds.

One way out of the determinist dilemma sidestepped by Godwin and the French thinkers was to imagine some cooperative element in the universe which collaborates with man in the work of redemption. This principle — necessity, grace, God, or "love, and beauty, and delight," as Shelley calls that which endures beyond change — beckons the strengthened will and imagination. Certainly the poet believed in some kind of shape in life's process on the side of moral and political good. It may well be that Shelley ultimately concluded that man is the partly unconscious agent of a force which emerges as a personal identity, a Thou, when the mythopoeic instincts are most fully alive (Bloom's thesis). At such times, the true revolution is attained.

The focus in Shelley as a poet of revolution was clearly on what must happen within the mind of man before the ideal revolution can be made actual, but this emphasis did not limit the attention which he gave to the immediate and practical reforms which exercise the will and give continuing life to the revolutionary ideals. In the very years that Shelley was creating his most refined and subtle delineations of ideal societies, his political views were marked by increasing practicality and concern with the details of arranging specific expedient reforms.

The mature Shelley was capable of making clear distinctions between the demands of theory and of practice. He acknowledged in "A Philosophical View of Reform," "All political science abounds with limitations and exceptions," in the course of developing the insight that equality in possessions was a moral rather than a political truth. Morals and politics may be united only in the visions of prophets like Christ, Plato, Rousseau, and Godwin. Equal ownership becomes a goal and a condition of a nobler society toward which it is our duty to tend and which may be partly created by our passionate desire to see it realized. "But our present business is with the difficult and unbending realities of actual life, and when we have drawn inspiration from the great object of our hopes it becomes us with patience and resolution to apply ourselves to accommodating our theories to immediate practice" (Clark ed., pp. 251, 254). Expediency cannot be neglected by the realistic reformer who wishes to make headway against conservative resistance.

While Shelley generally shared the moderate and reasonable views of his mentors, his own observation of a world in reaction against revolutionary hopes and ideals led him also to accept the idea of revolution. One may wait too long for tranquil change. Ideal enthusiasms must express themselves in action or die. The poet of the "Ode to the West Wind" never felt that destruction could be altogether avoided. There is action, even violent action, in all his revolutionary poems. "For so dear is power that the tyrants themselves neither then, nor now, nor ever, left or leave a path to freedom but through their own blood" ("A Philosophical View of Reform," Clark ed., p. 231). The violence of revolution ought to be diminished as much as possible. The way is to prepare the minds of men for the necessary changes. The mind which is able to attend to and comprehend a large number of ideas and relations will more easily grasp the necessity of social growth and reform than the conservative mind blunted by admiration of existent outdated forms. Men of inventive genius and imaginative vision seize new connections in thought and reality and then convey them persuasively. There may indeed be "interminable forms of thought" (Mrs. Shelley's note, Julian, V, ix) waiting as yet inconceivable progress in perception or creation. Progress, however, is not exclusively individual. There must be a community in the extension of perception. Minds and hearts united by love create special strength for the subduing of evil. Love, knowledge, and progress are linked. Feelings and ideas grow and strengthen under the agency of the imagination.

Sufficient knowledge to support revolutionary change exists and lies ready for use. When these truths, solvents of dogma, have been adequately conveyed to the active imagination of masses of men, the time of revolution may be short and relatively bloodless. Success may be surer and more enduring. "We want the creative faculty to imagine that which we know; we want the generous impulse to act that which we imagine" ("A Defence of Poetry," Clark ed., p. 293). Pure speculation and contemplation must move from the tower of knowledge to the world of action and being, from dream to reality. If the proper seeds are sown the harvest will come one day, though men must set up a number of intermediate goals and accept delays before the goals are attained, goals which the poets and prophets apprehend in vision now as humanity presses slowly on to realize them in the world of time and space.

The French Revolution seemed to demonstrate the fate of ideas in this world. An essential and perhaps irreconcilable conflict may exist between thought and experience. For Shelley the French Revolution was a powerful shaping force. It generated hopes and it revealed limitations. It gave Shelley his sense of mission. It instructed him in ways of moderating practical demands for reform and offered an outline for the ideal society. Shelley became a practical reformer and a poetic visionary as a result. He learned to maintain his faith by looking beyond the corrupt present, but he also returned to consider ways of getting started. He made connections between poetry, imagination, individual improvement, and reform which have been fully explored in this study. He adopted a theory of progressive perfectibility under the aegis of moral and creative imagination. There must be a revolution. The energy of ideas can be converted into action, as the French Revolution had demonstrated, but before it arrives, a true leadership, an aristocracy of the imagination, ought to be developed with the power to create and sustain the true revolution.

The scientist is guided by objects, the poet by his feelings. One obeys the laws of nature, the other the laws of mind and passion. The two must unite if the Promethean revolution is to succeed. At times the failure of the French Revolution and later reform movements drove Shelley into skeptical or subjective idealism. But his study of what had been achieved rekindled hopes of eventual success. So much ardor and experiment had changed the world and brought it closer to the poet's world of bright visions. There was an oscillation in Shelley's attitudes. His own experience and his study of the French Revolution altered somewhat his views of humanity, reality, and perfectibility. If humanity often seems hopelessly corrupt, if reality cannot be distinguished from illusion, and if perfectibility seems but another religious faith, what strong motives can one have for laboring for man?

The French Revolution had faltered. That was fact. Perhaps it was illusory to resist the lesson and insist on reviving the hopes it generated. Perhaps the world of revolutionary idealism, like any other construction of art, religion, or philosophy, must lose its power to motivate when a believer, puzzled by the ambiguities in man, confronts as he must the world of objects and events. The Revolution had itself degenerated into dogma. Faith, reason, and laws replaced flexibility and imagination.

The balance Shelley struck between practical and ideal reform in creating his image of progressive humanity would probably have held up under further experience for this lover of liberty, but the urgency, assurance, and resilient optimism could scarcely endure many such visions as *Hellas* and *The Triumph of Life*. Shelley might have learned, as Peacock suggested, to endow his characters with more reality, but the more realistic appraisal of human possibilities, social complexities, and natural resistance which a rounded view would entail could only have reduced somewhat the belief in and the visionary enthusiasm for the Golden Age to come.

Bibliography

Notes

Index

Bibliography

SHELLEY EDITIONS

Cameron, Kenneth Neill, ed. *Percy Bysshe Shelley. The Esdaile Notebook.* New York: Knopf, 1964.

Clark, D. L., ed. *Shelley's Prose.* Albuquerque, N.M.: University of New Mexico Press, 1966.

Hutchinson, Thomas, ed. *The Complete Poetical Works of Percy Bysshe Shelley.* London: Oxford University Press, 1947.

Ingpen, Roger, and Walter E. Peck, eds. *Complete Works,* Julian ed., 10 vols. New York: Scribner's, 1926–1930.

Jones, Frederick L., ed. *The Letters of Percy Bysshe Shelley.* 2 vols. Oxford: Clarendon Press, 1964.

Shawcross, John, ed. *Shelley's Literary and Philosophical Criticism.* London: Henry Frowde, 1909.

BOOKS, ESSAYS, AND ARTICLES ON SHELLEY

Angeli, Helen Rossetti. *Shelley and His Friends in Italy.* London: Methuen, 1911.

Aveling, Edward, and Eleanor Marx. *Shelley's Socialism,* reprint of 1888 edition by Leslie Preger. Manchester: Oxford Bookshop, 1947.

Baker, Carlos. *Shelley's Major Poetry.* Princeton, N.J.: Princeton University Press, 1948.

Barnard, Ellsworth. *Shelley's Religion.* Minneapolis: University of Minnesota Press, 1937.

Barrell, Joseph. *Shelley and the Thought of his Time*. New Haven, Conn.: Yale University Press, 1947.

Berry, Francis. "Shelley and the Action of Hope," *Orpheus*, II (1955), 83–98.

Bloom, Harold. *Shelley's Mythmaking*. New Haven, Conn.: Yale University Press, 1959.

Brailsford, H. N. *Shelley, Godwin and Their Circle*. London: Oxford University Press, 1949. (Home University Library.)

Cameron, Kenneth Neill. *The Young Shelley: Genesis of a Radical*. New York: Macmillan, 1950.

———— *Shelley and His Circle, 1773–1822*. Cambridge, Mass.: Harvard University Press, 1961.

———— "A Major Source of *The Revolt of Islam*," *PMLA*, LVI (March 1941), 175–206.

———— "Shelley and the *Conciones ad Populum*," *Modern Language Notes*, LVII (December 1942), 673–674.

———— "The Social Philosophy of Shelley," *Sewanee Review*, L (October–December 1942), 457–466.

———— "The Political Symbolism of *Prometheus Unbound*," *PMLA*, LVIII (September 1943), 728–753.

———— "Shelley, Cobbett, and the National Debt," *Journal of English and Germanic Philology*, XLII (1943), 197–209.

———— "Shelley and the Reformers," *ELH*, XII (March 1945), 62–85.

Dowden, Edward. *The Life of Percy Bysshe Shelley*. 2 vols. London: K. Paul, Trench & Co., 1886.

Evans, Frank B., III. "Shelley, Godwin, Hume, and the Doctrine of Necessity," *Studies in Philology*, XXXVII (October 1940), 632–640.

Fogle, Richard. *The Imagery of Keats and Shelley*. Chapel Hill, N.C.: University of North Carolina Press, 1949.

———— "Image and Imagelessness: A Limited Reading of *Prometheus Unbound*," *Keats–Shelley Journal*, I (January 1952), 25–36.

Gordon, George. *Shelley and the Oppressors of Mankind*. London, 1922. (Warton Lecture.)

Grabo, Carl. *The Magic Plant*. Chapel Hill, N.C.: University of North Carolina Press, 1936.

Guerard, Albert, Jr. "Prometheus and the Aeolian Lyre," *Yale Review*, XXXIII (March 1944), 482–497.

Houston, Ralph. "Shelley and the Principle of Association," *Essays in Criticism*, III (January 1953), 45–59.

Hughes, D. J. "Potentiality in *Prometheus Unbound*," *Studies in Romanticism*, II (Winter 1963), 107–126.

Johnson, R. Brimley. *Shelley – Leigh Hunt*. London: Ingpen and Grant, 1928.

Jones, Frederick L. "Shelley and Milton," *Studies in Philology*, XLIX (July 1952), 488–519.

—— "Canto I of *The Revolt of Islam*," *Keats – Shelley Journal*, IX (1960), 27–33.

Kapstein, I. J. "Meaning of 'Mont Blanc,'" *PMLA*, LXII (December 1947), 1046–1061.

King-Hele, Desmond. *Shelley: His Thought and Work*. London: Macmillan, 1960.

Knight, G. Wilson. *The Starlit Dome*. Oxford: Oxford University Press, 1941.

Kurtz, Benjamin P. *The Pursuit of Death*. New York: Oxford University Press, 1933.

Lea, F. A. *Shelley and the Romantic Revolution*. London: Routledge, 1945.

MacDonald, Daniel J. *The Radicalism of Shelley and Its Sources*. Washington, D.C.: Catholic Education Press, 1912.

Male, Roy R., Jr. "Young Shelley and the Ancient Moralists," *Keats – Shelley Journal*, V (1956), 81–86.

—— "Shelley and the Doctrine of Sympathy," *Studies in English* (University of Texas), XXIX (1950), 183–203.

Marshall, William Harvey. *Byron, Shelley, Hunt, and the Liberal*. Philadelphia: University of Pennsylvania Press, 1960.

Matthews, G. M. "A Volcano's Voice in Shelley," *ELH*, XXIV (September 1957), 191–228.

Medwin, Thomas. *The Life of Percy Bysshe Shelley*. Ed. by H. Buxton Forman. London: Oxford University Press, 1913.

Milgate, N., Ralph Houston, David V. Erdman, and Valerie Pitt. "Reading Shelley," *Essays in Criticism*, IV (January 1954), 87–103.

Notopoulos, James. *The Platonism of Shelley*. Durham, N.C.: Duke University Press, 1949.

Oras, Ants. "The Multitudinous Orb: Some Miltonic Elements in Shelley," *Modern Language Quarterly*, XVI (September 1955), 247–257.

Palacio, Jean L. de. "Music and Musical Themes in Shelley's Poetry," *Modern Language Review*, LIX (July 1964), 345–359.

Peck, Walter Edwin. "Shelley and the Abbé Barruel," *PMLA*, XXXVI (September 1921), 347–353.

Perkins, David. *The Quest for Permanence*. Cambridge, Mass.: Harvard University Press, 1959.

Peyre, Henri. *Shelley et la France*. Paris: E. Droz, 1935.

Pottle, Frederick A. "The Case of Shelley," *PMLA*, LXVII (September 1952), 589–608.

Pulos, C. E. *The Deep Truth*. Lincoln, Neb.: University of Nebraska Press, 1954.

Richards, I. A. "The Mystical Element in Shelley's Poetry," *Aryan Path*, XXX (June 1959), 250–256, and (July 1959), 290–295.

Ridenour, George M., ed. *Shelley: A Collection of Critical Essays*. Englewood Cliffs, N.J.: Prentice-Hall, 1965. (Spectrum.)

Rogers, Neville. *Shelley at Work*. Oxford: Clarendon Press, 1956.

Schulze, Earl J. *Shelley's Theory of Poetry: A Reappraisal*. The Hague: Mouton, 1966.

Scott, William O. "Shelley's Admiration for Bacon." *PMLA*, LXXIII (June 1958), 228–236.

Sen, Amiyakumar. *Studies in Shelley*. Calcutta: University of Calcutta, 1936.

Simpson, Louis. "Rehabilitations of an Angel," *Hudson Review*, XII (Winter 1959–60), 635–637.

Solve, Melvin T. *Shelley and His Theory of Poetry*. Chicago: University of Chicago Press, 1927.

Stovall, Floyd. *Desire and Restraint in Shelley*. Durham, N.C.: Duke University Press, 1931.

Strong, A. T. *Three Studies in Shelley*. London: Oxford University Press, 1922.

Turner, Paul. "Shelley and Lucretius," *Review of English Studies*, X (August 1959), 269–282.

Vivian, Charles H. "The One 'Mont Blanc,'" *Keats–Shelley Journal*, IV (1955), 55–65.

Walker, A. Stanley. "Peterloo, Shelley, and Reform," *PMLA*, XL (March 1925), 128–164.

White, Newman Ivey. *Shelley*. 2 vols. London: Secker and Warburg, 1947.

——— "*Swell-Foot the Tyrant* in Relation to Contemporary Political Satire," *PMLA*, XXXVI (September 1921), 332–346.

——— "Literature and the Law of Libel: Shelley and the Radicals of 1840–1842," *Studies in Philology*, XXII (January 1925), 34–47.

Wilson, Milton. *Shelley's Later Poetry*. New York: Columbia University Press, 1959.

——— "Romantic Heresy and Critical Orthodoxy." *University of Toronto Quarterly*, XXX (January 1961), 211–216.

Wolfe, Humbert, ed. *The Life of Percy Bysshe Shelley as Comprised in the Life of Shelley by Thomas Jefferson Hogg, The Recollections of Shelley and Byron by Edward John Trelawny, Memoirs of Shelley by Thomas Love Peacock*. 2 vols. London: J. M. Dent, 1933.

Woodhouse, C. M. "The Unacknowledged Legislators (Poets and Politics)," *Essays by Divers Hands*, XXVIII (1956), 48–74.

Woodman, Ross Greig. *The Apocalyptic Vision in the Poetry of Shelley*. Toronto: University of Toronto Press, 1964.

Yeats, William Butler. *Essays and Introductions*. New York: Macmillan, 1961.

OTHER SOURCES CONSULTED

Abrams, M. H. *The Mirror and the Lamp*. New York: W. W. Norton, 1958. (Norton Library.)

——— "The Correspondent Breeze: A Romantic Metaphor," *Kenyon Review*, XIX (Winter 1957), 113–130.

——— ed. *Literature and Belief*. New York: Columbia University Press, 1958.

Adams, M. Ray. *The Literary Background of English Radicalism*. Lancaster, Pa.: Franklin and Marshall College Studies, Number Five, 1947.

Adolphus, John. *Biographical Memoirs of the French Revolution*. 2 vols. London: Cadell and Davies, 1799.

Albrecht, William Price. *William Hazlitt and the Malthusian Controversy*. Albuquerque, N.M.: University of New Mexico Press, 1950.

Allen, B. S. "The Reaction Against William Godwin," *Modern Philology*, XVI (September 1918), 225–243.

Barruel, Abbé. *Memoirs Illustrating the History of Jacobinism*. Trans. by Robert Clifford. 4 vols. London: Burton, 1797–98.

Becker, Carl L. *The Heavenly City of the Eighteenth-Century Philosophers*. New Haven: Yale University Press, 1959.

Bentham, Jeremy. *Plan of Parliamentary Reform*. London, 1817.

Berkeley, George. *Essays, Principles, Dialogues*. Ed. by Mary Calkins. New York: Scribner's, 1929.

Bisson, L. A. "Rousseau and the Romantic Experience," *Modern Language Review*, XXXVII (January 1942), 37–49.

Bloom, Harold. "Napoleon and Prometheus: The Romantic Myth of Organic Energy," *Yale French Studies*, no. 26 (1960–61), pp. 79–82.

Blunden, Edmund. *Leigh Hunt's* Examiner *Examined*. New York: Harper, 1931.

Boner, Harold A. *Hungry Generations: The Nineteenth-Century Case against Malthusianism*. New York: Columbia University Press, 1955.

Brinton, Crane. *Political Ideas of the English Romanticists*. Oxford: Clarendon Press, 1926.

——— *The Jacobins*. New York: Macmillan, 1930.

——— *A Decade of Revolution, 1789–1799*. New York: Harper, 1934.

——— *The Anatomy of Revolution*. New York: Random House, 1960. (Vintage.)

Brown, Ford K. *Life of William Godwin*. London: Dent, 1926.

Brown, Philip Anthony. *The French Revolution in English History*. London: Crosby, Lockwood & Son, 1918.

Bruton, F. A. *The Story of Peterloo*. Manchester, England: Manchester University Press, 1916.

Byron's Works. Letters and Journals. Ed. by Rowland E. Prothero. 6 vols. London: John Murray, 1898–1901.

Lord Byron's Correspondence. Ed. by John Murray. 2 vols. New York: Scribner's, 1922.

Burke, Edmund. *Reflections on the Revolution in France.* Ed. by William B. Todd. New York: Rinehart, 1959.

Carnall, Geoffrey. *Southey and His Age.* Oxford: Clarendon Press, 1960.

Cartwright, Frances Dorothy. *Life and Correspondence of Major Cartwright.* 2 vols. London, 1826.

Cestre, Charles. *La Révolution Française et les poètes Anglais 1789-1809.* Paris: Hachette, 1906.

Cobban, Alfred. *Edmund Burke and the Revolt against the Eighteenth Century.* 2nd ed. London: Allen & Unwin, 1935.

———*A History of Modern France.* 2 vols. Baltimore: Penguin, 1963.

Cobbett, William. *Political Register.* London, 1802-1835.

———*Paper Against Gold.* London, 1828.

Cochin, Augustus. *Les Sociétés de pensée et la démocratie.* Paris: Librairie Plan, 1921.

Cole, G. D. H. *Life of William Cobbett.* 3rd ed. London: Home & Van Thal, 1947.

Coleridge, Samuel Taylor. *Essays on his Own Times.* London, 1850.

Collingwood, R. G. *The Idea of Nature.* New York: Oxford University Press, 1960. (Galaxy Book.)

Condorcet, Marquis de. *Esquisse d'un Tableau Historique des Progrès de l'Esprit Humain.* Ed. by O. H. Prior. Paris: Boivin, 1933.

Cornford, Francis M. *Plato's Theory of Knowledge.* New York: Liberal Arts Press, 1957.

Crocker, Lester G. *Age of Crisis: Man and World in Eighteenth-Century French Thought.* Baltimore: Johns Hopkins Press, 1959.

———*Nature and Culture: Ethical Thought in the French Enlightenment.* Baltimore: Johns Hopkins Press, 1963.

Darvall, Frank Ongley. *Popular Disturbances and Public Order in Regency England.* London: Oxford University Press, 1934.

Dicey, Albert Venn. *Lectures on the Relation between Law and Public Opinion in England during the Nineteenth Century.* London: Macmillan, 1926.

Dowden, Edward. *The French Revolution and English Literature.* New York: Scribner's, 1897.

Drummond, Sir William. *Academical Questions*. London, 1805.

Edwards, Bryan. *The History of the British Colonies in the West Indies*. 4th ed. 3 vols. London: Stockdale, 1807.

Eliot, T. S. *The Use of Poetry and the Use of Criticism*. London: Faber & Faber, 1933.

Erdman, David V. *Blake: Prophet Against Empire*. Princeton, N.J.: Princeton University Press, 1954.

Female Revolutionary Plutarch. 3 vols. London: John Murray, 1806.

Frye, Northrop. *Anatomy of Criticism*. Princeton, N.J.: Princeton University Press, 1957.

—— ed. *Romanticism Reconsidered*. New York: Columbia University Press, 1963.

Gershoy, Leo. *The French Revolution and Napoleon*. New York: Crofts, 1933.

Godwin, William. *Enquiry Concerning Political Justice and its Influence on Morals and Happiness*. Ed. by F. E. L. Priestley. Toronto: University of Toronto Press, 1946.

—— *Thoughts Occasioned by Dr. Parr's Spital Sermon*. London, 1801.

—— *Memoirs of Mary Wollstonecraft*. Ed. by W. Clark Durant. London: Constable, 1927.

—— *Fleetwood*. 3 vols. London, 1805.

Gottschalk, Louis R. *The Era of the French Revolution 1715–1805*. Cambridge, Mass.: Houghton Mifflin, 1929.

Halévy, Élie. *A History of the English People in the Nineteenth Century*. Vols. I, II. London: Benn, 1949.

—— *The Growth of Philosophic Radicalism*. Trans. Mary Morris. London: Faber & Faber, 1949.

Hammond, J. L. *Charles James Fox*. London: Methuen, 1903.

Hammond, J. L. and Barbara. *The Skilled Labourer, 1760–1832*. London: Longmans, Green, 1919.

—— *The Town Labourer, 1760–1832*. 2nd ed. London: Longmans, Green, 1925.

—— *The Village Labourer, 1760–1832*. 4th ed. London: Longmans, Green, 1927.

Hancock, A. E. *French Revolution and the English Poets*. New York: Holt, 1899.

The Complete Works of William Hazlitt. Ed. by P. P. Howe. 21 vols. London: J. M. Dent, 1931.

Helvétius, Claude. *De l'esprit.* Paris, 1758.

Hogg, Thomas Jefferson. *Memoirs of Prince Alexy Haimatoff.* Ed. by Sidney Scott. London: Folio Society, 1952.

D'Holbach, Baron Paul. *Système de la nature.* 2 vols. London, 1770.

Horsfield, Thomas. *The History, Antiquities and Topography of the County of Sussex.* 2 vols. London, 1835.

Howell, Thomas James. *A Complete Collection of State Trials.* Vol. XXXII, London, 1817; Vol. I, new series, London, 1888; *Trial of Henry Hunt and Others.* London, 1820.

Huizinga, Johan. *The Waning of the Middle Ages.* New York: Doubleday, 1954. (Anchor Books.)

Hume, David. *Treatise of Human Nature.* Ed. by L. A. Selby-Bigge. Oxford: Clarendon Press, 1949.

Hunt, Leigh. *The Examiner.* London, 1808–1821.

———*The Reformist's Answer.* London, 1810.

———*Autobiography.* Ed. by J. E. Morpurgo. London: Cresset Press, 1949.

James, William. *Selected Papers on Philosophy.* London: J. M. Dent, 1956. (Everyman's Library.)

Labaume, Eugene. *A Circumstantial Narrative of the Campaign in Russia.* Trans. E. Boyce. Hartford, Conn.: Silas Andrus, 1816.

Lacretelle, Jeune, Jean Charles de. *Histoire de la révolution Française.* 5 vols. Paris, 1801–1806.

Locke, John. *An Essay Concerning Human Understanding.* Ed. by A. S. Pringle-Pattison. Oxford: Clarendon Press, 1924.

Louvet de Couvrai, *Mémoires de Louvet de Couvrai sur La Révolution Française.* Ed. by F. A. Aulard. 2 vols. Paris: Librairie des Bibliophiles, 1889.

Lovell, Ernest J., Jr., ed. *His Very Self and Voice: Collected Conversations of Lord Byron.* New York: Macmillan, 1954.

Lullin de Chateauvieux, J. Fréderic. *Manuscrit venu de St. Hélène, d'une manière inconnue.* London, 1817.

MacCunn, F. J. *The Contemporary English View of Napoleon.* London: G. Bell, 1914.

Mackintosh, James. *Vindiciae Gallicae.* 3rd ed. London: G. G. and J. Robinson, 1791.

Malthus, Thomas Robert. *An Essay on the Principle of Population.* 3rd ed. 2 vols. London, 1806.

Marchand, Leslie. *Byron.* 3 vols. New York: Knopf, 1957.

Mathiez, Albert. *The French Revolution.* Trans. Catherine Philips. New York: Russell & Russell, 1962.

Moore, Dr. John. *A Journal During a Residence in France (1793–1794).* London: G. G. and J. Robinson, 1794.

Morgan, Lady (Sydney Owenson). *France.* 2nd ed. 2 vols. London: Henry Colburn, 1817.

Oldfield, T. H. B. *Representative History of Great Britain and Ireland.* 6 vols. London, 1816.

The Complete Writings of Thomas Paine. 2 vols. Ed. by Philip S. Foner. New York: Citadel Press, 1945.

Patterson, M. W. *Sir Francis Burdett and His Times.* 2 vols. London: Macmillan, 1931.

Paul, C. Kegan. *William Godwin.* 2 vols. London: Henry King, 1876.

Peacock, Thomas Love. *Works.* Ed. by H. F. B. Brett-Smith and C. E. Jones. 10 vols. London: Constable, 1924–34.

Rabaut Saint-Étienne, Jean Paul. *Précis Historique de la Révolution Française.* 5th ed. Paris, 1809.

Ringer, Alexander L. "J.-J. Barthelémy and Musical Utopia in Revolutionary France," *Journal of History of Ideas,* XXII (July–September 1961), 355–368.

Riouffe, Honoré. *Mémoires d'un détenu pour servir à l'histoire de la tyrannie de Robespierre.* A Louviers: Chaidron, 1795.

Roberts, Michael. *The Whig Party, 1807–1812.* London: Macmillan, 1939.

———— "Leigh Hunt's Place in the Reform Movement, 1808–1810," *Review of English Studies,* XI (January 1935), 58–65.

Schilling, B. N. "The English Case Against Voltaire: 1789–1800," *Journal of History of Ideas,* IV (April 1943), 193–216.

Schorer, Mark. *William Blake: The Politics of Vision.* New York: Vintage, 1959.

Sewell, Elizabeth. *The Orphic Voice.* New Haven: Yale University Press, 1960.

———— *The Human Metaphor.* South Bend, Ind.: Notre Dame University Press, 1964.

Letters of Mary W. Shelley. Ed. by Frederick L. Jones. 2 vols. Norman, Okla.: University of Oklahoma Press, 1944.

Mary Shelley's Journal. Ed. by Frederick L. Jones. Norman, Okla.: University of Oklahoma Press, 1947.

Shelley, Mary. *Valperga: or, The Life and Adventures of Castruccio, Prince of Lucca.* 3 vols. London: G. & W. B. Whittaker, 1823.

Shklar, Judith. *After Utopia.* Princeton, N.J.: Princeton University Press, 1957.

Southey, Charles Cuthbert. *Life and Correspondence of Robert Southey.* 6 vols. London, 1849.

Southey, Robert. *Essays, Moral and Political.* 2 vols. London: John Murray, 1832.

Spender, Stephen. *The Creative Element.* New York: British Book Center, 1954.

Spinoza, Benedict. *The Chief Works.* Ed. and trans. R. H. M. Elwes. 2 vols. London: George Bell & Sons, 1889.

Staël-Holstein, Anne Louise Germaine Necker (Mme. de Staël). *Considerations on the Principal Events of the French Revolution.* Ed. by Duke de Broglie and Baron de Staël. 2 vols. New York: James Eastburn, 1818.

Thompson, E. P. *The Making of the English Working Class.* New York: Random House, 1964.

Tiersot, Julien. *Les Fêtes et les chants de la Révolution Française.* Paris: Hachette, 1908.

Torrey, Norman L., ed. *Les Philosophes.* New York: Capricorn, 1960.

Trilling, Lionel. *The Liberal Imagination.* New York: Viking Press, 1950.

Tuveson, E. L. *Millennium and Utopia.* Berkeley, Calif.: University of California Press, 1949.

Twiss, Horace. *Life of Lord Chancellor Eldon.* 3 vols. London: John Murray, 1844.

Veitch, George Stead. *The Genesis of Parliamentary Reform.* London: Constable, 1913.

Volney, M. Constantin. *Les Ruines, ou méditations sur les empires.* Paris, 1791.

Wardle, Ralph M. *Mary Wollstonecraft.* Lawrence, Kans.: University of Kansas Press, 1951.

Wickwar, William H. *The Struggle for the Freedom of the Press, 1819–1832.* London: George Allen & Unwin, 1928.

——— *Baron D'Holbach: A Prelude to the French Revolution.* London: George Allen & Unwin, 1935.

Wilkie, Brian. *Romantic Poets and Epic Tradition.* Madison, Wis.: University of Wisconsin Press, 1965.

Willey, Basil. *The Eighteenth-Century Background.* London: Chatto-Windus, 1949.

Williams, David. "The Influence of Rousseau on Public Opinion, 1760–1795," *English Historical Review,* XLVIII (July 1933), 414–430.

Williams, Helen Maria. *Memoirs of the Reign of Robespierre.* London: John Hamilton, 1795.

——— *Sketches of the State of Manners and Opinions in the French Republic towards the Close of the Eighteenth Century in a Series of Letters.* 2 vols. London: G. G. and J. Robinson, 1801.

Wollstonecraft, Mary. *Vindication of the Rights of Woman.* Ed. by Mrs. Henry Fawcett. New York: Humboldt, n.d.

——— *A Vindication of the Rights of Men.* Facsimile reprod. with an introd. by Eleanor Nicholes. Gainesville, Fla.: Scholars Facsimiles and Reprints, 1960.

——— *An Historical and Moral View of the French Revolution and the Effect It Has Produced in Europe.* Vol. I (all published). London: G. G. and J. Robinson, 1794.

——— *The Love Letters of Mary Wollstonecraft to Gilbert Imlay.* Ed. by Roger Ingpen. Philadelphia: Lippincott, 1908.

Notes

I. Introduction

1. T. S. Eliot, *The Use of Poetry and the Use of Criticism* (London, 1933), p. 89.
2. Floyd Stovall, *Desire and Restraint in Shelley* (Durham, N.C., 1931), p. 41.
3. William James, *Selected Papers on Philosophy* (London, 1956), p. 209.
4. George M. Ridenour, "Shelley's Optimism," in *Shelley: A Collection of Critical Essays*, ed. George M. Ridenour (Englewood Cliffs, N.J., 1965), p. 3.
5. Elizabeth Sewell, *The Orphic Voice* (New Haven, 1960), p. 144.
6. Mary Shelley, *Letters*, ed. Frederick L. Jones (Norman, Okla., 1944), II, 124.

II. The Literature of Revolution

1. C. Kegan Paul, *William Godwin* (London, 1876), II, 207–208. A full account of Shelley's reading of Godwin, Condorcet, and Paine is available in Kenneth Neill Cameron, *The Young Shelley* (New York, 1950).
2. Marquis de Condorcet, *Esquisse d'un tableau historique*, ed. O. H. Prior (Paris, 1933), pp. 149, 168, 227, 239.
3. Edmund Burke, *Reflections on the Revolution in France*, ed. William B. Todd (New York, 1959), pp. 39, 91, 93.

4. James Mackintosh, *Vindiciae Gallicae* (London, 1791), pp. 31, 106–108, 124–125.

5. Helen Maria Williams, *Sketches of the State of Manners and Opinions in the French Republic* (London, 1801), I, 6, 9.

6. *Ibid.*, II, 25.

7. Lady Morgan, *France*, 2nd ed. (London, 1817), I, 5.

8. *Ibid.*, I, 49, 143.

9. *Ibid.*, II, 287, 289, 297.

10. *Ibid.*, I, 161–163, 178, 180.

11. *Ibid.*, II, appendix, cxxvii–ix, clxvii, clxxx.

12. *Works of Lord Byron: Letters and Journals*, ed. Rowland E. Prothero (London, 1898–1901), IV, 95.

13. Henri Peyre, *Shelley et la France* (Paris, 1935), p. 65.

14. Thomas Love Peacock, *Works*, ed. H. F. B. Brett-Smith and C. E. Jones (London, 1924–1934), VIII, 208.

15. Baroness de Staël, *Considerations on the Principal Events of the French Revolution* (New York, 1818), II, 308.

16. *Ibid.*, I, 43.

17. *Ibid.*, I, 27, 141.

18. Humbert Wolfe, ed. *The Life of Percy Bysshe Shelley* (London, 1933), I, 376. The influence of Barruel on Shelley is discussed in W. E. Peck, "Shelley and the Abbé Barruel," *PMLA*, XXXVI (1921), 347–353.

19. John Adolphus, *Biographical Memoirs of the French Revolution* (London, 1799), I, 238, 443–444; II, 139, 399.

20. Dr. John Moore, *A Journal During a Residence in France* (1793–1794), I, 321–322.

21. *Ibid.*, II, 449–453.

22. Honoré Riouffe, *Mémoires d'un détenu* (Paris, 1795), pp. ix–xi.

23. *Mémoires de Louvet de Couvrai*, ed. F. A. Aulard (1st ed.; Paris, 1889), I, 40, 43, 46; II, 54.

24. *Female Revolutionary Plutarch* (London, 1806), I, 176–177; II, 183, 185, 390.

25. Bryan Edwards, *The History of the British Colonies in the West Indies* (4th ed.; London, 1807), III, xvi, 15, 10, 207.

26. Jean Paul Rabaut Saint-Étienne, *Précis historique de la Révolution Française* (5th ed.; Paris, 1809), pp. 132–133, 151, 186–187, 398–399, 454.

27. Jean Charles de Lacretelle Jeune, *Histoire de la Révolution Française* (Paris, 1801–1806), V, 117.

28. Lady Morgan, I, 12, 136, 149–151.

29. Cameron, *The Young Shelley*, p. 150.

30. Milton Wilson, *Shelley's Later Poetry* (New York, 1959), p. 59.

31. *Ibid.*, pp. 66–67.

32. Thomas Robert Malthus, *An Essay on the Principle of Population* (3rd ed.; London, 1806), II, 373.

33. De Staël, I, 33, 46, 73, 209, 280.

34. *Ibid.*, I, 123, 176, 240.

35. *Ibid.*, II, 209.

36. Rabaut Saint-Étienne, pp. 408, 419–420.

37. Mackintosh, p. 163.

III. On His Own Times

1. J. L. and Barbara Hammond, *The Town Labourer* (2nd ed.; London, 1925), p. 94. The Hammond thesis is qualified and reinforced in E. P. Thompson, *The Making of the English Working Class* (New York, 1964), pp. 24, 56, 196–198.

2. T. H. B. Oldfield, *Representative History of Great Britain and Ireland* (London, 1816), V, 35–36.

3. Edward Dowden, *The Life of Percy Bysshe Shelley* (London, 1886), I, 133; Cameron, *The Young Shelley*, pp. 45–46, 85–87.

4. George Stead Veitch, *The Genesis of Parliamentary Reform* (London, 1913), p. 343. Burdett's shortcomings as a political leader are shrewdly analyzed by Thompson, pp. 458–459.

5. Michael Roberts, *The Whig Party, 1807–1812* (London, 1939), p. 295.

6. *Hansard*, XIII (March 15, 1809), 640.

7. *Letters*, I, 125.

8. *Hansard*, IV (new series; May 13, 1805), 785–787.

9. Roberts, p. 79.

10. Newman Ivey White, *Shelley* (London, 1947), I, 227.

11. J. L. and Barbara Hammond, *The Skilled Labourer* (London, 1919), p. 267. Thompson gives the best account of Luddism. See especially chapter XIV, "An Army of Redressers."

12. Frank Ongley Darvall, *Popular Disturbances and Public Disorder in Regency England* (London, 1934), p. 305.

13. Hammond, *Town Labourer*, p. 98.

14. Élie Halévy, *A History of the English People in the Nineteenth Century* (London, 1949), II, 17–18; Thompson, pp. 631–636.

15. *Letters*, I, 19.

16. *Ibid.*, I, 125.

17. *Works*, VIII, 199.

18. Leslie A. Marchand, *Byron* (New York, 1957), II, 533.

19. *Letters and Journals*, V, 242.

20. Marchand, II, 818–819, 842.

21. *Letters and Journals*, IV, 410–411.

22. Thomas James Howell, *A Complete Collection of State Trials*, I, 192.

23. R. Brimley Johnson, *Shelley – Leigh Hunt* (London, 1928), p. 290.

24. F. A. Bruton, *The Story of Peterloo* (Manchester, 1916), p. 42. The lasting significance of the Manchester tragedy is best discussed in Thompson, pp. 683–691, 709–710.

25. Horace Twiss, *Life of Lord Chancellor Eldon* (London, 1844), II, 348.

26. Hammond, *The Town Labourer*, p. 92.

27. G. D. H. Cole, *Life of William Cobbett* (3rd ed.; London, 1947), p. 239.

28. Halévy, *History*, II, 80–81; Thompson, pp. 700–709.

29. *Hansard*, II, new series, 213.

30. R. Brimley Johnson, pp. 138–139.

31. *Political Register* (July 29, 1820), p. 77.

32. Marchand, II, 864–865.

33. Halévy, *History*, II, 205.

34. *Letters and Journals*, IV, 358.

35. Kenneth Neill Cameron, "The Social Philosophy of Shelley," *Sewanee Review*, L (1942), 460.

36. *Letters and Journals*, V, 184.

37. *Ibid.*, V, 403.

38. *Works*, VI, 441.

39. *Lord Byron's Correspondence*, ed. John Murray (New York, 1922), II, 282.

IV. *Views on Practical Reform*

1. J. L. Hammond, *Charles James Fox* (London, 1903), p. 89.
2. Leigh Hunt, *Autobiography*, ed. J. E. Morpurgo (London, 1949), p. 175.
3. Ford K. Brown, *Life of William Godwin* (London, 1926), p. 337.
4. C. Kegan Paul, II, 266.
5. Roberts, *Whig Party*, p. 250.
6. Jean Jacques Rousseau, *The Social Contract*, in *Les Philosophes*, ed. Norman L. Torrey (New York, 1960), p. 156.
7. Leigh Hunt, *The Reformist's Answer* (London, 1810); and Michael Roberts, "Leigh Hunt's Place in the Reform Movement," *Review of English Studies*, XI (January 1935), 62–66.
8. February 16, 1817, p. 100. Shelley's financial ideas and their sources are studied in Kenneth Neill Cameron, "Shelley, Cobbett, and the National Debt," *Journal of English and Germanic Philology*, XLII (1943), 197–209.
9. William Cobbett, *Paper Against Gold* (1828 ed.), p. 251.
10. *The Examiner*, August 1, 1819, p. 481. Cobbett's contributions to the reform movement are fully assessed in Thompson, *The Making of the English Working Class*, pp. 744–763.
11. Lacretelle, III, 242.
12. January 3, 1820, p. 3.
13. *The Complete Works of William Hazlitt*, ed. P. P. Howe (London, 1931), VII, 224–225.
14. Marchand, II, 769.

V. *Program of Associations*

1. Crane Brinton, *A Decade of Revolution, 1789–1799* (New York, 1934), p. 5.
2. Adolphus, II, 117, 120.
3. Thomas Jefferson Hogg, *Memoirs of Prince Alexy Haimatoff*, ed. Sidney Scott (London, 1952), pp. 114, 128.
4. Augustin Cochin, *Les Sociétés de pensée et la démocratie* (Paris, 1921), pp. 78, 80, 83.

5. Crane Brinton, *The Jacobins* (New York, 1930), p. 240.
6. Crane Brinton, *The Anatomy of Revolution* (New York, 1960), pp. 42–43.
7. II, 372–373, 380.
8. Dowden, I, 244.
9. I, 269–270.
10. Riouffe, pp. vi, ix, xi.
11. I, 277–281.
12. *Esquisse*, p. 106.
13. Brinton, *Jacobins*, pp. 18–19.
14. C. Kegan Paul, *Godwin*, II, 204–205.
15. Edward Aveling and Eleanor Marx, *Shelley's Socialism* (reprint of 1888 ed., Manchester, 1947), p. 16.

VI. Revolutionary Ritual and Revolutionary Lyric

1. Carl L. Becker, *The Heavenly City of the Eighteenth-Century Philosophers* (New Haven, 1959), pp. 129, 155.
2. Riouffe, p. xii.
3. Brinton, *Decade of Revolution*, p. 154.
4. Lacretelle, IV, 196.
5. *Sociétés de pensée*, p. 83.
6. Julien Tiersot, *Les Fêtes et les chants de la Révolution Française* (Paris, 1908), p. xxvi.
7. Cochin, pp. 27–28, 30–31.
8. Tiersot, pp. xiv–xvi.
9. Williams, II, 289, 293–295.
10. *Works*, XIII, 120.
11. Adolphus, I, 171–175.
12. Rabaut, I, 272, 285–289.
13. Tiersot, pp. 107–110.
14. Adolphus, I, 491.
15. Tiersot, pp. 123, 128–130.
16. Adolphus, II, 430–433.
17. Tiersot, pp. 161, 165.
18. Adolphus, II, 444.
19. Tiersot, p. 171.
20. *Vindiciae Gallicae*, p. 80.

21. Tiersot, pp. 171, 242–243.

22. *Letters and Journals,* IV, 485.

23. Mary Wollstonecraft, *A Vindication of the Rights of Men* (1790), p. 38.

24. M. H. Abrams, *The Mirror and the Lamp* (New York, 1958), pp. 52–53.

25. William Godwin, *Fleetwood* (London, 1805), I, 141–142.

26. Wilson, *Shelley's Later Poetry,* p. 153.

27. *The Love Letters of Mary Wollstonecraft to Gilbert Imlay,* ed. Roger Ingpen (Philadelphia, 1908), p. 47.

28. Roy R. Male, Jr., "Shelley and the Doctrine of Sympathy," *Studies in English* (University of Texas), XXIX (1950), 193.

29. Harold Bloom, *Shelley's Mythmaking* (New Haven, 1959), p. 115.

30. *Ibid.,* p. 81.

31. I. J. Kapstein, "Meaning of 'Mont Blanc,'" *PMLA,* LXII (1947), 1058.

VII. Queen Mab

1. See Newman Ivey White, "Literature and the Law of Libel: Shelley and the Radicals of 1840–1842," *Studies in Philology,* XXII (January 1925), 34–47.

2. Peyre, *Shelley et la France,* p. 39.

3. Brinton, *Anatomy of Revolution,* p. 201.

4. *Ibid.,* pp. 201–202.

5. E. L. Tuveson, *Millennium and Utopia* (Berkeley, 1949), pp. 144, 146, 157.

VIII. The Problem of Evil

1. Ellsworth Barnard, *Shelley's Religion* (Minneapolis, 1937), p. 249.

2. Wilson, *Shelley's Later Poetry,* pp. 306–307.

3. Bloom, *Shelley's Mythmaking,* p. 112.

4. Malthus, *An Essay on the Principle of Population,* II, 99.

IX. The Doctrine of the Hero

1. De Staël, I, 17, 196, 209–210, 254–255.
2. Mary Wollstonecraft, *Vindication of the Rights of Woman*, ed. Mrs. Henry Fawcett (New York, n.d.), p. 168.
3. Eugene Labaume, *A Circumstantial Narrative of the Campaign in Russia*, trans. E. Boyce (Hartford, Conn., 1816), pp. 12–13.
4. *Manuscrit venu de St. Hélène* (London, 1817), pp. 34, 64.
5. Lacretelle, VI, 398.
6. Lady Morgan, II, 216.
7. Charles Cestre, *La Révolution Française et les poètes Anglais*, 1789–1809 (Paris, 1906), p. 56.
8. Mary Shelley, *Valperga* (London, 1823).
9. Marchand, II, 603, 611–612, 917.
10. Edward Dowden, *The French Revolution and English Literature* (New York, 1897), pp. 260, 263.
11. Leo Gershoy, *The French Revolution and Napoleon* (New York, 1933), p. 534.
12. Baron Paul D'Holbach, *Système de la nature* (London, 1770), I, 75.
13. Lacretelle, III, 60.
14. Wollstonecraft, *Rights of Woman*, pp. 89, 184.
15. Moore, II, 258–259.
16. Edwards, III, 43, 82–83.
17. Lacretelle, II, 249–250; III, 37, 260.
18. Williams, *Sketches*, II, 53, 55–56, 63–64.
19. Lacretelle, IV, 206–209; VI, 33.
20. *Esquisse*, p. 228.
21. William Godwin, *Memoirs of Mary Wollstonecraft*, ed. W. Clark Durant (London, 1927), pp. 124–125.
22. Wollstonecraft, *Rights of Woman*, pp. 59, 86–87, 197–198.
23. *Works*, III, 156.
24. Rabaut Saint Étienne, I, 69.
25. *Works*, XIII, 318.
26. Lady Morgan, *France*, II, xlv, xciii.
27. *Esquisse*, pp. 157, 198.

28. Robert Southey, *Essays, Moral and Political* (London, 1832), I, 210–211.

29. *Esquisse*, p. 60.

30. *Letters and Journals*, V, 190.

31. Benedict Spinoza, *Chief Works*, trans. R. H. M. Elwes (2nd ed.; London, 1889), I, 229.

X. The Revolt of Islam

1. *Vindiciae Gallicae*, pp. 53–55.

2. *Mémoires d'un détenu*, pp. 62–63.

3. *Mémoires de Louvet*, I, 116; II, 38–39, 66–68.

4. *Ibid.*, II, 56.

5. Tiersot, pp. 107–110.

6. Amiyakumar Sen, *Studies in Shelley* (Calcutta, 1936), pp. 309–310, 330.

7. *Ibid.*, p. 318.

8. *Letters and Journals*, V, 74.

XI. Prometheus Unbound

1. Stephen Spender, *The Creative Element* (New York, 1954), pp. 28–29. I learned a good deal about *Prometheus Unbound* from the discussion of the poem in Melvin Solve, *Shelley and His Theory of Poetry* (Chicago, 1927).

2. Northrop Frye, *Anatomy of Criticism* (Princeton, N.J., 1957), p. 155.

3. Kenneth Neill Cameron, "The Political Symbolism of *Prometheus Unbound*," *PMLA*, LVIII (September 1943), 747.

4. *France*, II, 313.

5. *Ibid.*, II, 40.

6. Bloom, *Shelley's Mythmaking*, p. 112.

7. Cameron, "Political Symbolism," pp. 749–751.

8. Carlos Baker, *Shelley's Major Poetry* (Princeton, N.J., 1948), p. 116.

9. Wilson, *Shelley's Later Poetry*, pp. 276–277.

10. "Political Symbolism," p. 744.

11. James Notopoulos, *The Platonism of Shelley* (Durham, N.C., 1949), p. 427.

12. Johan Huizinga, *The Waning of the Middle Ages* (New York, 1954), pp. 165–168.

13. Richard Harter Fogle, *The Imagery of Keats and Shelley* (Chapel Hill, N.C., 1949), pp. 215–218.

14. W. B. Yeats, *Essays and Introductions* (New York, 1961), p. 92.

15. G. Wilson Knight, *The Starlit Dome* (Oxford, 1941), p. 216.

16. D. J. Hughes, "Potentiality in *Prometheus Unbound,*" *Studies in Romanticism,* II (1963), 114.

XII. Hellas

1. Wilson, *Shelley's Later Poetry,* p. 183.

2. Wolfe ed., II, 359.

3. *Ibid.,* II, 230; and Ernest J. Lovell, Jr., ed., *His Very Self and Voice* (New York, 1954), pp. 321, 447.

4. Ross Greig Woodman, *The Apocalyptic Vision in the Poetry of Shelley* (Toronto, 1964), p. 189.

5. R. G. Collingwood, *The Idea of Nature* (New York, 1960), p. 70.

6. Lovell, p. 560.

XIII. Conclusion

1. C. Kegan Paul, *Godwin,* II, 207–208.

2. Becker, *The Heavenly City,* p. 111.

3. Carl Grabo, *The Magic Plant* (Chapel Hill, N.C., 1936), p. 424.